Carl Linder teaches Film Production at the University of California in Los Angeles. He has previously written for *Newsweek* magazine, and he is the founder and first editor of *Filmmakers Newsletter* magazine. His own films have received international recognition.

FILMMAKING

a practical guide

CARL LINDER

A SPECTRUM BOOK

Prentice-Hall, Inc., Englewood Cliffs, New Jersey

791.43
Lin

Library of Congress Cataloging in Publication Data

Linder, Carl.
    Filmmaking.

    (A Spectrum Book)
    Includes bibliographical references and index.
    1. Moving-pictures—Production and direction.
I. Title.
PN1995.9.P7L48   791.43'0232   75–31932
ISBN 0–13–314807–6
ISBN 0–13–314799–1 pbk.

© 1976 by Prentice-Hall, Inc., Englewood Cliffs, New Jersey

A Spectrum Book

10   9   8   7   6

Printed in the United States of America

Prentice-Hall International, Inc., *London*
Prentice-Hall of Australia Pty. Limited, *Sydney*
Prentice-Hall of Canada, Ltd., *Toronto*
Prentice-Hall of India Private Limited, *New Delhi*
Prentice-Hall of Japan, Inc., *Tokyo*
Prentice-Hall of South-East Asia Private Limited, *Singapore*

Contents

part I
THE TOOLS OF FILMMAKING

1

2

part II
THE DOCUMENTARY

6

7

8

part III
THE FICTIONAL NARRATIVE

9

This book is affectionately dedicated to my students—
who continue to learn filmmaking along with me.

ACKNOWLEDGEMENTS

I would like to give special thanks to the following: Paul Czirban of the Mother Rock Pottery Studio, L.A., who is the subject in the "potter" illustrations/ Cal Bernstein of Dove Productions, L. A. for his generous response to my storyboard problem/ Bruce Furst for his photographs of the potter/ Richard Kaplan who took excellent, but unflattering pictures of his beautiful wife/ Wendy Kaplan who posed for the unflattering pictures, even though she knew they would be/ Lori Katz who did the line drawings for the book/ James Boyer May for helping to edit and proofread the manuscript/ Pyramid Films, L.A. for making available stills from *Frogs*/ Charles Salmore for his assistance, generally, with all the production data relating to the making of his film *Frogs*/ Anita Schwaber for her efforts in helping me to get illustrations/ The Academy of Motion Picture Arts and Sciences for letting me use their library facilities.

WAYS TO USE THIS BOOK

I believe that a book should be read, and it should be *used*. By that I mean it should be a guide to experiences, in this case the experience of making a film. I am reminded of a beautiful, natural, tropical wilderness park in Miami, Florida, known as Matheson's Hammock. It is filled with hiking paths. Each path is a way to experience what the park has to offer—each is different, yet each one gives a feeling of the whole. Sometimes the paths unexpectedly intersect, and it is then that one becomes aware of a scheme, a degree of organization, a touch of man's hand amid the lush vegetation.

This book is not exquisite like that park yet its organization is somehow analogous. There are several paths here, and I invite you to take any one of them. Enter where you feel comfortable, and eventually you will encounter another path, beckoning you to change direction. You may wish to make a quick walk and return to your original direction—or you may wish to explore more fully the new one.

But what are some of these directions? The book is primarily designed to be read in sequence; that's the way it was written. And the parts are arranged as a logical progression of ideas that build upon one another. Most people who are beginners to filmmaking (and photography) will want to take this path, because it starts with the basics, "The Tools of Film," covering those items that make up the filmmaker's craft—much as a potter learns the mechanics of fashioning and controlling clay; the use of the wheel, types of glazes, and procedure in firing clay.

Next, the book endeavors to show how a "functional" type of film, the documentary, is made. To continue the potter analogy, making a documentary is a little like making functional pieces of pottery such as bowls, plates, and planters.

A discussion of the narrative story film follows because I see it as a stylization of the documentary mode. The story film is like the documentary, but with a greater condensation of sentiment and with greater "impact." It is less informational-oriented and more feeling-oriented, a little like the potter making his dinnerware more ornate, more decorative.

Finally, the part on the expressionistic film is similar to using the clay medium for the creation of abstract sculptural forms. It involves how to employ the film medium to serve *personal expression*, working with the bare materials of film itself.

A second path is to read the basics in Part One then proceed directly to a discussion of the type of film you would most like to make—documentary, narrative, or expressionistic.

Still another path (for the adventurous) is to read Part One and then turn to the "Suggested Projects" in the Appendix, taking each exercise in order—shooting a roll of film to illustrate each one. As the exercise is undertaken, the filmmaker is referred to additional, supplemental reading in the text (at the end of each exercise)—spot reading—for depth and dimension.

The exercises (Suggested Projects) serve both as a refresher for the experienced filmmaker, and as a primer for the beginner. Ideally, if one were to take the first path (each section of the book as it comes), the exercises would be taken up naturally in Part One, "Planning a Film."

Some people find it difficult to get into books, just because they're books, and I'm one of those people. I like to peruse a book for the specific subjects it has to offer, and so, frequently I will take a path through the index—reading every page under "lighting," for example, or every page under "Fellini." Then after I've satisfied myself that the book warrants my attention, I will surrender and begin with page one. You might try this approach here.

Now that you know some of the ways to use this book, I'd like to list some special things I had in mind while writing it.

After going over a lot of film books with a view toward using them in my classes, I found that there were none that approached filmmaking from my student filmmakers' point of view. Though I found many of the books to be excellent on the technical aspects, they were almost devoid of aesthetics. On the other hand, books that dealt with aesthetics were often dry and discursively philosophical. I needed a book that covered the technical essentials (but didn't overdo them), and one that talked to the beginning filmmaker with *his* aesthetic problems in mind, one that supplied the kind of aesthetic pointers that the average serious student would benefit from having.

So I set out to write a book that would satisfy the needs of my students. Few filmmaking books are written with students in mind. Maybe this is why I have trouble with most film books—because I don't feel they are "talking to me."

In any case, teaching some 3,500 students over the years has led me to understand better a few elusive areas in film education generally. Certainly the first, in my opinion, is *not* what is missing in the technical area. This ground has been covered again and again, and it has been trampled and made dusty, much as the plains in West Africa have been denuded by the beef herds of the Masai tribesmen. We traverse the same ground because it's there.

I found that most of my students could use the camera but didn't know how to *see* with it. In response to this obvious need I have devoted a considerable amount of space to "Seeing within the Rectangle" (Part One, Chapter II, Section 2).

I also found that a lot of beginners simply didn't know how to get started filming. They needed some suggested approaches, some ideas. So, in Part One I devote a chapter to "Planning a Film." It is replete with ideas for films and directs the reader to the "Suggested Projects" at the back of the book.

As a teacher, I've always tried to find new, fresh ways to express the dynamics of film. Out of this effort I coined a few terms and definitions. The most important of these is the concept of *gesture* and how it functions both in the filming and the editing process. I didn't invent the idea of gesture in film. I did, however, give it a name, a designation, so that it could be better understood. It is a tool that can aid the lay filmmaker's understanding. And in my opinion it is the most significant aspect of this book.

I have been fortunate in having an extreme diversity of interests among my students. I realize that their interests must be respected —and for their benefit, pursued, instead of trying to cast those interests in a single mold. Some people simply don't want to make abstract films, or story films. Their sensibilities may lean instead toward the documentary or training films. So, instead of turning my classes into what could easily have been a "tower of Babel" situation, with everyone speaking a different language, I utilized these differences to show how there are some basic things in approaching *all kinds* of filmmaking. Therefore, in the book I discuss as thoroughly as possible the three main film genres, comparing and contrasting them as I go along.

Something I've found lacking in most approaches to film education is an emphasis on editing. It's a hard subject to explain and communicate, and a good reason why in most books it is skirted if not avoided. (Most professional film editors learn through trial and error—or they have an intuitive feel for it.) It is a pet subject of mine, and so for me it is fairly easy. I discuss editing from different angles in every one of the four parts of this book.

In each part dealing respectively with the documentary, the narrative story film, and the expressionistic film, I go into the whys and wherefores of each way of working, the practical aspects of making these film types. In each part there are new words to frame old concepts—the "social" and "intimate" documentaries; the "running" and "situational" story films; the "collage" and "structural" expressionistic films.

Finally, perhaps unique to film books, are the "Suggested Projects"—exercises to help the beginnier integrate the vocabulary of film into practice. As an additional aid, I have included a listing of articles from the magazine *Filmmakers Newsletter* that bear on the material in this book. The articles, in a sense, are an extension of the text. If followed up, either through your library or bookstore, they will amplify specific subjects that cannot be covered fully here.

These then are some of the things I thought I'd especially like to see in a film book of this type. Good reading. And good filming, making your film.

CARL LINDER

part 1

THE TOOLS OF FILMMAKING

chapter 1

Getting Acquainted with the Camera

THE LENS

To do the best job, anyone engaged in filmmaking should first become familiar with his camera. Though there are many camera models of varying degrees of complexity, all can be compared with certain basic features of the lens and body.

Let's examine the lens first, because it is the "brain" of the camera, and because to some people its proper use is the most perplexing aspect of cinematography. The "zoom lens" is most frequently seen on cameras today, and it is generally assumed that, because many if not most cameras have them, they are the only ones to use. Seldom realized is the fact that professional film work, until about the mid-1950s, was done with what are known as "fixed focal length" (non-zoom) lenses. Though zooms are in wide use today, they have by no means supplanted the fixed focal length variety. Separate fixed lenses continue in use because they offer a broader range of focal lengths and produce a sharper focus than the zoom.

To understand what a zoom is and how it functions, it would be good to begin with an examination of its focal length components.

There are three basic positions: short focal length (wide angle); medium focal length (normal); and long focal length (telephoto). On Super 8 cameras the *normal* zoom position is 13mm. Less than 13mm (say 6 or 8mm) becomes *wide-angle,* and more than 13mm (say 30, 40, or 60mm) becomes *telephoto.*

Listed below are the three basic lens positions according to focal length, and their characteristics. These characteristics should be studied and kept in mind, because the focal length a filmmaker chooses can be one of the most crucial decisions he makes regarding the outcome of his filming efforts.

Lens Positions within the Zoom

THE NORMAL PART OF THE LENS

1. Is medium focal length, which is 13mm for Super 8 cameras. 2. Has a narrow angle of view (about 25 degrees). 3. Provides a slightly larger image of the subject. 4. Renders distance from the camera to subject fairly realistically. 5 Minimizes linear distortion (renders perspective normally). 6. Makes action toward or away from the camera appear normal. 7. Provides moderate depth of field (that area in front of and behind the subject on which the camera is being focused, which remains in acceptable sharp focus).

THE WIDE-ANGLE PART OF THE LENS

1. Is short focal length, which is less than 13mm for Super 8 cameras (10, 8, 6mm, etc.). 2. Has a wide angle of view (the human eye takes in about 180 degrees; wide-angle lenses take in more than 25 degrees, but generally less than 90 degrees). 3. Provides a smaller subject size than is perceived normally. 4. Lengthens distance (makes subjects appear farther away than they really are—and farther from one another). 5. Creates linear distortion (exaggerates perspective when using *extreme* wide angle, causing the horizontal and vertical lines to be curved, thus lending a convex appearance to the image. 6. Tends to speed up the action (subjects moving toward or away from the lens appear to be covering distance faster than they really are). 7. Provides good depth of field (increases the area in front of and behind the subject on which the camera is being focused, which remains in acceptable sharp focus).

THE TELEPHOTO PART OF THE LENS

1. Is long focal length, which is over 13mm for Super 8 cameras (30, 40, 60mm, etc.). 2. Has a very narrow angle of view (less than

25 degrees). 3. Creates a larger than normal subject size. 4. Shortens distance so that subjects appear closer to the camera and to one another than they really are. 5. Creates linear distortion (so that the perspective is flattened, curving the horizontal and vertical lines, thus producing a concave appearance. 6. Tends to slow down the action (subjects moving toward or away from the camera appear to be covering distance at less than the normal rate). 7. Provides shallow depth of field (decreases the area in front of and behind the subject on which the camera is being focused, which remains in acceptable sharp focus).

The zoom lens is variable in focal length—i.e., one lens does the work of all the fixed focal length lenses. The zoom can be thought of as a "bag of lenses." You can adjust from wide angle to normal to telephoto, and you can move the subject nearer (zooming in) or farther away (zooming out) without interrupting the shot.

How far you can zoom in or out depends on the focal length *range* of your lens. A low-price Super 8 camera may have a zoom range that goes from a slight wide-angle capability (such as 9mm) to a weak telephoto (perhaps only 27mm), whereas the zoom range for a more expensive camera might be somewhere on the order of an ample 7 to 56mm. *Very* expensive cameras may have a more than adequate zoom range, as high as 7 to 70mm, a 10 to 1 ratio.

But there is yet another aspect to lens focal lengths to consider. Since *extreme* wide-angle and telephoto lenses tend to produce optical distortion, they are limited to special uses. For this reason, it does not necessarily follow that "the bigger the zoom range, the better the lens." It is practical to have a zoom capacity on your camera that reflects *your* particular needs. But for most purposes, a zoom lens that falls roughly between 4 to 7mm (wide angle) and 40 to 70mm (telephoto) is quite adequate.

The zoom possesses the characteristics of fixed focal length lenses because it is made up of them. The various focal lengths are marked on the barrel of the zoom—usually, the last set of numbers nearest the camera body.

Inasmuch as the zoom has a variable focal length, it also provides a variable *depth of field,* which we defined as that area in front of and behind the subject on which the camera is being focused, which remains in acceptable sharp focus. Thus, from our preceding description of lens characteristics, we see that some focal lengths provide more depth of field than others—what we might think of as "bonus focus." Few people stop to think that they are often getting more in focus than they bargained for, and, conversely, that it is possible to get much less.

If you aim your camera lens at a subject and think you have focused on it, using the wide-angle part of your zoom, you may not be focused *precisely* on the subject at all. By precisely, I mean the "plane of critical focus," or that area of the picture frame that is sharpest, may be located in front of or behind your subject. The subject passed the sharpness test because it fell within the range of *acceptable* sharp focus. Since a wide-angle lens can have such a broad area that is exactly sharp (depth of focus) and another large area beyond that is in acceptable sharp focus (depth of field), everything looks just fine for the wide-angle shot. However, when zooming in, using the telephoto capability, the depth field and depth of focus shrink radically, blurring practically everything except that small area on the plane of critical focus.

Here is what happens. When an image registers on film, it is made up of many tiny dots that vary in size from minute points of light to large circles, known as "circles of confusion." The points and circles taken together resemble the dots that make up a newspaper photograph. The smallest points make up the critical plane of focus, and as they become larger, but still appearing to us as points, are included in that area known as depth of field. As the dots get still larger they become circles that overlap, creating a fuzzy or blurred image. As we look at the film image, we are seeing three areas in terms of sharpness: (1) the area in *critical* sharp focus (depth of focus); (2) the area in *acceptable* sharp focus (depth of field); and (3) the area considered out of focus.

In order to focus your zoom properly, follow this procedure. Whenever you are filming (and whatever you are filming) always *zoom in first* and focus on the subject. After you do that, the subject will remain in focus at other focal lengths, if it stays the same distance from the camera as when you began.

Also, when focusing on two or more separated subjects, focus on a point one-third of the distance behind the subject closest to the camera and two-thirds in front of the most distant subject. Don't focus midway between them.

Besides focal length, there are two additional considerations that affect depth of field—*lens aperture* and *distance.*

The lens aperture size is controlled by an iris diaphragm much the same as the iris of the eye. Its principal function is to regulate the amount of light passing through the lens. Most iris diaphragms on Super 8 cameras are automatic, and they are activated to open and shut by a photoelectric cell. Some older cameras have manual diaphragms, and all better cameras have both an automatic meter and manual override (a good arrangement). Many cameras have an aperture ring that is marked in "f/stops" and can be used to manually control the diaphragm setting (f/stops are numerical indications of how open or closed the aperture is). The larger the f/stop, the smaller the aperture. Generally speaking, the smaller the aperture (or larger the f/stop number), the greater the depth of field in the filmed image. It is important to remember that when the smallest f/stop number is set, such as f/1.2, the lens is "wide open"; and when the largest f/stop number is set, say f/22, the lens is "stopped all the way down." Also, even though a lens may be stopped down, it never completely closes. There is always at least a pinhole opening that admits light. This is why it is sometimes difficult to use the lens aperture to accomplish "fades" (making the image go completely dark), unless the filming is being done under low-light conditions. The lens aperture, then, regulates the amount of light entering the camera, and second, helps to regulate depth of field.

The distance setting on your camera is usually the second ring down on the lens barrel—or, between the aperture ring and the focal length ring. Generally, distance from the subject has a negligible effect on depth of field (except when filming under low light conditions, thus necessitating a larger aperture opening in which instance a farther distance from the subject rather than closer will contribute to greater depth of field).

In summary, the two most important conditions that yield best depth of field are short focal length of lens and large numerical f/stop.

In order to achieve the opposite of good depth of field—or *shallow focus*, simply reverse the above conditions.

Note: Even though f/22 will yield the greatest depth of field, it tends to degrade the image somewhat in terms of resolution. Film industry professionals prefer to use f/11 (or near it), which provides the greatest depth of field without loss in image quality.

Control over depth of field is first a technical act, but in the last analysis it is a creative decision. At first, one might leap to the conclusion that the more image in focus the better, and that out-of-focus areas of the picture should be shunned. Focus, like so much of cinematography, can and should be used as a method of selecting what it is you wish to be seen. It should be thought of as a means to emphasize elements of your picture. (For more on creative use of depth of field, refer to "Using Depth of Field for Emphasis," Chapter II.)

THE BODY

Practically all camera motors today are battery powered, and not much needs to be said about them except to warn the filmmaker to keep extra batteries handy.

The camera trigger (which activates the motor) usually has three settings: short run (camera starts when finger depresses trigger and stops when released); continuous run (trigger can be locked in position for continuous filming; allows the filmmaker to film himself); and single frame (takes one frame at a time—for animation, time lapse, or pixilation).

Many cameras have a dial (or switch) located on the side of the body for adjusting motor speeds, which is usually numbered 8, 12, 16, 18, 24, 32, 48, 64. These numbers indicate the number of frames of film per second (fps) passing through the film gate. These numbers let us know *how fast* the film is moving through the camera. The dial allows you to change the speed at will.

The normal frames per second for silent speed is 18 fps, and for sound speed, 24 fps. Most of the time you will be using 18 fps, for most filmmakers using Super 8 do not as yet apply sound directly to their films. (Footnote: However, Super 8 sound cameras and projectors are coming into wider use—such as the Canon, Sankyo, Elmo, and Beaulieu cameras—and the Kodak, Elmo, and Bolex projectors.) Eighteen fps is considered standard for silent speed because there is a minimum of "flicker" when the film is projected. The old standard used to be 16 fps, but was changed in the last few years for conversion to Super 8.

The "normal" filming speed is in direct relation to and determined by the speed of projection. If you were to film at 18 fps and project at, say, 64 fps, the action in the film would be speeded up. If, however, you were to film the action at 64 fps and project the same film at 64 fps, the action would appear perfectly normal. It should be stressed that if you decide to use this speed as standard, you would be needlessly wasting film. That is why the standard has been set at 18 fps for Super 8 as well as other gauge films; it offers both the greatest film economy and the best projection (without flicker).

At 24 fps it is another story. Here you must consider the sound quality as well as projection. Sound, peculiarly, must have a speed—both during recording and playback—that will yield an optimum tonal and frequency response. So when film has sound placed directly on it, as in the case of magnetic and optical sound tracks, the speed of the projected image must be taken into account and be sufficiently accommodated to the speed requirements of the sound track. Sound has a faster requirement for resolution than does the visual image; this is why sound film must be projected at 24 fps, as well as having been shot at 24 fps (to maintain normal motion). This standard for sound speed is universally accepted.

Filming at speeds that are not standard or normal will result in motion distortion—in what we call "slow motion" or "fast motion." Speeded up motion will occur in any film taken at less than the normal rate of 18 fps, but projected at 18 fps. (Filming at 6, 8, or 12 fps will create a fast motion effect, as in the old newsreels.) Likewise, when you film at a speed greater than 18 fps (and the projector is running at 18 fps), everything filmed above that speed (32, 48, 64 fps, etc.) will produce slow motion.

In general, the ability to vary frames per second is an asset, though its value has been greatly overrated, especially with regard to fast motion. Fast motion produces a comic effect, and few people ever have need for it. Slow motion can be more useful. The effect is often interpreted as poetic and lyrical. It is useful, too, in slowing down action for close examination, as in sports events. Finally, it can be effectively used as a method of transforming the filmed image for artistic purposes. Slow motion becomes most discernible when the film speed is 48 fps or over. Any speed less than that will be disappointing. In summary, an adjustable frames per second capability is useful.

Geared to the film transport motor (which governs frames per second) is the camera's shutter (which together with the lens aperture regulates the amount of light entering the camera and determines the sharpness of the image). In most Super 8 cameras, the "shutter speed" cannot be varied except by varying the motor speed. To put it another way, when the motor speed is increased, the shutter speed is also increased. On cameras with fixed shutters, the shutter speed always remains relative, in a constant relationship to the motor speed.

The shutter in many cameras is nothing more than a circular disc (a rotary shutter) with a pie-shaped window of about 180 degrees cut out of it. The disc is located in back of the lens and in front of the film plane. As each frame of film is pulled into place to be exposed, the disc spins synchronously to admit light through the window to each frame. When the frames per second rate is increased, the shutter speed is increased. The shutter speed when filming at 18 fps is approximately 1/35th of a second (for each frame). As the filming speed increases to, say, 24 fps, the shutter speed becomes approximately 1/50th of a second. Table 1 is a list of frames per second with their respective shutter speeds.

Table 1. *Approximate Shutter Speeds Relative to Frames per Second*

8 frames per second	= 1/15th of a second shutter speed
12 fps	= 1/25th
18 fps	= 1/35th
24 fps	= 1/50th
32 fps	= 1/65th
48 fps	= 1/95th
64 fps	= 1/130th

SHUTTER SPEED FORMULA

$$\text{shutter speed} = \frac{\text{shutter opening } (180°)}{\text{frames per second} \times 360°}$$

Since the shutter speed is one of two main factors which regulates the amount of light entering the camera (lens aperture is the other) it is an added concern for arriving at the correct f/stop during filming. As far as exposure manipulation is concerned, the motion picture camera is less versatile than a still camera, because the shutter speed must remain relative to the motor speed. The still camera, on the other hand, can be adjusted to accommodate the desired lens aperture. Most filmmakers get the lens aperture they want either by increasing or reducing the amount of light, or by choosing a film stock with the required emulsion speed.

One of the first concerns in photography is to have enough light to expose the film. Since the amount of light is regulated by the shutter and the lens aperture, one must often compensate for the other. Therefore, if the lens is stopped down (reducing the light to the film), the shutter speed has to be decreased (allowing more light to the film). If the lens aperture is more open (increasing the light) the shutter speed must be increased (decreasing the light). In addition to manipulating the amount of light to the film, both shutter and lens aperture are used by the filmmaker to gain image sharpness.

Motion pictures are really nothing more than a string of still pictures taken in extremely rapid succession. Each frame of film is an arrested moment in time, just as a single photograph is. We should add that the sharpness and clarity of each frame depends on how fast the action is relative to the shutter speed. Fast action and a slow shutter speed will produce a fuzzy frame, and the film, when projected, could appear blurred, depending on how severe the descrepancy is between shutter speed and the action. (We should point out that fuzziness in the action attributable to an inadequate shutter speed is much less noticeable when viewed projected than when seen as individual frames on a viewer.)

A good point to keep in mind, especially if you are manually controlling exposure, is to allow for a faster shutter speed when selecting an f/stop as you increase the frames per second. It may be helpful to know that when filming events such as horse racing or auto racing, a sharper image can be obtained by boosting the filming speed to 24 fps, instead of using the standard 18 fps, thus reaping the benefit of nearly double the shutter speed. The net result will be a barely noticeable slowed-down effect when projected at 18 fps. But each frame of picture (and the movie generally) will be sharper. Professionals customarily film fast-moving action at 24 fps in order to minimize blur. Be careful, however, not to use a faster fps *when panning with the camera*, because flicker becomes more noticeable as the result of the frames being sharper.

A good thing to have on your camera is a device that will enable you to wind back the film and reshoot it to create lap-dissolves (where one scene fades into another) or superimpositions (double exposures). In the past the device was usually a small crank that when inserted into the side of the camera and turned would wind back a portion of the already exposed film on to the feed spool. On many cameras now, it is automatic.

There is no trick to making at least double exposures with any Regular 8mm camera (and many larger-gauge professional cameras). With Regular 8 all you have to do is run the film through the camera twice. Since Regular 8 is on an open spool—and is double sprocketed—you can just keep flipping the film over, multiple exposing it as many times as you wish.

Lap-dissolving is another matter. In order to lap-dissolve you not only must be able to return part of the film to the feed spool, but also must be able to fade in and fade out. There are a number of Super 8 cameras now that have this feature.

The only Regular 8 camera able to make lap-dissolves is the Bolex, which was manufactured in several models. The small "P" and "K-1 and K-2" series were made in the early 1960s, as was the larger H8 Rex Bolex. These cameras came equipped with a "variable shutter" that allowed the shutter's pie-shaped opening to vary from wide open to closed. These models were probably the best 8mm cameras around, and still are if you don't mind shooting Regular 8—and if you can get one of these cameras second hand. These same cameras have the added great advantage of being able to film from 8 to 64 frames per second.

The film cartridge load of Super 8 cameras, however, will not return the film to the cartridge once it is exposed—at least, generally not more than ninety frames. In the face of this restriction, some camera manufacturers have included a wind-back device that will not wind the film back onto the cartridge spool but will stuff ninety frames or so of the exposed film back into the cartridge container. This is just enough film to provide for a moderate length lap-dissolve or a very short double exposure. Also, such cameras include a "fader" to help perform dissolves and fades. Both are handy conventional ways to smooth transitions between scenes.

All new cameras and most used ones feature what is known as "through the lens viewing," which is particularly valuable in close-up photography. Such a system often is an arrangement of mirrors and prisms that allows you to see what you are filming as the lens sees it. It has replaced the old, inferior viewfinder system, which is a separate entity from the lens and approximates only what is seen through the taking lens. Older cameras with viewfinders can be mounted with a Pan Cinor zoom lens that has a periscope viewer that allows you to see through the lens.

The eyepiece on a camera (the surface your eye rests against) should be adjusted to suit your eye before using the camera, especially after it has been used by someone else. Unless your camera manual suggests another method, set your lens focus ring on "infinity"; set your focal length at the highest number (or zoom all the way in); and, if possible, manually open the lens aperture to wide open. Next, take the camera out-of-doors and look through it at an object at infinity (a billboard, telephone pole, or tree about 100 feet away) and turn the eye-piece adjuster ring until the object you are viewing comes into sharp focus. These steps should correct the eyepiece for your vision.

Another feature on all new cameras is an automatic exposure meter. When it is working it is fairly reliable, but an exposure meter, built into the camera or not, can easily be thrown out of adjustment or broken. The only way to avoid possible malfunction is through a "manual override." Such a device will enable you to bypass the automatic meter and make adjustments and compensations as dictated by a hand-held meter, separate from the camera. It is always better to use a manual override whenever possible.

FILM FORMATS, RAW STOCKS, AND THEIR CHARACTERISTICS

The basic film gauges (film widths) in common use today are Regular 8 and Super 8mm, 16 and Super 16mm, 35mm, and 70mm. As each film size becomes larger, it doubles in size. For amateur use the gauge is Regular 8 and Super 8, though for instructional purposes Super 8 "print stock" is used to make reduction prints from larger-gauge films for cartridges in instructional machines that are used in libraries, doctors' and dentists' offices. For educational purposes (classroom films) 16 mm has been a standard and also is the gauge used by television news cameramen. The 35mm gauge is frequently used to make feature-length films, to film commercials, and often to shoot educational films (later reduced to 16mm projection prints).

Film Gauges

Several considerations govern the choice of film size. Primary among them is how the film is to be shown. If the projection distance is to be relatively short—the length of an average living-room or small classroom—then Super 8mm would suffice. The larger the projected image, the greater is the loss in picture quality. To overcome this problem, filmmakers go to a larger film format, which reduces this breakdown of the image. An auditorium would require 16mm, a theater 35mm, and a drive-in theater might necessitate 70mm. Films for television (other than newsfilm), including commercials, are generally shot in 35mm and reduced to

16mm, thus minimizing graininess and heightening sharpness. The same effect (achieving better picture quality) can be obtained by using a large projection format of, say, 35mm or 70mm and projecting it from a relatively short distance to a medium-size screen.

The choice of film gauges between 16mm and 35mm often boils down to the type of camera needed for the job. Until recently, the only easily portable lightweight field cameras were the 16mm Bolex, Arriflex, and Eclair. Now, many of these companies and a few others are making lightweight 35mm versions. In fact, there are presently so many options open to the filmmaker with respect to the gauge equipment available that, if he is a professional, he must decide on the basis of the market, or markets, for the film—and how much his film budget will allow—which gauge to choose. (Doubling the gauge often doubles the cost.)

The cost of film, laboratory processing, special effects, and printing all can effect the choice of film gauge. Though Super 8 has sufficient projectability for the filmmaker's non-professional needs, he must turn to 16mm to secure professional quality printing, special effects, and application of the sound track. Though camera manufacturers are constantly producing more versatile equipment, a satisfactory blend of technology and standardization is not expected till around 1980, perhaps even later. In spite of these difficulties, Super 8 is rapidly coming into its own and today it is the best hope for the average independent, non-professional filmmaker who wishes to explore film as a creative medium.

Many beginners want to know what "Super" means in Super 8 and Super 16. In both instances there is no change in actual *film size*. The difference between Regular 8 and Regular 16 and Super 8mm and Super 16mm involves a change in format that increases *picture size*. The sprocket holes are made smaller, spaced farther apart, and moved closer to the edge of the film, thus enlarging the picture area by one-third. This improves projectability. (Super 16 is used primarily when the picture original is to be enlarged, blown up to 35mm.)

Chemical Composition

The chemical composition of film stock is a clear, cellulose acetate base that has been coated with an emulsion of light-sensitive silver halides (compounds such as silver chloride, bromide and iodine) that create various colors. The emulsion's chemicals perform in a way similar to the anthocyanins found in certain leaves, which, when responding to light, produce brilliant red and purple colors. We look forward to this display in the fall when the autumn leaves turn. And almost all succulent plants will turn to vivid hues of yellow, red, purple, and blue when moved from shade or indirect sunlight to bright, direct sunlight.

The emulsion side of the film is generally dull, and the base side is shiny. Those filmmakers who use tape (or dry) splices in editing need not be so concerned over which side is which as those who are using wet splices (covered later in the section "Organizing and Splicing the Footage," Chapter V). When using tape splices, the Super 8 filmmaker need only look to see if the picture is going in the same direction, and line up the sprocket holes on the same side.

Films are made with different emulsion speeds to accommodate various needs. A fast film (with a high ASA Rating) is good for use under low-light conditions and thus is preferred by news cameramen and documentary filmmakers. Fast film, however, will often yield a "grainy effect" in which the projected image will appear to be made up of minuscule grains of sand. As a rule, the size of the grain is larger and more noticeable in fast film stocks than in slow ones. Not only is the grain more noticeable in a faster film, but there is a reduction in sharpness (resolution) of the image, as well as loss of contrast. For obtaining the best quality (low grain, high resolution, and good contrast), one would use a slower, moderately fast film whenever possible (when light conditions will permit).

For most purposes the best film today is manufactured by Eastman Kodak, chiefly because the controls used both in making and in processing the film are better than with other film makes. Color rendering, of course, is another matter and involves personal preference. Unlike European or Japanese film, Kodak film tends to reflect brighter, more intense colors. It has been theorized that cold-climate countries make color film stock that is more muted, and a bit heavier on the blue side, because of their distance from the equator, and that this type of rendering is more accurate to the overall natural perception of the inhabitants of those regions—truer to the way they "see."

Most color film stocks are made in an "indoor" and "outdoor" version to afford the best color balance. (A recent exception to this, however, is the Super 8, Kodak Ektachrome 160 Type G which can be used in any subdued light—outdoor or indoor—*without a filter.*) Tungsten light (artificial light) has different color properties from sunlight and is predominantly red, whereas sunlight is mainly bluish.Therefore, film designed to be used with photoflood bulbs or other artificial illumination will have an emulsion that is compensated with bluish rendering. By the same token, film designed to be used in predominantly blue sunlight will be compensated with a heavy reddish rendering.

If the tungsten (indoor film) is used out-of-doors in the sunlight, then a reddish (salmon colored) filter must be used to balance its heavy blue properties. All recent Super 8 cameras have a built-in filter to perform this conversion. In addition, there is a filter that is used to convert outdoor film to indoor use (which is bluish). It is used only with films other than Super 8, since the camera industry has agreed to accept one method of conversion, from indoor to outdoor, as the simplest standard for popular use.

Color Temperature

The color properties of light—whether bluish or reddish—are described in terms of *color temperature.* Just as hot and cold temperatures are measured in Fahrenheit degrees, so the blue and red properties of light are measured in Kelvin degrees. The bluer the light, the higher the Kelvin; the redder the light, the lower the Kelvin. Sunlight has a very high Kelvin rating, something on the order of 6,000 degrees at high noon. On the other hand, tungsten light, emitted from bulbs, has a much lower Kelvin, around 3,000 degrees or below.

As mentioned earlier, color film is balanced for the type of light recommended for use with it. Most Ektachrome film is balanced for use with 3,200-degree Kelvin bulbs. Kodachrome is balanced for 3,400-degree Kelvin light. Of course, the color temperature of light has no effect on black-and-white film.

Kodachrome and Ektachrome films have different characteristics. Kodachrome is made with a low ASA Rating (indoor 40, outdoor 25), and is a medium- to fine-grain film. However, it is a high-contrast film, which is especially good for rendering blacks and whites. It has a "red saturated" emulsion, which means that it is inclined to deliver red hues with purity and brilliance. Flesh tones are particularly beautiful in this film. Because it is a high-contrast film, it yields little detail in shadows, which is a drawback for some purposes.

Ektachrome now comes in several speeds, which offers the filmmaker a wide range of use under a variety of lighting conditions. Ektachrome 7241 and 7242, and other Ektachrome films, tend to be lower in contrast than Kodachrome—with off-whites and gray-blacks—but sharply define detail in shadows. These films tend to give good yellow and green rendition, but less intense red. Flesh tones are cooler.

Ektachrome 160 (and its companion, Ektachrome 40) deserves special mention, because it was especially developed with the popular market in mind. The 160 is a very fast film that enables the home moviemaker to shoot without special lights and with little of the expected color imbalance that comes with using unbalanced tungsten light from household bulbs.

When using these films (including black and white), it is important to first assess the conditions under which you will be filming, together with the overall intention of your film. For example, if the color rendition pleases you, and all other things are equal, Kodachrome will serve most needs of the filmmaker, even to interior filming with natural light. Ektachrome 40 will do just exactly the same thing. However, neither of these films is *best* for filming with natural light; neither is as good as the faster Ektachromes. The faster films, on the other hand, can be used only with difficulty under very bright light conditions—at the beach or in desert surroundings.

Black and white films, though not offering the illusion of depth and visual variety through color, are primarily desirable for factual shooting in which color would be distracting, or if the film is intended to be visually stark.

chapter 2

Looking at the Subject

LIGHTING

Lighting Hardware

For the beginner who, for one reason or another, does not want to invest a considerable sum of money in lighting, photoflood bulbs may be the answer. These are high-wattage bulbs balanced for color filming and have a color temperature of 3,200 K, or 3,400 K.

If you intend to invest in only a few lights, then it would be advisable to get at least 750-watt bulbs. When buying them you must designate whether you want 3,200 K bulbs for filming with Ektachrome or 3,400 K for Kodachrome. (Either bulbs are suitable for filming with black and white.)

Next, you must get sockets and reflectors. The most commonly used unit is a reflector that screws onto a socket, which connects to a clamp. The clamp is useful because it will attach to book cases, backs of chairs, doorknobs, etc. There are a few drawbacks to the photoflood as a light source. It has a relatively short life. As it starts to burn out the color balance drops off and it begins to emit a redder light (and this fact is not generally noticed by the filmmaker). The whole unit heats up, making the standard socket insulation inadequate, if not dangerous. In order to overcome these problems, it is best not to use the bulbs beyond their stated life (unless shooting black and white) and to use a *ceramic* clamp-on socket in place of the metal, paper-insulated one available in hardware or electrical supply stores.

Similar to the photofloods just described are the R40 photo-reflector bulbs used in connection with Lowell-Light hardware. The basic unit is a porcelain socket, swivel-mounted on a small metal plate that is notched to hang on a nail or door edge. It is frequently used with gaffer's tape, which is super strong and can be obtained at a camera rental agency such as the nationwide F&B CECO (Camera Equipment Co.). The cost for each unit and bulb is comparatively little.

A more expensive, but generally better, solution to lighting is the quartz-halogen lamp. Lightweight inexpensive units that sell for around $30 each and include bulbs, stands, and reflectors, ranging from 350 watts to 750 watts, are made by Smith Victor and by Hervic.

Heavier-duty and higher-wattage quartz lights used by many professionals are made by Colortran, Mole-Richardson, and Lowell-Quartz. In addition to providing more illumination, the lights can be obtained with "focusing heads" that allow a narrow or broad beam of light to be directed by moving a lever. These are highly portable, easy to set up, quite durable, and sell in the neighborhood of $135 for the stand, lamp-housing, and bulb.

For artificial light outdoors, a battery-powered light of the type made by Frizzolini (of New Jersey) can be used. These can be rented—and incidentally, are called "Frizzies."

Placement of Lights

Do not use a light mounted on a camera *unless* circumstances prevent doing otherwise. (These may include weddings, christenings, or bar mitzvahs.) One light is seldom sufficient to ensure a good result, especially when fixed on the camera. A set-up of this kind frequently produces "hot spots" that cause washed-out areas in the picture, harsh shadows, and reduction in picture depth.

A workable lighting set-up (see insert) requires a minimum of three lights. One is a *key light* (using a medium reflector), the major source of light, located near the camera lens. A *fill light*, located on the other side of the camera (using a broader reflector), lightens shadows and provides depth and detail. Finally, a *background light*, directed toward walls or other background areas, adds depth to the scene.

Types of Lighting

The lighting formula just described is truly basic, but it can serve for an infinite number of variations. Many professionals who must light with an artistic eye work with *back lighting* as well. Back lighting is directed toward the camera lens, silhouetting the subject and rimming it in a halo of light. *Cross-lighting* creates drama and interest by illuminating only half the subject. Still other types of lighting include *low key lighting*, whereby only special points of interest are illuminated. The effect it creates is somber and suspenseful, and it was a very popular lighting style in good theatrical films made during the 1940s. *High key lighting* uses overall illumination, and because it is especially suitable for comedy, is utilized for family television programs and talk shows. Many instructional and informational films also employ this technique, which affords peak visibility of the scene's components, demonstration models, etc. In *lighting for faces*, a soft, high-placed key light 45 degrees to the side of the camera, and a bright "kicker" light from behind and to the opposite side of the head, produces a pleasant modeling effect. (A kicker light is a small spotlight.) Kicker, or *rim lights*, are often used alone to outline the subject's form for a night effect and are usually placed to the left and right of the subject's head and above. To obtain *realistic lighting*, key lights should be placed so that illumination appears to be emanating from the direction of the windows, lamps, or other available light sources that are understood by the viewer to be present in the scene.

But to really learn lighting you should experiment with it. True professionals *light by eye*, and though this technique can be discouraging to the beginner because of technical slip-ups, the sooner one casts aside all aids and begins to *see* and interpret lighting effects, and lighting values, the better. Lighting by eye will help you to avoid becoming dependent on the light meter. The meter's chief function is to give a reading of the main light (key light), whereas the fill light, back light, and so on, are interpreted through the use of a contrast glass (a monocle used in evaluating contrast and shadows). But the non-professional can develop a feeling for lighting values, even without a contrast glass.

To get your eye used to working with light, it might be useful to film this experiment. Place your subject in a chair with your camera on a tripod directly in front of the subject. Frame the subject's face in the lens. While the camera is running, aim a single hand-held light close to the subject's head and walk slowly around him, at the same time raising and lowering the light, coming close with it, and moving away.

Viewing this filmed experiment should help you to become more aware of the brightness and shadow effects a main light source can create—and perhaps more important, the function of the key light in setting the mood for the entire scene. The key light is like the mainsail of a ship; all other lights are for "tack," modulation, and emphasis.

Lighting Ratio and Exposure Meters

Lighting ratio is the comparative brightness of the various lights used. The key light has a relative brightness to the fill light, and this difference is expressed in f/stops, which are indicated by an exposure meter reading. Kodak has established a light ratio (fill to key) for its color films, the optimum being 1:2 or 1:3, but not greater than 1:4. A ratio of 1:2, for instance, means that the key light is one f/stop brighter than the fill light.

For precise technical results, the conscientious filmmaker may take meter readings of each light to determine its brightness value relative to the other lights. However, in time, it is best to learn to judge light values by eye.

Color film affords more contrast than black-and-white in that it picks up and accurately reproduces a narrower range of lights and darks. Therefore, when using color film it is good to keep all lights within mid-range of brightness. In other words, eliminate hot spots (overly bright areas) and black shadows devoid of detail.

It is a good idea for any serious filmmaker to obtain a light meter—even if his camera is equipped with a reliable internal meter—if for no other reason than the higher accuracy it affords.

There are many meters on the market, but several have proven themselves over the years—the Weston, Lunasix (now called Luna-pro), Spectra and the Pentax Spot Meter. Both the Weston and Lunasix are dual *incident* and *reflected* light meters. The Spectra is largely used for measuring incident light, along with the Pantax Spot Meter, which is used mainly for measuring reflected light. For most purposes, even professional work, the Lunasix (Luna-pro) is quite adequate for the above-mentioned dual functions. It has the advantage of being sensitive to low-light conditions because it is battery powered, and it will read an area of the subject from 30 degrees or so (down to about 7 degrees with a spot-reading attachment). The Spectra and Spot Meter are for certain specialized uses. Space, here, will not permit a description of their function and uses. There are plenty of books already available that offer a thorough run-down on them (see list at end of text).

If you have a dual incident and reflected light meter, you must decide whether you are going to read source (incident) light or bounce (reflected) light. Most professionals prefer to take an incident reading first, because it averages *in the meter* the amount of illumination received by the camera lens. For most conditions a single incident reading would be reliable. It is especially useful, however, if the subject cannot be physically reached to take a reflected reading, as when filming from a moving vehicle or shooting a subject from a long distance (like across a river). The correct method of reading incident light is to hold the meter in front of the subject and aim it toward the camera lens.

If there is a sharp contrast between compositional elements in the same picture, such as filming in the shade of a tree surrounded by sunlight or filming two or more people with contrasting skin tones or while wearing very light and dark clothing, a reflected light reading of each contrasting element should be taken separately and averaged. A reflected reading would also be in order if there were very little available light—say from a candle—or an excessive amount of light—say at the beach or in the desert. Just remember that the reflected light meter is used either for measuring extremes in lighting contrast or as a method of checking and refining the evaluation taken from the incident reading. For greatest accuracy, it is best to use both methods, though such precision is seldom necessary. In taking a reflected light reading, aim the meter at the subject, holding it a few inches away and taking care not to read your own shadow.

To operate the meter, adjust the ASA scale to correspond to the scale of the film you are using (if Ektachrome 160, then set it at 160); take a reading and adjust the appropriate dial to correspond to the number at which the meter needle points; look on the dial for the shutter speed you are using (1/35 of a second if you are filming at 18 fps), and adjacent to it you will find the correct f/stop.

After having gotten the correct f/stop, you can do one of several things. (1) If you are content with the aperture opening the f/stop affords, you will set your camera accordingly (if you have manual control over the camera's internal meter) and begin filming. (2) If you need a smaller aperture for greater depth of field, you may wish to bring the lights closer to your subject, or simply add more lights. (3) You may wish to use the meter reading to check the f/stop against the camera meter reading. Such a comparison will reveal whether the camera's internal meter is in working order, or it may make the camera's reading more accurate.

Filming with Unbalanced Light

Until recently, filming with household bulbs as a light source would have been unthinkable because of their low light output and because they are unbalanced for color filming (producing a reddish cast over the entire scene). However, the recently marketed Ektachrome 160 to a great extent overcomes those drawbacks. It can be used with ordinary unbalanced bulbs, and it is possible to film with fluorescent light without getting as much of a cool, bluish cast as one would expect.

Even with a special film of this sort, using unbalanced light is an unsure proposition at best. Whenever a situation like this arises it is always a good idea to run tests before committing a good deal of money and time to a project. Often your own inventiveness is the only way out of a lighting problem in which light sources are mixed, such as part shade and part sunlight, part fluorescent light and household bulbs; or window light mixed with balanced light. In some instances a variety of filters may be tried, and in other cases predominantly reddish or bluish lights can be utilized to achieve balance. The success you get, finally, will depend on the accuracy of your tests—and your judgment.

Natural Lighting—Out-of-Doors

Two main problems crop up when using available light from the sun—harsh, sharp shadows created by the bright sunlight, and a flat undramatic lighting created by shade or overcast sky. Deep shadows created by bright sunlight can be filled in with light from a reflector of some sort, or with battery-powered lights. Reflectors can easily be made by covering large sheets of cardboard with household aluminum foil. Battery lights, though expensive, can be cheaply rented from a professional film equipment rental agency. Light from an overcast sky, or shade, can be livened-up with battery-powered lights.

Light, and the shadows it creates, should be controlled by the filmmaker as much as any other aspect of filmmaking. In the case of sunlight, where shadows—filled in or not—tend to have sharp lines, it may be desirable to use some kind of diffuser to soften them. A sheer piece of nylon stretched over a frame and held in the path of the sun will do it. One should keep in mind that devices for controlling light are best used creatively, for *selection* and *emphasis,* and that there is not just one "most pleasing" and "professional" approach to all filming. You may wish to preserve harsh shadows for the effect you want, or you may wish to eliminate them completely.

Another problem sometimes encountered is *too much sunlight.* If you are shooting in very bright sunlight with a film that has a high ASA rating (a fast film), you will need a *neutral density filter* to withhold a certain amount of light from the film. The filter is made with several values: $\frac{1}{2}$ f/stop, 1 f/stop, $1\frac{1}{2}$ f/stops, 2 f/stops, etc. However, one filter with a value of either $1\frac{1}{2}$ or 2 f/stops should be adequate for most uses. When filming with Ektachrome 160, it is best to take one of these filters along with you.

There are all kinds of filters used in filmmaking, but I would like to stress that much if not most filming by the non-professional can be done successfully without them. A *skylight* filter is good to help eliminate haze, and a *polarizing* filter is useful to cut down light glare from water or from the chrome on car bumpers. *Correction* filters, like the salmon-colored one (already built into your camera if you own a Super 8), are designed to change the color temperature of the light entering the camera. Finally, *color compensating* filters are used in the laboratory for printing color film. These filters come in primary and secondary colors in varying densities, the purpose of which is to correct initial color imbalance in the color "original."

Effects of Lighting

As has been mentioned, lighting allows the filmmaker to control what is to be seen, and how it is to be seen. It helps to establish the overall intentionality of the film. With more illumination, more can be seen—a simple but important point. And the more light, the more depth of field is possible with more in focus. (Both shallow and deep focus can be used as creative devices, as discussed in the next section.)

Though depth of field is an important selective device, the angle and positioning of the lights is another. The simple experiment previously described, in which the light is moved around a stationary subject, should clearly indicate how the angle and positioning of illumination directs our attention and creates mood.

Natural indoor lighting, generally from a window or skylight, can produce a feeling of intimacy, softness, and poetic lyricism. Though light of this type is bluish—off color—it can be justified by the inclusion of sunlight, often entering a room as orange "shafts" or "patches" that mix with the blue and provide an interesting color contrast.

Using colored lights is another way of achieving emphasis and mood. Colored lights mixed with color-balanced lights can be effective in bringing up warm skin tones (using red), or in cooling them down (using blue). Colored lights by themselves provide a fascinating opportunity for expressionistic approaches, especially when filming dance.

SEEING WITHIN THE RECTANGLE

Two major tenets of creative cinematography (and still photography) are *selection* and *emphasis*. The filmmaker selects the subject to be filmed and *how* it is to be filmed. And through selection he *transforms* the subject, producing *emphasis*. The subject is recorded on film in a transformed state, which becomes *the image*. The goal of the serious filmmaker is to understand and implement his transforming tools in order to create effective images.

So far I have discussed the working "machinery" of filmmaking —becoming acquainted with the camera, choosing film stock, and lighting, which are but preparations for even more important selective acts. *Seeing within the rectangle* is one of these acts.

To many people, viewing through the camera's rectangular window is simplistic and would seem to warrant little explanation. Yet the attitude the filmmaker adopts toward it can make the difference between a world for the viewer that is *seen* and one that is not, an image that is alive and experienced and one that is "so what."

In order to establish a method of seeing, one must first divorce himself from the notion that he is viewing only a piece of the world through the rectangle. A good attitude to adopt would be, "The world does not exist until it enters the frame!" Though in fact the rectangle is a window, one should not think of it as such. Ideally, the filmmaker should limit his awareness of things going on outside the frame, the way one thinks of the space in a painting or still photograph. The reason for this self-induced illusion (that the frame's contents is all there is) is to sensitize the filmmaker's awareness of the *visual content* in the frame and to exclude the *psychological content* existing outside the frame. When one sees through the rectangle this way, it is possible to almost magically transform the subject and create an image.

Cinematic and Theatrical Presence

What the filmmaker strives for, most importantly, is the creation of a *cinematic presence* from the *theatrical presence* of everyday reality. It is the difference between simply making a filmed record of an event, and making *a film* of it. Whenever the transforming tools of filmmaking are used, consciously and intentionally, cinematic presence can be created.

To better grasp the idea, let us say that everything that takes place around us, seen in our three-dimensional, 180-degree, wrap-around vision and accompanied by multiphonic, never-ceasing sound, has theatrical presence. It is a rudimentary form of theater, and we are both participants in it and spectators of it.

Things or people that have a high degree of uniformity in real life, that look and act the same, have an especially strong theatrical presence—Little League baseball players, policemen, bankers in business suits, animals, surfers, all sports in which the range of expressive activity is limited to uniform gestures—boating, skiing, hang-gliding, skating, etc. I have a pet name for these things. I call them "intractable subjects," because it takes a special effort to shape them, to inflect them, to overcome the cliché.

Cinematic presence occurs when theatrical subjects (nearly all subjects) are filmed using cinematic devices to create an image, interpret the subject, rather than simply to imitate it.

To illustrate this point—almost everyone at one time or other has seen a film of/and about sculpture. It matters not whether the sculpture is African, seventeenth-century Italian, or Pre-Columbian; it happens that sculpture is one of the intractable subjects I have just described. It is one of the most extreme types of theatrical subjects imaginable, partly because it is designed to exist in space, to be experienced in space, and was created specifically as a controlled theatrical experience (as differentiated from a "freer" theater, as in group therapy, swingers' parties, the classroom, and on the street). Automatically, sculpture becomes a difficult subject, because film is a two-dimensional medium. And making it doubly difficult as a subject is sculpture's static quality in terms of *actual* motion.

How, then, is sculpture to be transformed from a theatrical to a cinematic state? Merely filming it will not suffice. As you have noticed, in the best of films about sculpture, at least several standard cinematic devices are used. The subject is often placed on a revolving pedestal so that it can be turned, allowing it to be seen from all sides. It is lighted so that the three-dimensionality, the depth of the piece, will be seen and its mood imitated. As the subject turns, the camera stationed at a high, medium, or low position will zoom in on it, calling attention to details; or it may zoom out from a small, visually poignant area to reveal the harmonious totality of the piece. The camera itself may move in relation to the revolving sculpture—panning vertically—or lights may be manipulated to subtly alter the intensity and angle of shadows. These are but a few basic ways by which cinematic transformation can be brought about.

The Rectangle

Seldom recognized is the mysterious potency of the rectangle itself. It could be considered the parent of practically all that we perceive as the cinematic experience. Its chief power is in permitting or denying the viewer access to the subject. It is this supreme control over what is seen that should be recognized by the filmmaker as his primary selecting device for emphasis and transformation.

The edges (or sides) of the rectangle can be thought of as "magic" delineations that contain the subject—similar to the illusionistic space of the theater stage. This arbitrary sense of containment can be made to seem "real" if the filmmaker creates his visual world within it. This approach is opposite to that of the filmmaker who uses the rectangle to casually, unintentionally, obtain a "slice of life." The filmmaker who constructs within the rectangle *includes only intended visual material,* primarily by limiting the view only to that which he wants to be seen by the simple act of positioning or moving the camera.

Furthermore, since all of what is included in the rectangle is important, whatever enters or leaves the frame is equally important. Because the sides of the frame are in fact doors to the space, *the dividing lines between what is seen and what isn't becomes critical.*

In *The Servant,* Joseph Losey amply uses the picture frame throughout, frequently directing his camera to allow the performers to hover near the frame's edges, rather than centering them. There is no doubt but what their near proximity to the frame's edges suggest the possibility of a sudden exit, creating a feeling of "cat and mouse," much like the feeling generated by the perverse characters themselves.

Practically everyone has noticed how extremely sensitive a cat can be to the sudden appearance or disappearance of an object. It loves to play hide and seek. In a sense, the rectangle, by arbitrarily limiting what we see, sensitizes us in much the same way, so that we become extremely, visually attuned to entrances and exits from the space, aware of what is included and what is not. The ordinary subject that may hold only passing interest for us as an uncontrolled theatrical event, when filmed, selected by the rectangle, can be heightened in importance because it is ordered within the space. The rectangle, then, governs all events and movement that take place within it.

Subject Size: Close-ups and Long Shots

Subject size is perhaps the first thing we notice when we look through the camera lens and is in direct relation to the rectangular space. In film, the subject size is referred to as a close-up, medium, or long shot.

How one defines a close-up is relative to two things: the subject size, and the overall size of all the subjects as a matter of style throughout any given film. Generally speaking, if the subject pretty much fills the picture frame, or comes in close proximity to the frame's top and bottom edges, it could be regarded as a close-up.

However, with extremely large and extremely small subjects, this definition can be modified—as in the case of an insect in contrast to a human. A close-up of a fly may fill only half the frame, whereas a close-up of a person may be regarded as anything from waist high to a full-face shot. A close-up of a large building, for example, may feature only details—a few windows, a door, and so forth.

The style of a film can dictate the "closeness" of a close-up. Most theatrical films made for large screens seldom portray people closer than from the shoulders up, and the bulk are medium shots no closer than waist-high. Films made for television, on the other hand, are replete with close-ups of the full face, because of the smallness of the viewing screen. Expressionistic films made by independent, nonprofessional filmmakers and students, get even closer to the subject, often for poetic, artistic emphasis. In such films it is not unusual for a person's eye, mouth, or other details of the body, such as pores or the navel, to fill the screen.

Close-ups, whether in theatrical films, televison, or avant-garde films, tend to create an immediacy of feeling. The sheer unfamiliarity of subject size can generate a feeling of awe and curiosity, resulting in greater viewer involvement.

As the size of the subject is made larger, its context is reduced, and by virtue of this, its meaning is transformed. The less associative visual material that accompanies the subject, the more *generally defined* it becomes. In generalizing the subject's meaning it becomes more ambiguous, and hence freer to contain a multiplicity of meanings and feelings. Thus, the face of a person which fills the frame, minus the background—perhaps a backyard—can easily be "placed" in a different context in the editing—in the context of a beach scene if desired. In this case, when the surrounding background is eliminated through the close-up, it frees the subject from associative visual material, such as trees, houses, other people, and so forth. The same technique can be applied to close-ups of a face, where only the mouth, nose or eyes are included in the frame. Minus associations of gender and age, the facial features tend to become generalized or symbolic. Instead of a teenage girl's eye, what we see becomes simply a human eye.

Because of this quality of "disembodiment," the close-up can provide, in editing, what is known as a *cutaway*. The cutaway (discussed in later sections on editing) is frequently a detail of a scene, sometimes a close-up, which allows the editor to compress time by cutting away from the main action and returning to it at a later time, leaving out many unnecessary parts of the action.

Close-ups call attention to details, for clarity and emphasis. Documentaries, especially, which depend on the accurate visual conveyance of detail often relating to complicated activities— sports, crafts, science, etc.—use the close-up for descriptive purposes. Point of view is frequently established in social documentaries through the inclusion of selected details provided by close-ups. A character's emotional response in the form of reaction shots is another use of the close-up.

Close-ups can have a certain shock value—punctuate a scene, or provide a visual change of pace. Used in this manner, the close-up is similar to *rhetorical emphasis* in writing, notably the uppercasing or italicizing of selected words.

There are several optical means used to achieve close-ups; and because there is a choice, some confusion may ensue. One method uses the telephoto lens, which allows the close-up to be obtained from a long distance. By standing back from his subject, the filmmaker can unobtrusively get "tight" shots—often used (as well as over-used) to film children candidly, or in any situation where the presence of the camera, if noticed by the subject, could become an obstacle to filming. Other uses of the telephoto close-up occur when the subject is "out-of-reach" of the camera—where physical closeness between filmmaker and subject is prevented—or in a case where the filmmaker wishes to avoid getting in the way of his own light.

But there are drawbacks to using the telephoto for close-ups. One gets shallow depth of field; there is some light loss in the optics; there are spatial and linear distortions; and, perhaps most objectionably, the shaky or jiggling camera is vastly accentuated. If one does use the telephoto for close-ups, it is recommended that filming be done under bright light conditions, and that a camera brace or tripod be used.

Another common method of shooting close-ups is simply to get as near to the subject as possible. In this case, either the wide angle or normal part of the lens is used (thus minimizing camera movement). But with this procedure, a very large subject size is not possible. If subject size is insufficient, then a close-up attachment must be obtained (called a plus diopter)—usually one or more of a set of auxiliary lenses obtainable from most camera stores for about $15. These lenses attach to the front of the zoom lens and can be used individually or in groups of two or three, giving greater or less magnification.

Many people employ diopters while using the longest focal length part of the zoom. This slightly magnifies the image already provided by the zoom (by allowing closer proximity to the subject), but at the same time it proportionally increases problems with depth of field, light loss, shaking camera, and so forth. Generally, it is much better to use the diopters on the normal part of the lens, while physically moving closer to the subject.

The "macro-zoom" is another way of obtaining close-ups. (Unlike the plus diopter the macrozoom close-up capability does not degrade lens quality because it is integrated into the lens itself.) The macrozoom necessitates getting extremely close to the subject —perhaps only a few inches. Though this can produce a spectacularly large subject size, it has the gross disadvantage of extreme light loss through the complex optics—as well as the possibility of blocking the light on the subject while filming, because of the close proximity. Another difficulty arises from accentuated camera shakiness (the same problem as with the telephoto). But these difficulties can be overcome with some equipment and a little planning.

The chief advantage of the macro-close-up is in the filmmaker's ability to select and manipulate very small details of the subject, or to take a tiny subject, such as an ant, and enlarge it to fill the screen. Macrophotography is most useful in filming for scientific detail, or in transforming natural reality for artistic purposes.

Let's turn now to the *long shot.* It is opposite to the close-up in many ways. For example, control over what is seen in the rectangle is largely dependent upon the subject. Unlike the close-up, where all the control of the shot is in the camera, the long shot, because of the broad view, depends on the keenness of the subject's identifiable qualities.

To better illustrate this point, let us examine a working formula for the structural composition of the long shot. First, the subject, that may be a person, must be far away from the camera, but not so far away that he "loses identity." If the subject is a woman, she should be identifiable as such—and if she's a particular woman, it should be clear who she is. Next, the surrounding should not detract from nor obscure her identity. People, automobiles, children, things in motion—anything which might visually confuse the main subject with the surrounding—should be avoided. For the most effective long shot, the surrounding should contribute to the mood of the shot yet be somewhat neutral. Shore lines, rolling hills, desert dunes (*Lawrence of Arabia*), cliffs, farmlands, fields, the ocean, sky: all have the right kind of character and neutrality. In addition, the subject should contrast with the setting in color and density—a lone, bright yellow tractor in a wheat field, a red kite against the sky. If the subject is a person, sometimes a brightly colored hat or scarf will do the trick. The point is that the subject should be easily identified. Color accent can do this, and it may also be compositionally pleasing.

Along with the more obvious benefit of establishing geographical setting, creation of mood is one of the chief attributes of the long shot. The emotional feeling generated by this kind of shot depends, of course, upon its context in the edited film. Generally, one could say that the mood is meditative, calm, "intimate." Since shots like this are often dominated by nature, a feeling of oneness with nature combined with an awe of its geographic scale tends to create, in the viewer, a mental state of resolved paradox. Because long shots do lend themselves well to showing off natural locations, they are used frequently in travelogues and documentaries (*Endless Summer*) or story films (especially in some of David Lean's films such as *Ryan's Daughter*) where landscape contributes meaningfully to the story.

When one seeks a feeling of subject smallness in comparison to the largeness of a setting, use of the wide angle part of the zoom lens is recommended. In addition, movement by either subject or camera can be a significant contribution to this type of shot. The camera can pan close to the subject; and if the camera is stationary, a zoom from close-up to long shot, or vice versa, can be effective. The subject could be walking, riding a horse, or water skiing: If the subject is the only thing moving, it easily stands out in the surroundings.

The "panoramic" type of long shot is self-explanatory. It is a shot from a long distance of a city, mountains, or an ocean in which the main purpose is to convey a general impression of what is there. My only suggestions about using this device are to sharpen your eye for what is interesting when composing your shot, and to use a tripod if there is an extensive pan involved.

Using Depth of Field for Emphasis

"That part of the picture area, in front of and behind the subject focused on, which remains in acceptable sharp focus" is known as depth of field. Because it is one of the factors in cinematography which controls what is seen, it is an important tool for selecting and emphasizing the filmed subject.

Until a few decades ago, the art of motion pictures in America had striven for absolute clarity and sharpness of detail in commercial films intended for the public. This trend came to be known generally as the "deep focus school," most prevalent in the first quarter of the century, and again in the 1940s and evidenced in the work of such directors as D. W. Griffith, and later, John Ford and Orson Welles. The reasons behind using maximum focus came about, in part, because of an overall movement toward greater realism. The camera served as a recording mechanism as opposed to a transforming one. In the interests of competing with the novel as an art form on the one hand, and in trying to create more believable realism for the escape-seeking public on the other, it became desirable to cast the camera in the role of invisible documentarian. In keeping with this approach, any deviation from the way we would see in actuality, or reality, was shunned. (Also in the interest of realism, the subject (actor) before the camera was kept in the center of the picture in order to avoid any emphatic suggestion of artificial framing by the edges of the rectangular frame.)

Deep focus (maximum depth of field) is most beneficial as a preserver of realism. For this reason it is especially effective in documentary filming, or at any time when the subject itself, rather than the camera, becomes the main source of artistic emphasis. Here, the camera's chief function may be that of recorder rather than interpreter, especially where natural settings have such an overwhelming expressive quality in themselves—as with mountains, jungles, the desert, the ocean—and particularly when the settings for a film—the costumes, props, and sets—are complex and lavish.

Greatest depth of field can be achieved by using an extreme wide-angle lens and adjusting it to the smallest aperture. In order to obtain such a small lens aperture, the filmmaker must either be using a "fast" film, or he must be filming under bright light conditions.

Where deep focus allows the subject, or performer, to control emphasis (as in the case of the long shot), *shallow focus* is strictly a camera-oriented method of selection and expression. By controlling depth of field, and setting up a *plane of focus,* irrelevant or distracting details in a scene can be eliminated—or at least de-emphasized—

while leaving only main points of interest in sharp focus. This technique is coming into wider use in American films, especially in television ads, although it has been an expressive device used in foreign films for some time.

Shallow focus is best achieved by using an extreme telephoto lens, with the largest aperture (smallest numerical f/stop). A large aperture is obtained through the use of a slow film (having a small ASA rating) or by filming under low light conditions.

Camera Position

A problem plaguing nearly all beginning filmmakers is that of not being able to view the subject expressively. In a general way, this problem involves all ways of seeing through the rectangle. However, one specific way to solve the problem is through *camera position*.

Filming a subject from a variety of angles—low and high, back, sides, and front—is not the way we see things in the everyday sense. When we see realistically, the subject is usually viewed *frontally*; and this frontality is frequently an arbitrary matter, determined largely by the way people are used to viewing. Thus, the front of a table becomes, in reality, its top. And when filming what is on a table, we usually aim the camera downward. Seldom does one stop to think that objects on a table can be filmed from the side, shooting along the table's surface. People, for example, are usually filmed from the front, face view, ready to engage the eyes; occasionally, however, they are seen from the side, and even more rarely, from the rear, or from above or below the face. In using only conventional angles the filmmaker's range of expressive power is needlessly limited. The camera can offer new ways of seeing things, not only by showing us a freshly structured image but by inflecting its meaning in a different way.

Before or during filming, as many angles as possible should be considered for their expressive potential, whether or not they seem appropriate at the time. Yet it is also important to be aware of the pitfall of over-intellectualizing before filming, of making judgments before actually experiencing the angle of view in the rectangle. One can never exactly anticipate circumstances, vis-à-vis lighting, subject, setting, and so forth, until the visual event is registered and experienced through the camera lens.

Two of the most frequently used camera positions are *camera* point of view, and *subject* point of view. The camera view sees omnisciently—whatever and from whatever it chooses. Such a point of view, understandably, allows the greatest freedom for interpretation, for it implies that the filmmaker (acting in the audience's place) is selecting the subject and how it is to be seen, thus putting him at liberty to emphasize what he wishes. The omniscient camera is free to interpret realistically too; and by this token it is found in all kinds of films, frequently mixed with the more restricting technique of subject point of view.

Subject view means that the camera sees as the subject would see—literally from his view—so that it is the subject who directs what the camera sees. In its most uncomplicated form it is used in informational and documentary films where an activity carried on by the subject—from watchmaking to playing football—is filmed so that the subject's hands are seen performing the activity—probing a watch or catching a ball. In a theatrical film, the subject may walk to a window and look out: The camera then affords us a view of what he sees. In a case like this, the subject's face may be slightly in the frame to the left or right foreground.

A dramatic and engaging angle with respect to subject movement is achieved when the camera is positioned to receive the action toward the lens—as with a gymnastic activity—swinging in a swing, sliding onto first base, catching a ball, and so forth. This view is opposite in feeling to a movement "cross-screen," which does not have the high degree of audience involvement and intensity gained from toward-camera movement.

The camera positioned above, looking down on the subject, places the viewer as overseer by putting the subject in an "inferior" position; and this angle can suggest scrutiny, manipulation, and control of the subject. The camera positioned below, looking up on the subject, suggests the subject's power, majesty, nobility, or command.

Filming the subject from the "rear" places the viewer in the voyeur's seat, suggesting eavesdropping, and this angle can connote the subject's disregard, disdain, or unawareness of the camera. The latter point of view is seen frequently in documentaries showing slums, skid rows, native market places, and so forth. Finally, a side or profile shot often creates a feeling of detachment and objectivity in the viewer, because the subject is neither pointed toward nor away from the camera.

Framing and Composition of Elements

Though much of what has already been discussed bears on composition in one way or another (as does the material in succeeding sections), the spatial relationship of the foreground, background, and sides of the picture frame to the subject within that frame deserves special mention.

The projected film is a two-dimensional experience much the same as painting. Since depth does not actually exist in film, it must be suggested in an illusory manner.

It should be stressed that the need for a feeling of realistic depth is usually associated with realistic filmmaking such as documentaries and most narrative story films. In these, it is felt that actual spatial relationships should be suggested in order to preserve believability. Yet, as we can see in paintings and other visual art forms, an exact imitation of *real* space is often unnecessary in sustaining the realistic *effect* of the work. This holds true for film also.

Distance can quite effectively be suggested by filming a subject "through" or "past" some foreground material. This is called *framing the subject*. If out-of-doors, tree branches or leaves may be used. If filming a dinner scene, glasses and hands of the guests in the foreground will suggest depth. (When only hands or parts of heads are shown, it is called *extending the image,* because you are getting the feeling of a lot of people without actually showing their entire bodies. The possibilities are, of course, limitless, depending upon the available elements in the setting. If, as just mentioned, the extreme foreground elements are out-of-focus, the viewer's attention will be drawn beyond the foreground to the main subject that is in focus. If, however, the foreground subject is in focus, we tend to refer to it visually because it is larger than the subject in the background, and because it is sharply defined. Generally, sharpness of the subject and/or its proximity to the camera (near or far) will aid in controlling the point of attention relative to composition. It should be added that contrast in terms of black and white or color (as in the case of the long shot previously described) is a major compositional element. For instance, color is more suggestive of depth than is black and white.

Near and distant *levels of the action* suggest depth also, as well as a greater complexity of the action. Such a technique is skillfully used in *The Desperate Hours* with Humphrey Bogart. At night, as Fredric March walks spotlighted down the walkway of his home toward the door to speak to the kidnappers, a uniformed policeman looking on and holding a shotgun is framed, silhouetted in the foreground. A similar technique is used in many of Hitchcock's films, notably *Rear Window*. In *The Servant*, Joseph Losey positions two of his main characters in the medium foreground of a restaurant scene, while another couple can be seen through a space in a partition, much smaller in size, and located in the background, slightly to the rear of the main characters. The effect is something like a "mirroring" of episodes.

In a more recent film, *The French Connection*, there is a hide-and-seek scene on a subway platform where the detective tailing the French dope smuggler dodges in and out of a waiting subway. Both foreground and background are used as action levels, heightening tension more than if the scene had been filmed with the action levels cross-screen.

Levels of the action create a more complex image, although such an image tends to be somewhat more theatrical than cinematic. The burden of the performance rests heavily with the actors here, for the camera has much less control over what is seen.

Deep composition offers the possibility of great psychological tension *within the frame;* and this technique differs from a similar effect created through cuts. It relies on perfect timing of the actors, and could be risky when retakes are not possible. This technique requires consummate directing skill. The overall effect is less filmic because it seems to deny some of the editorial craft usually used to create psychological tension. It is a technique suitable to a stage-oriented director.

Motion and Time

The aesthetic elements of film so far discussed are not peculiar to cinematography alone. Indeed, they bear importantly upon the media of still photography and painting, as well as upon other "pictorial" modes. But special to motion pictures (and video tape) are two aesthetic elements that are uniquely characteristic. Motion and Time. The full meaning of the former way be grasped far more immediately than the latter because it can be demonstrated explicitly. When motion occurs we can "see" it. Yet, by itself, time is something only experienced implictly and abstractly. When there is no motion, then we have no real way to "mark" time; and thus time "passes" unseen, only measurable by our feelings of either attention or boredom. In film, motion always *includes* the element of time; but there are occasions when an immobile image is projected on the screen. The viewer watches this image, acutely aware of the time it is being projected, because he knows that the image is bounded by the *fixed length* of that scene and by that piece of film. The time of the scene is pre-determined by the number of frames that make it up, running at either 18 or 24 frames per second. Thus, time is integral to the medium of motion pictures, as in no other medium.

Let us take up some aspects of motion and its ramifications. Movement, *motion*, in film can be thought of as having divisions that separate one "act" from another—in other words, "activities" can be partitioned into segments. They can be regarded, in a sense, as *gestures* which have terminal points, marking the beginning and culmination of each.

Furthermore, each of these gestures can be thought of as a continuous, extended image—unlike the motionless image of a still picture. The image in film, then, always stretches over a period of time, and is frequently, though not always, in motion. On the other hand, the still picture is perceived instantaneously. The information it offers—its graphics and its feeling or tone—makes a sudden impression. The image in motion pictures is a continuous, developing phenomenon, a linear experience quite closely related to the written language. (Film has a great deal more in common with the written language than this, including the montage-collage juxtapositioning of images and rhetorical devices using comparison and contrast, metaphor, analogy, and so forth. These similarities are explored in later sections.)

The image extended is what we are dealing with in film; and in terms of motion it may be created from two major sources—subject movement or camera movement. Arbitrary though these categories may seem, they none the less afford us with clear working areas for examination.

SUBJECT MOVEMENT

The subject can be defined as the main point of interest in the picture frame. Although, in a general sense, there are other ways of thinking of the subject, I will for the time being refer to the simplest of concepts—that "something" toward which the camera is pointed. It could be a person, a flower, or a building; the sky, the ocean, or hills. Subject movement occurs whenever that "something"—which is the point of interest, and upon which the camera's attention is held—moves.

As was pointed out earlier (in The Lens), the focal length of the lens affects our perception of movement and of whether it is toward or away from the camera. A short focal length lens accelerates the feeling of subject motion toward and away from the camera, and a long focal length lens causes the subject to appear to move at less than the normal rate. Fight scenes are made especially dynamic when the brawler's punches are thrown in the direction of a wide angle lens. Near the last scene of Mike Nichol's *The Graduate,* Dustin Hoffman's sense of futility in trying to get to the church was emphasized by filming it with a very long telephoto lens.

Also affecting "sense of movement" is the direction of the action. Cross-frame movement is more noticeable than movement toward or away from the camera because the sides of the picture frame act as spatial reference points. Similarly, other elements in the frame may also function as reference points. An airplane shown flying in an empty sky will convey less sense of movement than when it is seen flying through a cloud or past tall buildings.

Although cross-frame movement appears especially exaggerated when filmed in close-up, it appears muted when occurring at a distance. This is because the magnitude of the action in relation to the frame space is greater in a close-up than in a long shot. Hence, rapid acts closely filmed, such as hammering a nail or sawing, may be visually disturbing. To remedy this, the filmmaker can either direct the subject to slow down his activity, or the normal movement can be filmed at a slightly higher speed—perhaps 24 frames per second—which will smooth out the action but not slow it down discernibly (this is with the projection speed at 18 frames per second). From an aesthetic point of view it would follow that an activity of low movement intensity can be dramatized by filming it in close-up, and, conversely, that an activity surprising in itself, like a karate kick, could sustain itself in a more distant, medium shot.

As was mentioned earlier, movement deep into the picture frame—away from the camera—is more suggestive of depth than when it is cross-frame either horizontally or vertically; and this is a good thing to keep in mind, especially for realistic filmmaking. Movement *toward* the camera, particularly if it is sudden, will tend to be more arresting; while movement away from it, if slow and deliberate, will evoke more reflective feelings in the viewer.

When filming movement, it is useful to be aware of its *directionality* and *rate* for editing purposes. In matching the action—making parts of the action logically related, in terms of direction—it is important to be conscious of the "way" a subject is moving. Especially when a subject is filmed at different intervals, the speed with which it is traveling can change; when this happens, the scenes representing differing rates will be mismatched in the editing. For instance, if the director (especially the director of a realistic film) is not alert, his performers may unconsciously alter their own pace of moving or gesturing, resulting in a ludicrous change in the action that can alter the mood of the sequence.

In discussing film composition it has already been pointed out that the delineations of the picture frame act, at the same time, both as *containers* of the space and as *doors* to it. A subject is held into the frame (given a "formal" space by its perimeter), while the edges are understood passageways for the subject. It is because of the ambiguous nature of the frame's demarcations that they are areas of tension and great interest. The closer the subject is to the frame edge, the greater the tension the viewer experiences—partly because the frame edge divides the *seen* from the *unseen*. In manipulating his subject, the filmmaker can make good use of the frame as a ready-made tension-producer.

This principle can be easily demonstrated by filming someone bouncing a ball out of the picture frame and then catching it when it appears in the frame. As the ball leaves, our interest heightens, and as it re-enters the frame, we experience relief.

Some film aestheticians have pointed out that the film rectangle is a disadvantage: because it reminds the viewer that he is watching a movie, the frame theoretically disenchants the viewer and works against his *illusion* of reality. Although this may have some foundation if one considers the entire film medium as one that serves and promotes unadulterated reality, this attitude seems to me barely justifiable if film is to be used as more than a mere copying medium. Luckily, for the further growth of film as an *expressive* vehicle, new filmmakers are rejecting this highly limiting view.

If, on the other hand, the picture frame is thought of as a kind of stage—and if the viewer is induced to accept it as such, if he is shown that it is being used as a space for emphasis—then the subject's potential for meaningful movement is enormously increased.

CAMERA MOVEMENT

The Pan. If subject movement contributes to the developing, extended image by acting like a "performer" in creative filming, then camera movement—as the "counter-performer"—contributes equally to the image. In other words, the camera should be thought of as a performer with as much expressive potential as the subject.

Of all camera functions, perhaps the most important one is *to select*, to be a discriminating eye. The *pan*, which is a pivotal movement of the camera, either horizontally or vertically, is most often used to keep the subject in frame when it is moving; and by virtue of doing so, the panning shot may express the option of staying with the subject. After all, the camera can stop at any time and "choose" to let the subject walk out of the frame. By this token it selects through its co-operation with the subject.

The pan is also used to *reveal* the subject—to allow the viewer to see certain details, and in a certain order. It could be an ordinary pan of a landscape or a crowd, or of objects and pictures in a room. The effect is frequently suspenseful, because there is new, unseen material of an uncertain nature entering the picture frame. (It is also being *brought into* the frame.) Here, the camera functions as a discovering, probing eye.

The pan may be used to shift from one point of interest to another, of equal or greater interest—or it may serve as a transitional device to get from one locale to another. The "swish pan," for example, is a very fast horizontal movement where the "in-between" visual material is blurred in order to convey a sensation of traveling. The pan may also be used to describe a subject's point of view, so that as he looks in various directions, the camera imitates his gestures, and we feel that what the camera sees is what he sees.

Finally, the pan may simulate the "camera in motion"; this effect is achieved when the camera is pivoted on a tripod while using a long focus lens. Such a panning shot most nearly approximates the feeling of the camera moving alongside a subject.

The Mobile Camera. When the camera itself becomes mobile, the result is perhaps one of the most dramatic, yet most neglected, forms of camera movement. This highly expressive technique has been slighted—especially lately—in the interests of economy and convenience by low-budget, independent filmmakers because putting the camera in motion requires some sort of vehicle and the people to control it. The simplest and least cumbersome of these is a wheel chair, requiring only one person to push it as the cameraman films while seated on it. A more complicated version is the "dolly"—a contraption with wheels, sometimes equipped with hydraulic lifts and extensions—which usually requires a crew of several to power and guide it. Scenes filmed from any kind of moving vehicle, or even those filmed as the camera is being "walked in," are generally called "dolly shots."

There are several standard types of dolly shots, among which are the following: the camera moving in on a subject; the camera moving behind or alongside a subject; the camera moving through or past a subject. The move-in on a subject is often used in studio work on theatrical films where heavy dollying equipment is readily available. A movement of this type creates a feeling of immediacy by calling attention to actions or facial expressions, thus heightening dramatic tension. The camera moving alongside or behind a subject is frequently used in chase sequences—notably in countless westerns where, for instance, the stagecoach is shown, wildly out of control. Camera movement through or past a subject is a technique used to show the emotions of a crowd of people; to go ahead of an explorer moving through a jungle; or, in underwater filming, to show a feeling of depth.

On the whole, the mobile camera has a number of aesthetic advantages: It imparts to the image a feeling of immediacy, tension, high drama, depth, and fluidity—all of which serve to heighten audience involvement. On many occasions a zoom shot is made to substitute for the mobile camera; but because of optical distortion it will lose a sense of depth and perspective.

An ambulatory or walking movement, when controlled to prevent unwanted shaking, can be a quite useful technique and is sometimes indispensable when shooting documentaries, where vehicles would intrude on and complicate spontaneous reactions from subjects. Because walking in on the subject and moving around it can be regulated instantly according to what is seen through the lens while filming, the movement tends to take on a more responsive, deliberate feeling. Walking the camera evenly necessitates good balance as well as sighting the path of movement in order not to trip or bump into things. Through practice and concentration, however, a technique can be successfully developed.

When there is an interplay of both camera and subject movement—as in the case of a dolly shot alongside a subject that is moving, or under any other conditions when both are moving at the same time—the image becomes more complex. The viewer feels more like a participant than a spectator. This method is especially useful in certain documentary films where an activity may be "described" by a moving camera from several angles, and where the point of view is constantly changing.

Using the Zoom.   Other forms of camera movement are created through the use of the zoom lens. The zoom lens will bring a subject close, enlarging it, and "push" it away, reducing its size. When zooming in, interest in the subject is heightened (this is similar to dollying in), not only in the mysteriously fluid alteration of the subject, but in the change to a larger subject size, which amplifies detail. Zooming out, on the other hand, is a movement that, in a continuous way, includes, and reveals, more and more of the subject and other compositional elements within the picture frame.

In addition, the zoom can be thought of as a transitional kind of movement that directs attention from a point of general interest to a more specific one, and vice versa. It is subtler than a simple cut from a long shot to a close-up because it eases the viewer into the change. It can also function as a transitional device in the editing, where a zoom (in or out) may terminate a scene. And a zoom may also be used for punctuation, for picking up the pace of a scene by moving in, or slowing it down by moving out. Lastly, a slow zoom, if done very slowly and deliberately, can build tension.

chapter 3

Planning a Film

GETTING STARTED

I have discovered that beginning filmmakers universally agree on one thing: They want to make films. But the similarity ends there. All would-be filmmakers are in varying states of preparation, from those with no experience with a camera, to those who have been making "films" for a few years and are dissatisfied with their output. In every case, except for those few who already have very specific film projects in mind, the problem of *how to begin* is paramount.

The most obvious solution—taking the camera out and filming with it until one gets an idea or an inspiration—is the method usually tried in lieu of some other guidance. In many cases, this approach works well: The inspiration does come, and good films are made from little more than the determination to film and make films. Yet even people of this sturdy stripe have to start *somewhere*; they must have, at the very least, a vague notion of a subject, of a place to begin.

Using Suggested Projects

In filmmaking, at least two things are needed to get a successful start: a subject—*a reason to film*; and a method—*a way to film*. Realizing that for many people, searching for a film idea could become a stymieing, time-consuming obstacle, I have devised a series of exercises or suggested projects that will enable the beginnner to launch immediately into the process of filming. Momentarily, these exercises will act as substitutes for his original direction; hopefully, allowing him to find a direction. Of course, the actual subject of these exercises can be whatever he finds involving, something that is convenient and practical to film. A subject can be anything from a family hiking trip to an outing on a boat, from a son or daughter at play, to a friend's interesting occupation.

Although the exercises are outlined in the Appendixes of the book, I should like to mention here that each represents a separate way to view the subject, and each offers a thorough experience with one of several cinematic approaches: lighting, movement, close-ups, working with the picture frame, seeking expressive angles, and so forth. They are arranged in an order which will advance the beginner quickly, and they can be thought of as weekly projects.

On the other hand, the person who has his own idea for a first film, when left alone to pursue it on his own terms, will probably have success with it. Yet in the process, he will probably not be exposed to as full a range of cinematic expression as he might have had he been directed to use certain methods while filming. The point here is simply that the beginner often cannot consider the full range of options open to him in terms of filmic approach because the alternatives just don't occur to him; and, as a consequence, his learning how to make films with aesthetic emphasis frequently becomes a needlessly drawn-out process. The exercises, then, are an effort to compress the learning process that make the *means* of filming the very end itself. They can be applied, as has already been suggested, to random subjects or to an over-all theme. For those who begin by filming subjects at random (a little of this and a little of that), suggestions are given on how to put the film together using montage or collage. (See the sections on Putting Your Film Together and The Expressionistic Film.)

Getting an Idea

If, however, the beginner wishes to use a theme instead of shooting in a more free-form way, here is a list of some possible ideas. Bear in mind that an idea may be nothing more than an approach or a beginning: a repetitive element, an image which threads the film, or a recurrence of similar scenes. Here are some of the things that could inspire a film:

1. A film can evolve from a single broad theme you want to say something about—such as pollution of the environment, violence, love, alienation, youth, old age, and so forth.

2. A film can be based upon some commemorative occasion, such as a street fair or festival, or a display or some special exhibit.

3. You may have seen a movie that gave you an idea to make a film like it or that made you desire to elaborate on some facet of it.

4. A personal experience can set off your imagination. Rush-hour on the freeway; being vandalized; being in some holocaust such as a flood, an earthquake, or a great fire: one of these may inspire you to recreate it in a story, or to film an activity that symbolizes or parallels the event.

5. A recurring dream you have had may suggest a story or a theme. (Fellini has made his reputation this way.)

6. A friend may have an interesting role or activity that might prompt you to explore it as an intimate documentary. Perhaps the person is a boatbuilder, a potter, or a fashion model.

7. The lyrics to a piece of music can suggest a framework for a story—or the music itself might conjure up visual images.

8. A poem, short story, or even a novel can provide a useful structure for interpretation, or for adding your own emphasis.

9. You might have started a film and never finished it, or you may have film footage left from several uncompleted projects. You may want to take a fresh look at it, to re-interpret your efforts, or even to use some of the best footage as a basis for renewed shooting.

10. Finally, you might wish to base your film upon an aesthetic problem peculiar to the film medium—such as lighting, motion, time, transformation—letting one of these serve as both the *subject* and the *method* of the film.

Above all, your idea should be something you find involving, something important to you—and in making a film about it, something from which you expect to learn.

POINT OF VIEW

When an idea for a film is conceived, how it will be approached and developed becomes a part of the total conception. Therefore, a knowledge of the possible methods of treating a film idea may help to render it in a way that best suits your feeling toward the subject. For instance, let us say that you have a friend who is a stained glass window-maker and that his unusual occupation has been a source of fascination to you. You feel that the subject would be excellent: First, because you are personally involved with the person and with what he does; and second, from a visual standpoint, his work would lend itself particularly well to film.

The initial impulse of most filmmakers is to "document" an activity such as this, to film all the intriguing *processes*: making a diagram of the proposed window, cutting and buffing the glass, fitting it according to the drawing, "leading it in," and, finally, installing the finished work. Very well and good. So far, the approach is simple, *informational*, and it has considerable visual appeal—a "how-to-do-it film."

It is possible, however, that one might choose to go deeper into it, probing the source of the creative activity and revealing something of the man—his motivations in choosing his work and the special joy he derives from it. Finally, one might wish to show how his artistic occupation relates to our lives—how it enriches our environment and how it adds to us personally. Such a film would have depth and feeling, and it would be what is sometimes called an Intimate Documentary (see the separate chapter on this subject in Part two).

In contrast to the *informational* approach, which features the activity, making us keenly aware of all the procedural details, and stops at that, the *intimate* documentary approach is an exploration of the man's particular *way* of going about his work. It features his facial expressions, filmed from imaginative angles, and uses lighting that evokes a mood, thus giving us greater depth and complexity of expression. (It should be noted, however, that the intimate documentary sacrifices some of the purely informational aspects of film in order to convey a deeper feeling and attitude.)

Where the informational film would possibly have a "narrator" describe the craft aspects of stained glass window-making, the documentary might use the window-maker's own voice instead: we might hear him discussing experiences peripheral to the work itself, revealing his attitudes and feelings.

In addition, the stained glass window-maker's circumstances can be thought of as providing a germ for a *fictional story*—the activity and situation from which a simple narrative plot can be woven. Let us imagine the window-maker sitting at his bench, carefully and methodically going about his work. Finally finished, he takes the piece out of his studio to a church where he is to install it. He sits on a high scaffold, preparing the place for the glass to be fitted. His face and hands are seen from outside the church, shot through the space into which the window will be placed. Suddenly, some small boys come into foreground view, and they appear to be taunting the man. Now the boys are seen from the man's view, as they stand below, yelling and gesturing. The man places the window in the space and steps back to admire his handiwork. We see how beautiful the window is with the light shining through it. Now we see the boys from outside as one picks up a stone and throws it, smashing the window. They try to run but are caught by a priest who had been watching them, and who holds onto their arms. The window-maker goes outside and confronts the boys. The priest is angry and wants to turn them over to the authorities immediately. The window-maker persuades the priest to give him custody of the boys, and he takes them into the church. The priest is apprehensive lest they be even more destructive. The window-maker shows them the splendor of the other windows. They walk quietly around, looking—enthralled by the colors. Finally, the man hands pieces of the broken window to the boys and invites them to go outside to look at them in the sunlight; he points out the leading that holds the pieces together. The boys are interested, and the man gives them the pieces of glass to take with them. Next, he is seen returning to the church with another window. From outside we see it being fitted into place. From inside we see him admiring his work. Then we see the two boys in the church: sitting, looking at the window, their faces reflecting its meaning. (For more on the Fictional Narrative form, see Part Three.)

Another, wholly different treatment of the same subject might be the use of the stained glass window-maker's studio as only *an occasion* to create interesting abstract images. These may have little if any direct relationship to the process of the art, to the actual tools, to the pieces of glass in themselves, or to the man as an artist. The main reason for creating images such as these is to enjoy their pure form, color, and movement. What gives a film like this unity is the mood generated by the images.

In this instance, the filmmaker goes to the window-maker's studio with the idea of transforming all that he sees—of using a close-up or a macro-lens to film the items he wishes to change into a world of free forms and color. He picks up pieces of glass and holds them to the light in front of the camera lens, and turns each piece, watching "what it does," making it "perform" by moving and turning it. Perhaps he films the window-maker's eye, his mouth, his hands—seeing them as dramatic disembodied symbols that he will intercut with the pure movement of colored forms. The resulting film will be a series of abstract impressions gathered from the raw materials of the studio. It will represent another world—that of the filmmaker and of his spontaneous, unrestrained responses to the visual effects he designs. He "scores" his visual music as he goes, "writing" his movie as he films it. The ordering principle of the film will be in its flow of images and in the use of film as a painterly medium, where its effectiveness is in the sensual, kinetic experience it provides, in its almost visual counterpart to music.

Still another way to view the stained glass window-maker is as an *occasion* to film, using the images of him and of the studio, poetically, as metaphor. This is similar to the foregoing, pure abstract approach, except that the images are not totally transformed. Here, images of his face, of his hands, and of his work are not so changed that we cannot tell what they are, yet they are altered to the extent that they become generalized in meaning, enough so that they will fit into a not-so-specific context, in much the same way that words are used in a poem. These images may be used along with a host of others either drawn from distant unrelated situations or taken over a long period of time—vastly different images that will compare and contrast with the ones taken in the window-maker's studio. In other words, this is a collage film that constitutes a composite of life made from all sorts of footage strung together in such a way that meaning is *generated* and feelings are *suggested*. These disparate images are unified—given continuity and a context—through their kinetic structural properties of form, movement, and color as well as through the intrinsic, connotative, or inferential meaning of the images. (For more on these two last-mentioned film forms see Part Four, The Expressionistic Film.)

These, then, are only a few of several ways the same film idea may be viewed for approach and development.

A WORD ON SCRIPTING

The planning of a film can be simple or complicated, quick or drawn-out. A good deal of the planning lies in outlining the steps to be taken in the actual filming, and this is called a script. It should be emphasized that under-planning as well as over-planning can be a pitfall. The former will get in the way of creative filming because it will not have anticipated enough of what is needed for a film: it may result in much good energy wasted on hand-wringing disappointments. The latter can stifle creativity because a too well-scripted film can easily become a blueprint that, in its detailing, will not permit the creative modifications of either inspiration or changed circumstances. As the poet, Ezra Pound, has said, beware of "over-preparing the event." Don't forget: spontaneity, and, often, unforeseen circumstances may unexpectedly provide the life for your film. A script should be an orderly list of things *you must include*. These are things you don't want to forget while filming; and, in a rudimentary sense, this is what a script is all about. Ideally, it should free you, not chain you.

There are films that must have scripts, ones that need none, and still others that cannot be scripted at all. A fictional narrative, for example, *must be* scripted. In fact, there are time-honored forms for this process which are covered in detail in Part Three.

By now it should be clear that, in general, there are no hard and fast rules for the scripting of films. One should, above all, be tuned to necessity. Whether you should script at all, or how far you should go with it, should be a purely pragmatic decision. Is it necessary? And how much of a script is needed to do the best possible job?

chapter 4

Shooting Your Film

GESTURE: VISUAL PHRASING

In the preceding sections, many standard methods of approaching a subject filmically are discussed at length. A variety of film situations are covered, as well as the uses of lighting, image size, depth of field, angle of view, framing, composition, and movement. All of these aspects involve ways of seeing the subject and interpreting it.

There is yet another way to see the subject: in terms of *gesture.*

Structural and Inferential Aspects

Previously, the elements discussed were presented showing how both form and content worked simultaneously. When I mention a pan, for instance, I tell how it is accomplished and what effect it has in producing feeling. Now, I should like to regard these components of the image separately. When the purely physical dynamics of an image are viewed independently of the meaning they evoke, we are considering their value as *structural gestures.* On the other hand, when the pan is seen as a way to generate feelings perhaps of mystery or discovery (viewed independently of structural considerations) these are inferential components or *inferential gestures* of the image. Therefore, every image can be seen as having two aspects: a structural aspect—what it is in terms of form, color, and movement; and an inferential aspect—what conclusions or inferences can be drawn from the image. Of course, this dichotomy is arbitrary. The distinctions do not, in fact, exist separately; yet a separation can be made in order to see more clearly how the two aspects function, sometimes independently, and sometimes wedded.

The reason for introducing the concepts of gesture here (for they are discussed in relation to specific types of film forms later) is because they do have a bearing upon the way the subject is seen and filmed. They also have a significant influence on decisions made during editing.

Briefly, let us examine just a few types of gesture from the structural aspect. Any movement, whether by the subject or the camera, can be considered a structural gesture. A pan, a mobile camera movement, a zoom: all are gestures. Likewise, any direction of movement by the subject—cross-screen, toward or away from the camera, or up or down—is a gesture. Forms in themselves (even immobile forms) can function as structural gestures because of the *ways* in which they fill the picture space: geometric, organic, round, angular, potato-shaped forms. Colors are particularly important as structural gestures, for sometimes an image is characterized by the dominating color within the picture frame.

Gestures which can be called inferential are ones where the image's connotative aspect overrides our perception of the structural aspect. Thus an automobile accident filmed at night, where a car is turned over and burning, will impress the viewer most forcibly by thoughts of injury, death, and horror before he is able to appreciate the color and motion of the orange, leaping flames.

However, fire being emitted harmlessly from the stack of an oil refinery will likely impress us with its torch-like form (as in a quite beautiful scene from Antonioni's *Red Desert*). To illustrate further: A close-up of a child crying, her face filling the frame, may be devoid of any particular gestural configuration or color (unless she is wearing a brightly colored scarf, or has a striking hair color). In this case, we tend to "tune in" on the inferential aspects of the scene: Crying is generally an unhappy event; why is she crying? And so on.

Now that the basic difference between structural and inferential gestures has been established, how is this information important to you while filming? To begin with, what you film is what you must work with when you begin to edit. Knowing, for example, that having a good supply of clear, discernible gestures included in the footage will make your job easier (and more effective), you can plan to obtain those shots during the filming stage. Though all structural gestures have inferential content, it is important to determine, while filming, the dominant aspect of the image you are creating. The key to successful filming and editing is always to be sure that your film is either visually (structurally) strong, or strong in terms of feeling (inferentially) strong.

Once your stock of images has been gathered, they can be related gesturally when juxtaposed in the editing. But how is this done?

Certain timeless rhetorical devices are quite the same for film as they are for other *linear* media such as the written language, music, or drama. Comparison and contrast, rhythm, denotation, metaphor: All provide unity and emphasis, either structurally or inferentially.

Ultimately, the less abstract problem of "where to cut the film," will lead to a more easily reachable understanding of the abstract systems and rhetorical uses in film mentioned above. These "methods" can be thought of as *rule systems*. (These are covered in succeeding sections.)

How, then, is gesture cut? In other words, where do you cut an image for greatest effectiveness? When editing intuitively, most filmmakers simply include as much of a gesture or a series of gestures as they feel is necessary in order to convey the desired information and feeling. This is well and good, provided that the editor has a finely developed intuition. However, for those beginning to develop a feeling for cutting and juxtaposing scenes, it might be helpful to tackle editing problems from what we know we can clearly illustrate.

Active and Passive Gestures

Let us imagine that these two aspects to an image—structural and inferential gestures—are like two sides to the same coin. It's the same coin, but each side informs us in a different way. Furthermore, it should be noted that the structural side of the coin can be subdivided into two predominate aspects—*active* or *passive*.

Active gestures, as the term implies, are in motion or undergoing a change. In order to qualify as an active gesture, the physical motion, or change in mood, should have a discernible configuration. The configuration can be seen to have—more or less—a beginning, an apex, and a dissipation phase. Imagine, if you will, something like the shape of an ocean wave as it gathers and builds, reaches its peak, and then breaks apart. All movements or "moods" start somewhere, go somewhere, and cease. This, then, is the basis for isolating an active gesture.

Here are a few examples of movements with discernible configurations. On a playground, a child is running toward a slide; he climbs it, and then slides down. This could be thought of as a series of three separate gestures: (1.) running toward the slide; (2.) climbing to the top; (3.) sliding down. Although these can be regarded as separate activities, they are also *denotative* in that they grow out of one another. They fit together in a series we think of as a unit. Gestural segments are somewhat like movements in a dance. Each movement is begun and completed; and each, in turn, leads into the next. The greater the number of denotative segments left intact and in succession, the more of a "story" develops.

One could include, with the segments just described, the gesture of the child as he runs back to his mother's waiting arms. This, then, would be a suitable scene for a story film or a documentary; and we might include still more denotative gestures, depending on the variety of the available material and the established pace of the film.

In a collage film, however, it is conceivable that a filmmaker may use only *one* of the four gestural segments, or that he might use all four, placing them separately at different points throughout the film. The important point here is that gestures may be isolated—indeed, they should be, at times, for their most effective use. They can be used separately, or sequentially, depending upon the requirements of the film. In collage or montage the segments can be used separately, as in advertising films and short poetic film statements. They are used in more of a unit—say, four or five gestures together—in a documentary, educational, or training film. Still longer units that might continue for several minutes at a time are found frequently in the story film.

Cutting on the Action

In cutting an active gesture, one simply separates it from the unit of denotative parts (according to the needs of the film's statement) just as one breaks off squares from a chocolate bar. When you snip the film, it is important to be sure that you *cut on the action*. Don't leave tag ends on your scene that are not part of the action movement either at its beginning or its end. This is where so many people fall down in the editing process. They leave little hiatuses of inactivity between scenes; and these create boredom in the viewer and slow down the entire pace of the film. In order to cut on the action, just move the scene back and forth in the editor-viewer until you begin to see some motion: That is where you mark the frame to be cut. The same procedure is used in trimming the end of the scene: Cut at the point where the motion ceases. Pauses can be used for punctuation (or as separate passive gestures), but they should be used intentionally.

Active gestures can have a way of "canceling themselves out." That is, they can erase their own effectiveness if they are misused. A canceling out occurs when a gesture is repeated with very little variation. For instance, if the child in our illustration, instead of running into his mother's arms, were to go back to the slide for another try at it—including this repeated gesture might tend to cancel the effect of the preceding one. This is what is referred to in English rhetoric as "redundancy." Seeing the same thing again tends to generate boredom, unless there is either something special about the child—or if he were to come down the slide *differently*.

Let us suppose that the mother is in the foreground after the child's first trip down the slide, and that she is trying to persuade him it is time to leave and have lunch. If we know this by seeing her motioning him to leave, it adds an element of interest to the child's return trip: We see him, "trying" his mother's patience. It is good, though, to be watchful of repeat gestures and to eliminate them if possible, lest they show us something already seen and thus risk losing the viewer's attention. There are exceptions to this rule, of course. Just remember, the key to taking exception to any aesthetic rule is "intention." If you intend to repeat the gesture, then there is probably justification, and that is another matter.

The concept of active gesture takes in camera movement as well as subject movement. Pans, dolly shots, zooms—all of these possess a discernible configuration that begins and ends. The pan starts—it is in motion—and stops. Here, as in the illustration with the child, unless there is an important gestural follow up, another image capable of sustaining interest, then there will be an empty space, a let-down. The filmmaker must be as diligent about cutting on camera movement as on subject movement. It all adds up to the same thing: maintaining a flow of information and feeling at a pace that will sustain the viewer's interest and involvement. When this flow is violated, the film is rather like a string of moving railroad cars being unhitched in the middle—and everything in the rear gets left behind.

The key to identifying the *passive structural gesture,* on the other hand, is that it has no discernible configurative movement. A close-up of a sewing machine needle in motion would qualify as a passive gesture because we cannot effectively see its movement. Its repetitious activity seems to blur into an event, simplistic and without direction at any given moment. In a slow motion version of the same action, however, the up and down thrusts of the needle become readily discernible, qualifying each movement as a separate, *active* gesture. Other repetitious, rapidly executed actions are also considered passive, such as running in place (jogging), the turning wheels of a moving car, rustling of tree leaves in the wind, the moving lips of a person talking, and so forth.

Images *not in motion* are also passive gestures. Motionless shots of signs—such as ONE WAY, DO NOT ENTER, EAT AT JOE'S PLACE, or of sculptural objects, buildings, or a cat lying still on the floor—are passive, as are things moving only slightly—like a close-up of a flower jostled by the wind.

Now that we know what a passive gesture is, what determines how long it should be left on the screen? With an active gesture, terminal points can be seen. But this is not the case with a repetitive or motionless event. What has to become the determining factor is *time,* pure and simple.

The length of time the image is left on the screen (e.g., the length of the scene included in the film) should be determined by how rapidly the *information* and *feeling* content of the image can be perceived. If the image is dynamic and complex it will bear a longer viewing than one that is simple in structure and/or vapid in feeling. Other deciding factors are whether we have seen images like it previously in the same film or whether or not the image is familiar to our general experience. Also of critical importance is how the image is juxtaposed with other images.

What I'm saying here about active and passive gestures is tacitly understood by skilled professional editors. But in lieu of such experience, these principles are offered to the beginner as a kind of crash course in what usually takes talent and a decade of experience to master. However you feel about the concepts of gesture—structural and inferential; active and passive—I urge that you read on in the other sections to see how these ideas are applied to specific film genres. Also, I should like to encourage any and all would-be filmmakers to study with an assiduous eye the better filmed ads on television, as well as all good films, in order to ferret out and understand cutting techniques as they are professionally applied.

FILMING WITH GESTURE FOR COHERENT EDITING: WORKING WITH SYNTAX

Now that gesture, both structural and inferential, has been described and its use in editing suggested, let us back-track for a moment, returning to the *filming* process.

Since "gesture" and "image" are somewhat similar concepts, it would be clearer, perhaps, to say that gesture is really a way of characterizing a part of an image. A pan, for example, has a gestural configuration (a movement cross-screen), but it also has feeling. These elements taken together could be considered *the image*. And it is possible that a cluster of gestures may make up a single image. So when filming, one may emphasize one or more of the image's gestures for the purpose of editing. To speak of the process simply of gathering images does not give a clear, concrete basis for analysis and discussion. Therefore it may be helpful to think of the filming process as the *gathering of gestures*.

Stylistically, how a film feels is determined by one, or by a group of, dominant gestures. A film with a lot of pans in it, and many zooms, might tend to generate feelings of searching, peering, and scrutinizing. It will be a film which is largely *camera interpretive*, as opposed to *subject interpretive* (where the subject does the moving). On the other hand, a lot of passive gestures may suggest a more serene, less restless attitude, and the film would then take on an inward feeling. I am not implying that all films should have a predominant gestural style (filmic approach)—only that style is another way to achieve cinematic unity.

Some Basic Transitional and Continuity Devices

Not only will a lot of similar gestures lend style as well as continuity to your film, but they will lend transitional unity to the editing. Film style is like the literary style of an author. Hemingway uses short, terse, punchy, journalistic sentences. Aldous Huxley uses complex sentences filled with lumbering Latinisms. Transitional unity, on the other hand, has to do with how well the "phrases" go together—or, in film terms, how effortlessly the scenes seem to fit.

The fitting together of scenes in a sequence is, of course, mechanically performed through "cuts," "lap dissolves," or "fades." Although the use of fades (where the scene goes black or vice versa) is practically obsolete as a transitional device, cuts (the abrupt joining of two scenes) and dissolves (a simultaneous fade out of one scene and fade in of another) are still rudimentary and indispensable. In fact, lap dissolves seem to be used more these days than cuts. The "quick dissolve," especially, is so fast that it almost appears to be a cut, and yet it retains the softness of the dissolve, easing the eye into the adjoining scene. Although traditionally the dissolve has been used to indicate the passage of time or a changed locale, it is now used more and more in advertising commercials to join montage elements (distantly related images).

As noted earlier, there are Super 8 cameras that will provide lap dissolves and fades between scenes. In professional work, however, these effects are usually performed in the laboratory during printing. This service is not generally available to those who are having Super 8 prints made, mainly because the necessary equipment is not manufactured; and there is, at present, little demand for fades and dissolves in this film gauge. In time, it is predicted that the facilities and equipment now available for larger gauge films will also be standard for Super 8. Those who wish to perform dissolves and fades with their cameras will find that the amount of planning and preparation demanded by a dissolve somewhat inhibits spontaneity as well as slows down the filming process.

More on Cutting on the Action

We have seen how scenes are joined; next we will explore how the cutting and content of scenes can affect transitions. If an abrupt cut is used between two scenes, it will work better if the cuts in the adjoining scenes are made *on the action.* If the film records a passive gesture, the cut should have the correct "timing." It is possible that even if the scenes do not have a denotational relationship—a logical succession where one action is the off-shoot of another (as in the illustration where the child goes up the slide and runs into his mother's arms)—the scenes will appear to fit together. Let us imagine a film montage composed of beach scenes (a series of unrelated shots) which might go something like this: A person runs into the surf; someone throws a beach ball; close-up of a girl turning her head; a man in striped long-johns jogs down the beach; a child comes down a slide; a couple on a blanket are kissing; a person walks out of the surf, and so on. If each of these shots is cut on the action—just as it begins and as soon as it ends—they will all join together with a feeling of "rightness," and they will most assuredly provide a visually exciting beach montage.

In the above illustration I purposely included the shot, "a couple are kissing," because it is a passive gesture. Even though a passive gesture involves no discernible, configurative action, it can be cut on the gesture as that gesture is delineated by "time" rather than movement. If the right amount of time is allotted for that gesture, the cut will work much the same as if there were configurative movement involved. Since an element of time is central to both movement and non-movement, sensitive use of timing can sustain tension and provide flow within the film. This way, scenes joined by a cut will seem appropriate because they will have a relaying effect on each other (where one scene leaves off another begins).

The relaying effect can be made even more forceful through the selective use of *kinds* of movement, forms, and colors within the adjoining scenes. Thus, rhetorical use of images through comparison and contrast, rhythm, and metaphor is made possible. In other words, the use of scene content itself (or rather, a manipulation of it) becomes a transitional refinement that promotes an even flow of images.

Directionality of Movement

Returning to the just-illustrated montage of a beach scene where the transitions are aided by joining the scenes as the gesture begins and ends, let us now see what happens when the *directionality* of the gesture is considered, including its *rate of motion*; the relative *size of the subject in the frame;* and its *color, form,* and *texture.*

Suppose we begin the montage with a shot of a person running into the surf, filmed from the side so that the action crosses the screen from right to left; then we follow this with a shot of a beach ball being thrown from right to left also; and after that we show a shot of a child coming down a slide from the same screen direction as the other shots. Now, we shall punctuate this sequence with the passive, non-directional shot of the couple on a blanket kissing. We follow this with a sequence of active gestures, except that this time they will be going in the opposite direction cross-screen. We start with a shot of a girl turning her head from left to right; then a man jogs down the beach, also left to right; finally, we film a person walking out of the surf in the same direction cross-screen.

This order of images is slightly different from the first montage arrangement: It places the passive gesture where it will accent the flow of images and orders the bulk of the shots so that, in terms of their connotations (inferential gestures), they are first "ascending" and then "descending."

For clarification, let us see how the first group of three images connote a feeling of anticipated joy. The bather enters the water; this leads to the engaged, energetic activity of the ball-thrower; then we see the child having fun on the slide and move directly to the lovers' kiss. These could be read as a series of up-beat images. Now I have followed this sequence with the girl (who looks serious) turning her head, opposing the direction of the previous actions; significantly, the shot of the girl follows the scene with the lovers, suggesting that she is turning her head away from what has gone before. Reinforcing this is the action of the jogger in his funny, clown-like outfit (yet he seems dispirited as if he would like to call it quits); and, finally, a bather exits from the surf, a little tired, yet smiling. This last group is descending, let-down—and works toward a resolution of the cycle.

Role and Rule Systems

It can be seen that directionality, if used intentionally, can reinforce the feeling of the images as well as our acceptance of the statement that the sequence represents. The sequence—the arrangement of gestural scenes—constitutes the *rule system* of the film. Structurally and inferentially, the rhythm and emphasis, patterned to form a "set" of expectations and anticipations, become the keys to the viewer's acceptance of the film experience. Ultimately, the arrangement of the gestures is dictated by the content, or *role*, of each image, which, by virtue of placing it in a context, further defines that role. The dynamics of both rule and role systems are interdependent. The important thing to remember, both in filming and in editing, is that the role, or content, of the image is decided *first*. It is that which gives a clue to its possible use in a rule-system context—an arrangement. These concepts are elaborated upon in Part Four.

Although the montage of gestural scenes just illustrated is solely subject-interpretive (i.e., the subject moves), I should like to add that *camera-interpretive* gestures (where the camera moves) will inter-cut very well with other directional gestures. If, for example, a person is running in a certain direction cross-screen, such movement can be complemented when followed or preceded by a camera pan, say, in the same direction.

Especially when putting together subject gestures, one must consider the relative size of the subject, not only in relation to the picture frame but in relation to preceding subjects. This, as well as the rate of subject motion, are crucial to successful, effective juxtapositioning of images.

For instance, in the beach montage where the bodies of the subjects are in motion, they should be (1.) large enough in the picture frame to dominate our view; (2.) comparative in size. The girl who turns her head, however, will have to be larger than the other subjects so that her movement will have effect. Finally (3.), the rate of motion should compare, and the "energy and vitality" of the subjects should match. (Along with this, one should remember that a close-up of a subject amplifies *the feeling* of its rate of motion.)

So far, I have placed a lot of emphasis on movement as a structural gesture. Less dynamic, perhaps, are other types of structural gesture that deserve consideration: These are *color, form,* and *texture*—which can be manipulated too. Although each can provide a source of structural unity, color seems easiest to control, and is more noticeable to the viewer than form and texture. A dominant color will easily carry over from one shot to the next, provided that it is made conspicuous. Color does not become elevated to the intensity of a gesture until it becomes dominant. And this is equally true with form and texture. The problem with the latter two is the difficulty in raising them to the intensity needed for them to appear as major structural elements.

When color is dominant it can be quite visually engaging, so much so it becomes almost "active." The image of a person wearing a yellow hat (filmed relatively close-up) will compare with yellow flowers, a yellow car, a yellow traffic sign, and so forth.

However, in order to notice *form,* one needs a simple image in the picture frame, such as a flat ocean below a huge, orange, setting sun. A form like this might compare successfully with other round forms—a basketball, an orange, or even someone's round belly. If used, the forms would have to be repeated clearly, as well as being comparative in size within the frame. The same is true with texture. An image of a person with an "electric head" or a wild and frizzy "afro" hairdo might compare with the twiggy branches of a tree in fall, a tumbleweed, or the Statue of Liberty's head.

Since much filming is of a documentary nature (at carnivals, festivals, and public gathering places), structural gestures can offer a handy source of unity for what might otherwise be a hodgepodge of shots. These same basic principles can be applied to other film genres, discussed later. I have said comparatively little about the unity provided through inferential gesture; but this is the main substance of succeeding chapters, and particularly Chapter 13, page 225.

chapter 5

Putting Your Film Together

ORGANIZING AND SPLICING THE FOOTAGE

Once you have planned your film and shot it, you are ready to begin a separate creative act. You are ready to don the editor's hat—a role that calls upon you to suspend all the prejudicial feelings you may have acquired while engaged in planning and shooting. You must, in other words, be prepared to enter this process as innocently as you can and with as few predispositions about your film as possible.

The need for this frame of mind is simple. What you have in front of you should be your current source of inspiration. You are no longer working with *subjects*—you are now working with *images*. The images may or may not resemble your subjects, depending on the kind of film you are making. It is what these images communicate to you, now, which you must interpret. You must listen to them, "read" them, allow them to convey their potential for statement. Every image has a part or role to play which in turn will be suggestive of some kind of rule system.

Although you may have worked with a script, further changes are always needed in its interpretation through editing. The editor should be prepared to make these adjustments in the interest of the film's greater effectiveness. Flexibility and receptivity, above all, should be the bywords. Therefore, the first act in the editing process should be to review what you have in the way of footage.

Getting Organized

The first thing to do is to see what you have. The best way to do this is to look at the footage projected. You may wish to screen it several times; and while viewing the film you should take notes on provocative images, on gestures with potential, and on moments in the footage where the camera shakes or where an image is spoiled. During these screenings you may begin to get an idea for a sequence of images—perhaps even for a beginning and an ending.

The process of weeding out the good from the bad footage is one of the primary steps in editing any film, whether documentary, narrative, or expressionistic. The film's "words and phrases" have to be sorted out. One way is to note the more spectacular images (those that shout their effectiveness)—ones that are innately structural or inferentially powerful. Dynamic, action shots fall into this category, as do shots which are strong in lighting, in the use of color, in unusual framing, or in the use of form for comparison or rhythm. Inferential gestures that convey emotion should also be noted. Then there are the subtler images that convey information about place, characterization, or activity—images that are essential to the film's overall statement. Next, separate out images that reinforce or accent the material you have decided to use. During this time of sorting out the images, you can be weighing the utility and effectiveness of each in your mind. In a sense, you have been involved in finding and selecting the image's possible roles.

A role of an image is either arrived at through its discovery or through assigning a role to the image. (For further elaboration on roles and rules, see Part Four.) Knowing what an image is—what it is capable of expressing—is to have at least an inkling of its potential use in the rule system of which it will become a part. Therefore, during the initial phase of "sorting," you may also be noting some ideas for the order of the shots.

The relative positioning of your shots may be dictated in part by the overall content of the film. If you are making a film about someone building a boat, the process from beginning to end will suggest an order for the images. If you are working from song lyrics, their order will provide a framework. But if you are making a film with a freer form, one which depends upon an inner coherence dictated by what the images themselves suggest, then the structure will have to be *arrived at* intuitively.

Even if you are working from a "plan," you should consider alternative departures from it. It could prove vitalizing to the original conception in a way not anticipated. The point is to leave yourself as open as possible to various ways of relating your images. This holds true for even the most prestructured type of film.

Cutting the Film

After you have made a decision about the images, you are ready to "break the film down." Physically separate the shots. The best way to do this is to run your film through an editor-viewer. The viewer is a mechanism that allows the film to be seen projected on a small rear projection screen (usually about a $4'' \times 5''$ piece of ground glass). It allows you to control what you are seeing by forward- or backward-winding—one frame at a time or very fast. At any point, you can stop and mark a frame of the film where you want to cut. As you come to scenes you have decided to pull off the roll, the beginning and ending can be marked with a pin-hole punch located on the viewer, and then cut with scissors.

An editor-viewer should be selected with several things in mind. It should have a bright screen for easy viewing, even in a semi-darkened room; and it should have a transport system that allows easy access for threading and removing the film. The transport system should also have as few "contact points" for the film as possible in order to minimize scratching. Although some scratching of the film over a period of time, through constant use in the viewer as well as in a projector, is unavoidable, it can be reduced with good equipment. Splicers sometimes come with the viewers, but often they are badly made and don't hold up. It is better to buy a splicer separately; and if you choose to buy a tape splicer, try to get one with a simple, straight-across cut. Although they cost more initially, I find the guillotine type to be the best designed; and, in the long run, they are more economical and less troublesome than many other types.

Once a scene is isolated from the main roll, it should be labeled and catalogued in a notebook, called a "log book." The piece of film can be rolled tightly and held with a piece of masking tape, which can be used for labeling, too. Or the scenes can be hung from pins with the ends dangling into a sheet-lined waste basket or laundry hamper. If the scenes are hung up, a common method is to tape them to a white wall or to a white plywood sheet. In any case, the film should be hung in an area that is clean and won't scratch.

The professionals use an editing bin. It is nothing more than a metal frame that provides support for a sack-like canvas container. The frame is perhaps two and one-half feet wide and four feet long—and the canvas part is about three feet deep. Above the frame is a horizontal bar with hook-like projections in a row along it. The film scenes are hung from a sprocket hole on a series of hooks, which are often numbered to aid in cataloguing.

It should be noted that professional filmmakers working with larger gauge films have a "workprint" made of their original footage. Only this print is used for viewing and editing. Once the workprint has been assembled, only then is the original touched. The original, called the "negative," is then "conformed" to the arrangement of scenes matching the workprint. Cutting the negative is done by a trained "cutter," and is done with scrupulous care in order to prevent scratches and dirt from getting on the film. But for the beginner, having a workprint made can prove to be an unnecessarily time-consuming and costly step. This means that care in handling the film—viewing, projecting, splicing—should be a primary consideration.

In order to join the ends of your scenes together, you will need a splicer. "Tape splicers" are slightly different from "wet splicers," but the principle is essentially the same. The chief advantages of a tape splice over a wet splice are the ease with which it can be made and its "holding" dependability. (A poorly-made wet splice will come apart at the most unexpected times.) Some disadvantages to the tape splice include the facts that joined ends tend to pull slightly away from each other over a period of time and that the tape itself can become brittle with age and break. But it may take five to ten years for these defects to occur.

But the wet splice, on the other hand, conjures up a host of possible flubs and abortive attempts for the beginner. Although this is the splice most often used by professionals, those who make wet splices usually work with the finest equipment. (A splicer alone can cost $300 and up.) Not only that, but professionals have the advantage of skill developed through long practice. Some factors which govern making a good wet splice are: a good piece of equipment; a brand of cement that will do the job well; practice in applying the correct amount of cement; and timing in allowing the cement to weld. It should be noted that a *good* wet splice is stronger than any unspliced portion of the film.

Titling

To some beginners titling a film may seem superfluous, whereas to others it may be a necessary and important phase. Whether or not you have immediate use for hints on titling, some of the procedures might be good to know for future reference.

Once you know what you want to call your film, how do you film the title? The most common way is to use lettering against a background of some sort. The lettering is either laid on the background, held in front of it, or adhered to it. A light background requires dark lettering and vice versa. It is generally agreed that white lettering against a dark background is more pleasing and readable than the other way around.

All manner of type faces can be purchased from art supply stores for a nominal fee. Usually, these are designed to adhere to a poster board backing, which comes in colors; and although putting on the letters takes patience, they are easily applied. Once a titling board is prepared, the next step is to film it. Since most lettering is large enough to have the camera at a distance, it might be desirable to attach the board to a wall with some masking tape. Place a light to either side aimed toward the title board, being careful to avoid glare. Place the camera on a tripod away from the titles so that the end of the credits falls just within the left and right sides of the picture frame. This will give the largest, most legible reproduction.

It is always advisable to try different approaches to filming the titles—zooming out, panning across, fading in, and dissolving them. If you have a manual exposure control, you may want to try several exposure versions: first filming at the correct exposure, next at one f/stop higher (stopping the lens down one stop), and then taking still another shot at two f/stops higher. As the f/stops are increased, the color of the background will become richer and darker, and the lettering will have more contrast, and will be, to some extent, more legible. One of the versions is bound to be just right.

Another method of titling is to integrate the title with the film itself. The title may be a road sign or another kind of sign appearing in the locale of the film; or lettering can be superimposed over a scene—a technique for which many cameras now are especially equipped. The title of the film may be written on or attached to something—the sand if it is a beach or desert film. Or one might use body paints on a portion of a person's anatomy if one were making a dance film.

A FURTHER WORD ON EDITING

Aside from the mechanical act of cutting the film, there are the creative decisions relating to "where to cut," and where to position the pieces, both of which go toward making up a *completed film*. This decision-making process is really at the core of editing.

The most elementary view of editing is comparable to what an editor on a magazine or newspaper does. His job is to shorten the text, to substitute words or to rewrite a phrase or two if necessary. I notice that a good many film students have the impression that film editing is similar. In fact it is, except that there is much more to it.

I would say that the editor's most creative role is in his ability to "build" rather than to pare away. An editor builds scenes; he constructs films. He works from the raw footage, seeking its potential for a sturdy, effective construction. Selecting what is effective from what is not is only half the job. Selecting with a form in mind, and then making that form from the footage is the other half. In other words, the filmmaker is architect and builder both in the filming process and during the editing.

We can see this most clearly in making a rudimentary montage film (See the previous chapter on filming and editing with gesture). The most simple impressionistic sequences are filmed—and arranged—in order to achieve: (1.) a sense of continuity (wholeness); and (2.) emphasis (amplifying selected information and feeling). Out of the basic tenets of editing spring sophisticated terms for polished units of film form: expansion and compression of time; parallel cutting; cutting on the action; mastering the use of the cut-away. The jargon of editing sounds like a foreign language, but it is really quite simple, much easier than learning a language. With the information offered here and in subsequent chapters, you should be able to edit *any* kind of film competently.

INTRODUCTION TO SOUND

Sound can probably be the most powerful of all methods of unifying a film. It must be remembered, though, that it is a nonvisual component, and because of this many beginning filmmakers tend to over-rely on it to "carry" their film in terms of meaning and impact.

We sometimes forget that some of the most stirring film poetry ever made is silent. Between 1908 and 1913, D. W. Griffith made almost 500 short films, many of which are mini-masterpieces, which played in storefront nickelodeons and which hadn't a smidgen of sound accompaniment.

A film can virtually lack camera or subject interpretation and still succeed on the basis of the sound track. A strictly informational classroom film, for example, is sustained mostly by the accompanying narration. Here, straight documentation with little or no interpretive emphasis is sufficient; sound is easily half the total experience.

Sound has the effect of "binding" images—giving them justification—and of clarifying what is seen. The same is true with some of the older Hollywood films, where the plot is reinforced and clarified by dialogue, music, and sound effects. Where would the Busby Berkeley spectaculars be without sound? And those heavily plotted backstage melodramas? Where would Al Jolson be without film sound? Of course, without sound, most of what we see today would be a total loss. Most films are made with sound in mind.

Unfortunately, when it is realized that a film doesn't have to be "visual" in order to succeed, the beginning filmmaker can easily make the mistake of ignoring the interpretive potential of the camera. But to reason this way is shallow—a sort of ends-justifies-the-means way of thinking.

A less utilitarian view would acknowledge that a film statement could very well be *more effective* if the visuals were given equal weight with sound. The validity of this point has been proven again and again, first by the European and Japanese filmmakers of the last two decades, and now by independent filmmakers in this country.

I have always stressed the value of making films which speak as eloquently as possible on the visual level. All this, of course, presumes that the filmmaker genuinely desires to learn all of the ways in which film can be expressive—and that his purpose extends beyond the most basic utilitarian goals.

But what are some of these "magic," compelling things sound can do? On the most general level, sound-on-film acts as an "indicator" to the ultimate, or *real*, meaning intended by the images. It acts as a kind of "pointer" to the image's main meaning. In a film, if a woman hears a mysterious sound outside her window, we will know that we are to expect something ominous. And in educational films, the narrator tells the viewer what he is supposed to look for. Sound, therefore, has the effect of specifying feeling as well as directing our attention.

Sound Aesthetics

Sound falls somewhat conveniently into two broad categories: (1.) that which *reinforces* the visual image; and (2.) that which works obliquely to it, or *against* it. I call the second category *antithetical sound.*

The majority of films we see have sound tracks that are reinforcing: The sound works *with* the feeling of the image. If it is a love scene, we hear soft romantic music; and if it is a chase scene, there is loud adventurous music. In the same way, sound effects reinforce what is seen. We hear doors open and close and cars start. And of course, the most reinforcing sound of all—dialogue—gives an extra dimension to the characters and to their presence. It fills in where visual material is sparse, often substituting for filmed material.

Antithetical sound has a more dramatic relationship to the image than reinforcing sound, it plays off against the image, creating a kind of "sense gap" that the viewer must complete for himself. In an effort to resolve the difference between what he sees and what he hears, the viewer perceives fresh relationships, and meaning *takes on a poignancy.* Although this technique must be used cautiously in story films and documentaries, there are a few, especially those made by more imaginative filmmakers, that use antithetical sound. In practically all of Stanley Kubrick's films, there are moments when the sound does not quite seem to fit the prevailing mood of the images. In *2001: A Space Odyssey*, Kubrick uses a Strauss waltz next to scenes of a space shuttle rendezvous with an Earth-orbiting space station. The effect is satirical, humorous, and wistfully beautiful. In his *Clockwork Orange*, a rape scene goes on during some romping, gay-sounding music, which also accompanies other scenes of even more brutal violence. The effect here is to salve the shocked feelings of the viewer, reducing an otherwise horrendous occasion to one of farce and satire. Add to this a touch of irony. Another rape scene in Orson Welles' *Touch of Evil* is accompanied by some jazzy boogie-woogie music. More satire.

In these instances, the sound examples I've used are in a way more "oblique" to the image than "opposite" to it. The reason is that the story film form will tolerate less of a sound departure than will, say, an expressionistic or an experimental film. The story film is predicated upon the "fulfillment of anticipation" idea; and because of this, diameterically opposed sound could very well rupture the viewer's relationship with the familiar progression of events.

To reinforce the image with sound is to intensify it and to amplify its existing meaning. But to use a sound mood that is distant from the image sets up a resistance to familiar associations and establishes an abrasive perception. Here, the viewer is struggling to reconcile an unfamiliar relationship. The result, if it is used skillfully and if it works, generates fresh meaning. However, if the technique is employed awkwardly, and if the sound is impossible to reconcile, the result will be low comedy instead of resonance and irony.

Obtaining Sound Recordings: Use of Microphones

Music and sound effects for your film are available from several sources. The record store is the place most of us think of first; and it should serve well, provided that it is well stocked and offers variety. To supplement the average record store's general offering, it is possible to find interesting and unusual records at stores in ethnic neighborhoods where, for example, traditional and popular Italian, Mexican, and Japanese, music may be found. Often, highly unusual recordings, like that of the Japanese bamboo flute or Pre-Columbian bells, can be purchased through mail-order houses.

A much overlooked source of sound is the daily panoply of music and sound effects that pours out over the airways. These sounds can be "collected" by jacking-in a tape machine to the output of your AM-FM tuner. In this manner, recording is via a jack cable rather than trying to record off the speaker system with a mike.

The flexibility you have in recording sound, and, ultimately, in preparing it to go with your film, is determined by the tape machine you use. Cassette machines, for example, do not have the fidelity of reel to reel ¼ inch tape machines: Their greatest drawback is that the cartridges will not allow the tape to be edited. It is best to obtain a good ¼ inch monaural or stereo tape machine of the Wollensak or Sony variety. For the price, around $200, these machines afford good fidelity for most uses, and have easily accessible tape heads for editing, with in-put and out-put systems for recording and transfer.

Once the tape has been edited it can always be transferred to a cassette cartridge for convenient portable use if you are playing the tape in conjunction with the film. In most cases, the tape will require editing in order to shorten, extend, or intersperse spoken words with music or to eliminate unwanted portions.

You can create your own sound effects and record them. One way is to tape sounds at a high speed and re-record them at a much lower speed. The difference in speed lowers the pitch of the sound and elongates the sound pattern, sometimes transforming it into an entirely different sound. When, for instance, a human cough, recorded at a high speed, is slowed down, it comes across like a lion's roar, and, using the same technique, ordinary bird calls become the sounds of jungle apes.

For most "live" recording purposes it is best to use a unidirectional microphone, which will cut out most of the ambient noise, allowing, for the most part, only the intended sound to be recorded. Unidirectional mikes have to be especially obtained, as most mikes purchased with tape machines are omnidirectional. The omnidirectional mike is useful in picking up general sounds, such as those of a busy city street or of panel discussions. Whenever the sounds to be recorded come from several different directions, an omnidirectional mike is an essential.

Live recording should be done holding the microphone as close to the sound source as possible (six to eight inches). This will add "presence" to the recording and will, at the same time, eliminate much unwanted, ambient noise.

Narration can be recorded directly on a print of the film as it is being projected (on a projector that will record sound) or it can be recorded on a tape and either applied to the film print later or simply played in "rough sync" on a tape machine with the projected image. A portable "sound booth" can be improvised from a thick cardboard box lined inside with egg crates or other acoustical materials. A small window may be cut in the side to permit the narrator to see the projected image as he is being recorded. A piece of glass or clear plastic can be taped over the window to help shut out projector noise. The narrator can sit at a table with the booth resting on it and enclosing his head and shoulders. The mike should be attached to his shirt or lapel (if it is a lavalier mike), or else put on some soft unreverberative material such as a pillow or a folded blanket, and placed as close to the speaker's mouth as possible. (If the mike is too close, of course, breath will produce popping sounds, particularly if you are using a very sensitive mike.) At the rear of the booth, behind the narrator, a blanket or rug should be hung in order to improve sound acoustics.

After sound has been recorded for use as a sound track—whether narration, music or effects—there are always adjustments to be made. The tape will have to be edited.

Editing Sound Tape

Because the sound image cannot be seen, editing a tape may seem formidable to some people. It shouldn't be, provided you are working with a tape machine that will allow you some advantages. First of all, you need to have access to the tape playback head (usually the one on the extreme left); and secondly, you should use a machine that will allow you to move the tape back and forth *manually*, by turning the reels. At the same time, you should be able to activate the play-back head, so that what is passing by it can be heard. This latter aspect is extremely important. Some tape machines allow the motor to be disengaged and retain play-back monitoring when the "break" is depressed. But many machines do not have this breaking feature. When this is the case, other ways of disengaging the motor (and simultaneously activating the play-back head) must be found.

In order to edit a tape you must first locate the section to be removed. This can be done by locating the *start* of the passage in question. Once it is located, the machine's motors must be disengaged to allow manual turning of the reels, and the tape advanced by hand (sometimes moving it back and forth) until the first note of music or the first spoken syllable of the desired section is found. When the section is pin-pointed, simply snip the tape at that spot with a pair of scissors, being careful to allow perhaps a half inch to the right of the beginning in order to permit splicing space. After the first cut has been made, the section to be removed can either be run out on the floor or taken up on an auxiliary spool. When the end of the sound passage is reached, a second cut is made. Now the original feed and take-up spool must be rejoined with a splice, until another passage is found to select out.

Although joining the ends of sound tape is usually performed with a "splicing block" (costing $10 or so), the operation can be performed without one. To make a tape splice all you need is a pair of scissors and a small roll of $\frac{1}{4}$ inch sound-splicing tape. Being careful to align the edges exactly, overlap the ends of tape by about a half inch. Then make a through, diagonal cut (at about a 45° angle) with the scissors. Next, place *half* of an inch-long strip of the white splicing tape on one of the two ends of sound to be spliced, laying it on the shiny (base) side, and pressing gently to make it adhere. Then, on a flat surface, preferably dark, "navigate" the other sound tape end under the overlapping end of white splicing tape until the two diagonal sound tape ends meet and the two pieces fit together exactly. Press the loose end of splicing tape, completing the joining of the two sound tape ends. Now, with the back of your fingernail, rub the tiny bubbles out from under the white splicing tape, securing the weld. The splice is made. If there is any white splicing tape extending beyond the top or bottom of the sound tape, it should be trimmed away with scissors.

After the sound track tape has been roughly edited, the next step is to play it with the projected film. You may discover that you need to shorten or lengthen it to correspond to the playing time of the film. If you find that certain passages in the tape would be more effective if they "fell" adjacent to specific visual images, you may wish to jockey those sections around until they are the way you want them.

Generally, it is better to have a little more sound track than you need. This is because sometimes, during the final phase of transferring the sound to the film—since there is a differential in motor speeds between projector and tape machine—you may wish to take sound out; and in many cases, this is a bit easier than having to add sound. Also, if the tape sound track is only intended to be roughly synchronized with the film—to be played separately with it—then having more sound than is needed will allow you to turn the volume down, fading out the sound as the film ends.

To make sound editing simpler, it is recommended that a few well-placed pauses be included. This will allow for shortening or lengthening the spaces where needed. A similar technique is to include music with many codas or refrains or to use other sounds that are repetitious or continuous, such as drones, buzzes, bells tolling, and so forth. Although it is difficult to cut music unless there are pauses between symphony movements or song verses, a continuous sound can be cut any place. Speech is exceptionally easy to cut because of the natural pauses between utterances. Sound editing can be a lot of fun, and is one of the more important areas where emphasis can be achieved in the filmmaking process.

Synching Sound with Film

As has been mentioned, the sound track tape, once made, can be played along with the film or it can be transferred to the film itself by recording on a "sound stripe" that has been applied to the edge of the film (opposite the sprocket holes). A sound stripe is little more than a thin tape-like strip, either laminated or squeezed out onto the film by machine.

Original Super 8 film raw stock can be purchased with a sound stripe on it. This is usually for use in cameras that are designed to record sound *in the camera* as the film is being shot. However, when you wish to transfer an independently made and edited sound tape to the film, this is usually done after a regular roll of film has been developed and edited: At that time, the sound stripe is applied either to it or to a print of the original.

The next step is to buy, rent, or borrow a Super 8 *sound projector.* The edited sound tape is played in conjunction with the film as it is being projected in order to see if any adjustments in tape length need to be made. This projection can also serve as a rehearsal for starting and stopping both machines synchronously.

As the two machines are "jacked in" to each other by a cable, and you are doing a run-through, you can also check the sound level on the projector. After you have adjusted tape and film to finish together, and sound levels are accounted for, you are ready to record.

It should be remembered that narration can be placed directly on the film as it is running through the sound projector—without pre-recording it on tape. Although this allows more precise synchronization and timing, ways must be found to stifle projector sound. Some sort of sound booth, such as the one described earlier, should be used to enclose the narrator.

LEVELS OF FILMIC REALITY

It is a commonly held feeling that once you turn the movie camera on and begin filming—that's it. Control is surrendered to the ineffable mysteries of the camera itself, and the image—what happens in front of the camera—is what is going to be recorded on film, and what will be the final result. This is seldom the case. It is doubtful that the projected, finished film ever really duplicates the visual experience one feels at the moment of documentation. If the filmmaker claims that the film is accurate in every respect to what he saw, then he is rationalizing. He is accepting "what is" for what he thought "was." This discrepancy between what was and what is demonstrates the concept of levels of *filmic reality*.

Let us assume that Janie, a neighbor girl, or your daughter is the subject of the film you're about to make. You've seen her when she's sweet and when she's bad, when she's beautiful and when her flaws are showing. You've experienced her in her many moods. On top of that, she is a youthful reflection of you. You feel preeminently qualified to make the definitive film of Janie because, after all, you are her mother. You have loaded your camera and are about to make a film, about HER.

What you are experiencing is the reality of your subject prior to filming. It is the *a priori* reality—before the fact of filming—with which you have so saturated your expectations. In short, Janie has a very real existence *outside* the film you are about to make. Why outside the film? Because Janie has not yet been experienced *in a film*. In other words, the three-dimensional Janie is of questionable importance to the two-dimensional Janie we will see in the film. They are two distinct children, like twins, who might look alike, but whose behavior is different. There are reasons for this.

One very important reason is that when we get in front of a camera our normal behavior changes. It does so because we, somehow perhaps as humans, intuit that what is being seen "of us"—our self-concept, the image we are conscious of projecting—will be ascertained and evaluated by others in a much shorter time than in real life. Judgments will be passed on us in haste. Therefore, we offer a stylized version of ourselves—our essence, distilled.

Suddenly we become performers of ourselves—caricatures, impressions of our self-images.

Should exception be taken that the film of Janie was made when she wasn't aware of the camera, then very likely she will give us a low key version of herself, because she didn't know anyone was paying attention. She will appear to be Janie *at rest*, inward and not particularly expressive. The film will be so candid that it may be dull.

So, Janie just isn't going to meet our expectations. This is the first level of filmic reality: the live subject, together with what we know about it. It is extremely difficult to transfer this level of reality to film.

The second level of filmic reality is what we experience within the rectangle at the moment of filming. This is perhaps the most important level, for it is then that the primary magic of the filmic experience is obtained. The rectangle is the stage, and what occurs there is crucial. Above all, it is a radical alteration of what we experience of the subject prior to filming. It is another distinct phase in shaping the image. For more in detail on this subject, review "Seeing within the Rectangle" in Part One, and "Understanding the Documentary," and "Exploring the Subject," in Part Two.

Unfortunately, what is being experienced, seen, and designed for film may very well not be recorded as we are seeing it because of mechanical problems with the camera, because of the age of the film, or, perhaps, because of nothing more than the type of film we are using.

We may think we are filming a beautiful, composed sequence; but if the exposure meter of the camera is not working, nothing of value will be recorded. This, sad as it may seem, is the third level of reality, when the film comes back from the lab completely black. Or there may be a light leak in the camera that exposes the entire film, resulting in little more than slightly tinted clear acetate. Again, no image. Or, let us say your pin registration is not working: The camera runs, but the film fails to advance. These are but a few of the mildly terrifying possibilities that could exercise control over what *you think* you are getting on film.

After all is done—the film has been shot, and it has been sent to the laboratory for processing—the image of Janie is ready to be developed by technicians who don't know who you are and probably could care less. To state it simply: The fourth level of filmic reality is what you get back from the lab—WHATEVER YOU

GET BACK. Anything from scratches to change of normal color and to outright, inadvertent destruction of the film can, and does occur.

Now you are ready to sit down and edit. During this process you will be able to see *the image* of Janie pass through a further phase of evolution. At this time you will again be able to exercise bold strokes of creative vision. But whatever else happens, the image could again change radically from the way you had seen Janie before you started to film. How the shots of her are juxtaposed in the editing will determine how her "film presence" is emphasized and developed. This constitutes a fifth level of filmic reality.

After the film has been edited and you are ready to put sound with the film, you are high on the ladder of metaphysical creation. During this sixth level, sound can have a profound effect on your film.

Perhaps now you want to have your film original printed. So it's back to the lab, perhaps, for more alterations of Janie's image. In this process, the print made at the lab can be filtered and faded, coated and cured. Many of these changes can be made at your request. In fact, if you have the time, money, and patience, the lab can create an entirely different film for you with wipes and dissolves, freeze frames and fades—even a "face job" can be done. What color would you like Janie's face? A sickly yellow-green urban pallor or a robust, warm Catalina tan? Regardless of such possibilities, however, most people will settle for a print as nearly accurate to the original as possible. But, unless elaborate and costly processes are used, the print *never* looks exactly like the original—in this seventh level of filmic reality.

At last! You are ready to project your film of Janie for an audience. At this point you would think your film beyond more changes; you would think that it would remain pristine in its last crucial test—but not so. You must yet meet the challenge of the eighth and last significant level of reality—projection.

Some projectors run fast and some run slowly, thus affecting both the movement of the image and the pitch of the sound. Some projectors have long focal length lenses and some have short ones, and this factor affects the size and brightness of the picture. Some projection screens have a high reflectability while others have a low reflectability. The projector may be too close to the screen or too far away; and it may make a noise that competes with your sound track. The house current could fail, or a projection bulb could blow, thus terminating the show. Or if all goes well mechanically, the audience could be drunk or hostile; even worse, they could be saccharine and patronizing. The list is endless. Just remember, these considerations can affect *the way* a film is seen, thus affecting the meaning of the film. Therefore, do not think that your film is impervious to change. You are involved in change whether you like it or not—from the moment you decide to make a film.

At the root of the matter is the fact that film is a medium that does not record as faithfully as some might think. Though most of the changes just mentioned are not good, indeed, many others are desirable—when intended. These take place in the crafting of the filmed image, and without which, the film would be pointless and unimaginative. The simple arbitrary placing of a subject in a rectangular frame, itself, is a transformational act. No matter how realistic a subject may appear on the theater screen—by the time you see it—it has undergone a lot of "unrealistic" rendering. A major emphasis of this book is how to recognize types of *creative* transformations—and to encourage you to utilize them to make better films. We can do without the problems posed by the "levels of filmic reality," but we can't do without *intentional,* controlled transformations as a valid part of the filmmaker's craft.

HOW THE PROCESS OF MUTUAL INFORMATION WORKS

Mutual information is the organic route to creating. Instead of the map route—the process of scripting—the organic route allows whatever directions have been taken to be changed according to aesthetic necessity and desirability. Mutual information operates, or should operate, during the process of filming, and again in the editing.

Mutual, in this case, means a sharing. It works like this. You pick your subject and begin moving around it with the camera. As you move, you begin to see interesting angles and relationships with the light you hadn't anticipated. But you do see them now. You are beginning to receive the visual information afforded by your subject; and you are reacting to it in a way that will emphasize the effect you have discovered. By directing this emphasis or exaggeration, you essentially "re-inform" your subject; or, more accurately, you start to shape the image on film. In turn, you react to the subject, the re-informed image, and further refine your approach by making still more adjustments in your movement as well as in the placement of the subject with respect to light and the camera. This give and take, modulating your activity and filmic selection, is the process of mutual information.

This is a more organic method than scripting because the visual image is allowed to "grow out of itself." All the filming is "experienced" in the rectangle; and decisions are made on the basis of what is seen there, rather than on what has been completely decided on a piece of paper prior to the filming act.

Of course, there are many instances where the use of this method is impractical, notably in the making of story films, where time and other considerations may prohibit an appreciable amount of experimentation with the subject. Besides, in story filming, every angle and every lighting situation will have been chosen for the emotion it will elicit. Excursions with the camera, such as the ones undertaken through the mutual information method, might very well unearth feelings not anticipated by a story format; these feelings would be useless to a type of "purpose film." (I consider films made for commercial, instructional, or entertainment purposes as purpose films.)

On the other hand, the on-the-spot inventiveness that can result from using the technique of mutual information can and often does produce startling and remarkably unpredictable results. It is a good route to originality, and a way to evoke truth both in your subject and in yourself. The expressionistic film does exact this kind of truthfulness from the materials and techniques used to make it up; and, to a large extent, so does the documentary. I am using "truth" here to mean "accuracy." To be true is to be accurate; and use of the organic technique is the greatest insurance for obtaining what is true.

Mutual information is something that all artists and scientists understand and employ in their endeavors as a matter of course. It is the process of listening, watching, and then shaping. It is a dialogue between yourself and your materials—between your necessity to shape and form images and the innate possibilities *of the basis* for the image with which you are working.

Lastly, when you sit down to edit and are confronted with a variety of images that you must unify and work into a system or context that will give them meaning, you must again "listen" to your materials. Perhaps it is here, even more than in the gathering of the images, that you will have to be intensely aware of and sensitive to what your images are saying and suggesting.

part II

THE DOCUMENTARY

chapter 6

Understanding the Documentary

INTRODUCTION

In order to understand the *nature* of the documentary film, it may be helpful to compare it first to some of its early predecessors. The primitive cave drawings are probably the oldest demonstration of humans attempting to record circumstances making up their environment. Although the Bible has gained its reputation largely as religious scripture, it has been a major source of documentary information about people and events in ancient history. During the Greek and Roman Empires, the bards and rhapsodists reported in their songs on the lives and deeds of their contemporaries, some of which were collected in *The Iliad*, *The Odyssey*, and in the works of Clearchus, Herodotus, Athenaeus, Petronius, and Juvenal. In a more recent time, *Moll Flanders*, *The Adventures of Tom Jones*, and *Fanny Hill* are novels that draw heavily from the real lives of people (many of whom were in jail) who received a fee for telling their experiences to writers. Charles Dickens, of course, was well known for his penchant for probing into social institutions for the blind, the disabled, the insane, and the orphaned. In a way, he was a sort of nineteenth-century Ralph Nader. Today, Truman Capote rediscovered a similar documentary technique in writing his novel *In Cold Blood*. While most of these "life experiences" derive from factual accounts, all are embellished and stylized by both the teller and the writer. The written word offered much freedom to the would-be documentarian of the past: He might alter events and the characterizations of his subjects in order to generate interest and meaning.

On the other hand, film, unlike words, is a much more faithful recorder of actuality, because its literal visual impressions leave little room for ambiguity. Used without intention, film records as objectively as anything can, and because it can copy so well, it is a strong tool for gathering socially useful information. Yet as a medium of expression it is no more creative than words are when they are used for their own sakes.

The value of film for the preservation of history is undisputed; but because the documentarian can capture uncontrived life events with great fidelity, filmmakers have rejoiced in this new and excellent means to achieve objectivity, not realizing that it can be delusory. Indeed, the *value* in an objectively recorded subject is frequently not obvious to the viewer. It is a little understood fact that, in order to perceive the subject with meaning, it must be ordered within a *context*—whether one as specific as the composition of a single frame or one arising the linear context of juxtaposed frames (of images). The uncontrolled context of randomly ordered images that the pure, objective approach produces (where the subject controls all that we see) must rely on a subject that is interesting or sensational enough to be self-evidently meaningful. The burden is laid on the subject to speak for itself; and the viewer, it is thought, will provide the context. But all too often, when the subject is shown with no accompanying interpretation whatsoever (i.e., out of a meaningful context), it leaves the viewer aroused by what he has seen, but unsatisfied as to the film's meaning. It is akin to what we experience when watching newsfilm on television with nothing but a commentator's drone to order our perceptions: we seem to hear an anonymous voice speaking into a void. Although sometimes exciting and entertaining, it is nearly always of questionable lasting value.

How, then, can a documentary film provide more meaning? It can—through an orderly presentation of its material; or, to put it another way, through the creation of images. To do this, the documentarian must see selectively and with a purpose. He must see meaning and experience it for himself first; then he can communicate it to others.

The main difference between the documentary and fictional narrative forms is that in the former, "life examples" for the construction of meaning are found in a natural state, and in the latter, life examples are "staged" and shaped in fine detail. The aim of documentary and fiction is the same—an *intentional presentation* of life examples. In the process, life becomes stylized or idealized. The two forms differ both in the methods by which the material is obtained and in its *degree* of stylization.

Many people make the mistake of thinking that the documentary is just a *copy* of reality and of actual events. This simply need not be the case. The form may be saddled with this reputation because documentarians in the past have believed it. Many, therefore, have used the medium badly. This, luckily, is not as true today, particularly since we have the films of Pennebaker, Wolper, Leacock, and the Maysles brothers. But even though these men offer a bright promise, their work is frequently too careful and puristic. The myth that the documentary is either sensational or boring becomes self-serving and self-fulfilling.

There are a few people graduating from film schools who frequently teethe on the documentary, using it to test their skills; then move on to the more lucrative area of theatrical films, where the arena of competition is more exciting. We find such a person in Charles Salmore, whose prize-winning mini-documentary *Frogs* is discussed in a later section. This is to say that the documentary may be the worst used, most poorly represented of film forms; and yet it is the one with the most undiscovered potential for statement. It has been a workhorse for the news media, educators, and combat armies, and has been used as a dry tool for sociologists. But it can be more than that; it can be as powerful as fictional narrative.

Certainly one of the hopes of the beginning 1970s was Joseph Salzman, a young TV documentary writer-producer, who made some stunning reportorial films and a few that were genuinely moving. You may never hear of the titles or see the films because they were made for local Los Angeles viewing and they are owned by CBS-KNXT, the station he worked for. His film on breast cancer, *Why Me?*, one about *The Junior High School*, another on the Watts ghetto, *Black on Black*, and a dolefully moving film about a person who just wasn't ready to die, *The Very Personal Death of Elizabeth Schell Holt-Hartford*, stand as monuments to a persistent will to say something important. I use the past tense for Salzman because, after having made his films, he is going back to his first love, teaching journalism. His reasons for retiring when he was doing so well are his to say. But there is no doubt that his films dignify the art of the documentary. Just what this art is—as apart from travelogues, newsfilms, and informational wildlife studies—is what this chapter aims, at least in part, to illuminate.

One can work toward the goal of the artful documentary by simply understanding where its center of emphasis and its strength lie. That strength comes from uncovering the significance of real life examples and ordering them in a meaningful way. In doing so, it is true that the filmmaker subjects others to his interpretations; but he is also providing them with life examples, offering ways to see them through his eyes and with his experience.

THE DOCUMENTARY AND ITS RELATIVES

The term documentary can be applied to any film form. In the broadest sense, every type of filmmaking, from the story film to the abstract film, uses the camera as a tool to document whatever is before the lens. Yet when people use the term in a strict sense they usually refer to a type of filmmaking which is largely *a recording of unfictionalized events.* That is, the film medium is used to document a real activity, event, or occasion. A host of film modes fall into the category of "pure" documentation.

Early film records show that the filmmaker's first impulse was to "record" all manner of events transpiring around him: parades, inaugurals, exhibits—even operas and stage plays. Film's primary value was seen to be utilitarian; it was simply a documenting device for the dissemination of information. This important use of film persists today in several forms.

Newsfilm

The newsfilm is the simplest of related documentary forms. Pure, "objective," news coverage—such as that of the President's arrival from a summit conference abroad—becomes the documenting of an event in perhaps the most objective way *possible.* Such a situation is not open to much interpretation in the visual sense. Circumstances preclude getting anything "telling" or unusual because the whole thing is carefully staged; in fact, such coverage is often referred to as "managed" news. In this case, the camera obediently sits there, grinding helplessly away, gorging its lens eye with every visual tidbit irrespective of its relevance or truth. I often think of uncreative newsfilm reportage as just a tiny step removed from the most objective of all visual automatons—the so-called surveillance video cameras stationed in banks. Of course, the news media in this country prides itself on objectivity, so much so that it is frequently impossible to see the relevance in what we are watching.

In our time, news coverage is an information-gathering and an information-presenting activity. It should be understood that what is meant by "information" here is the what-actually-happens aspect or the strictly factual view that presents details of happenings essentially free from comment or interpretation (except for that interpretation emanating from the subject itself). It is an expository form. It might be useful to keep the above definition for handy reference, because the gathering of information is *the primary* aspect of all documentary forms.

Feature Newsfilm

Besides the newsfilm, there is the "feature" newsfilm, a form that is more organized and more interpretive. Where the straight newsfilm takes its organization primarily from the *event,* the feature is more of a wedding of the filmmaking process with the subject, one which brings selection and emphasis to the film through camera work and editing. Its objectives are to explore the subject "in depth," going further than objective news coverage, and to present the subject "with relevance," often as a slice-of-life relating to a single individual or a group of people. Features of this sort are typified by the familiar network news specials of Charles Kuralt On the Road.

Such a feature may choose to explore the activities and motivations, say, of an artist who has chosen to sculpt a mountain with the aid of his entire family, using bulldozers and explosives. Still another one may deal with the plight of aerospace engineers in Oregon who are out of work and on welfare. The personal level to which I have referred is dubbed "human interest" in journalistic argot. It shows what happens in an informational way, and relates it to people in a personal way, too. There is another aspect to which these features aspire—a universal appeal. In the case of the artist who labors over his monumental work, it is pointed out through narration and the artist's own words how this effort relates to man's general striving to master nature and shape it in his image.

It should be pointed out that the feature news special, when only a few minutes long, cannot possibly be very thorough. At best, it gives an impression, an outline. However, more thorough hybrids of the news feature have come along, among which are ones with a "magazine" format like *60 Minutes* and *Chronolog*, where each topic is given ten minutes or so in coverage. The ultimate expansion on this idea, of course, is the hour-long documentary "special." It is here that the filmmaker, when given an adequate amount of freedom (and if he has the ability), can come up with a truly superior film. Joseph Salzman's films, mentioned earlier, are examples. Because more time and effort can be given to them, they are frequently quite substantial from the standpoint of depth coverage. And once in a while they are even memorable, like the acclaimed Edward R. Murrow documentary on the travails of the migrant farm laborer, *Harvest of Shame*. For the student of the documentary, news features of the type just described are good models to illustrate the more standard methods of gathering and presenting information.

The Informational-Instructional Film

Another relative of the documentary is the informational-instructional film which, like the news film, has as its purpose presenting information as an end in itself.

Types of informational films can have a wide range. Some have instructional value through simple exposition much like the travelogue. The purpose of such a film is to expose, to reveal, to acquaint—and perhaps to entertain (which can be instructional too).

A school may wish to have a film made of its experimental, special studies program with a view to presenting it to the school board as a kind of progress report. Or, members of a botanical society may wish to have a film made to show their world-wide membership what is being done regionally in the way of field trips and collecting specimens.

Perhaps the most common informational films of all are the home movie and the travelogue, both of which are intended to record events and places. Even though it has been disparaged by "serious" filmmakers as a form that is awkward and inept—and worse, boring—the home movie need not fit any of these descriptions. Good film techniques insure the success of *any* film form, whatever the subject. (Both the home movie and travelogue are less complex manifestations of the "intimate" and "social" approaches to the documentary, two major forms which are discussed in the next sections.)

The *instructional film*, sometimes called an educational film, is a highly structured and stylized presentation of factual material, the aim of which is to teach. Such films are used widely in schools, and have become practically unparalleled as successful supplementary teaching tools.

The instructional film is much more concerned with an orderly presentation of facts than is the purely informational film. One wanting to learn the basic techniques of presenting filmed material for instruction might begin by documenting an activity that involves a process or procedure—such as boatbuilding, pottery-making, or leather-working. Crafts lend themselves well to this kind of film. The process is followed, or covered, by the camera and the film is assembled in the editing so that the how-to-do-it aspects can be clearly grasped by the viewer. "Training films" sometimes fall into this category, although the term is usually applied to films designed specifically to prepare the viewer for some procedural task related to institutional training—as in the military service, civil service, hospitals, and so forth.

Promotional and Propagandistic Films

When a film's purpose is to *sell* or *persuade* the viewer, it becomes a promotional or propagandistic film. Some documentaries intended to persuade are: films made around election time to boost political candidates; films made to promote activities such as healthful exercise, travel, or cleaning up the environment; films made to gain sponsorship of a bond issue (as for school earthquake safety); or, in a single example, a film made to enlist support for a linguistics program for minority children. These films, although strongly informational, are often slanted by a specific point of view. They are related to the documentary in that they are supposed to be based upon facts, yet the structure is highly stylized (fictionalized) and interpretive. The persuasive documentary is a type of film that endeavors to manipulate feeling and attitudes in order to evoke some form of action by the viewer.

The documentary, like most of the other film forms, has its analogues in the written medium. The newsfilm finds its equivalent in the assortment of items on the front page of a newspaper; a promotional film is like the many brochures we get in the mail touting a product or a service, or it may resemble a company progress report, or an annual summary to the stockholders. The informational film is like articles and books on travel, or newsletters, or industrial "house organs." And the instructional film closely parallels the textbook or hobby magazine.

The more complex documentary film—what I call the "prototypical documentary" because it brings together *all* of the important aspects of such a film—is the main focus of the succeeding sections. The complex documentary incorporates three main aspects: the *informational level* (the principal emphasis in the film types just discussed), the *personal* level, and the *universal* level. The documentary prototype goes beyond the informational level. It probes deeper, and it is more revealing of life and its meaning than its simpler relatives. The prototypical documentary comes closest to raising the form to an art. It is, I believe, the most profound approach one can take to this genre.

THE CREATIVE INVESTIGATIVE FILM

The documentary prototype can be subdivided into two main parts. One, the *social documentary,* makes its statement about a group of people who are related to one another racially or ethnically, or through occupation, custom, or common interest. The other— *intimate documentary,* is centered around a single individual whose social affiliations are only brought out incidentally.

The Social Documentary

In the social documentary, a common denominator binds the group as a unit. That the subjects of a film are city-dwellers or glass blowers, surfers, Eskimos, cat-fanciers, soldiers, politicians or racing-car drivers is of primary importance. In a film of this sort we tend to view the people as they are affected socially rather than personally, that is, what brings them together. An investigation into group involvement, then, is the featured aspect of the social documentary.

For instance, in D. A. Pennebaker's *Monterey Pop*, the throngs that were filmed at the Monterey Pop Festival in 1964 came to share music as an experience—and that sharing is the lens, so to speak, through which both performers and spectators are seen. A more recent example is Charles Salmore's incisive and humorous film about a group's devotion to frogs for eating, sport, and profit. The film is called *Frogs*, and was made in 1972.

In Lewis Mumford's 1938 classic, *Cities*, urbanites are shown impotently trapped in the city's "core" because of their economic and social immobility. Or, as another example, *Glass* is a film that points up the sensitivity of the glass blower as he practices his art and that contrasts him with the depersonalized attitude of employees in a bottle manufacturing plant. *Endless Summer*, by Bruce Brown, is an odyssey of a group of young surfers who go off around the world in search of "the perfect wave."

Characteristic of films like these is a greater attention focused on the *activities* of the group (what the people are doing and how they do it) than on any one person's unique reaction to a situation. In almost every instance, the group subjects of social documentaries are *doing something*, engaging in an activity which dramatizes their common bond. Performers and audience interact at the music festival; frog devotees are filmed at frog-jumps, and while hunting frogs and frying frogs; and the surfers are seen riding the waves. As will be shown in more detail later, *some form* of subject activity is essential to all documentaries, whether the emphasis is on a group or on a single individual.

The logistics involved in making a social documentary are often extremely complicated and necessitate organization and planning to a considerable degree. The extent to which this is needed is determined by how ambitious the film is, and, often literally, by how much ground it will cover. How many people are involved as subjects, where the film is to be shot and under what kinds of circumstances, and how many people are assisting in the making of the film are all factors that determine the size and complexity of the task. (The *intimate documentary*, discussed next, bypasses much of this preparation.)

It is easy to see, then, that in filming a social documentary organization is paramount. For an example of this organization, one only has to examine cursorily what went into the making of Michael Wadleigh's film, *Woodstock*, which is about a musical "happening," and also about the beginning of the end of a youth culture and life style.

There were 400,000 youngsters at Woodstock, New York, in August of 1969. The documentary was to be filmed in a single weekend, and for this, Wadleigh had assembled an eighty-man crew and fifteen cameramen. He returned from Woodstock with 120 hours of film (or 315,000 feet of exposed 16mm footage). During the filming he frequently had as many as eight cameras going at the same time. So tight was the schedule, and so hectic were the conditions, that synchronization of the sound ("slating" each take on the spot) became impossible. The technical problems in an undertaking of this magnitude are complex enough; but, when added to the unpredictable agenda of events and to the various problems connected with managing a crowd, care in planning is the only thing that will insure the film's completion. As it turned out, the enormous amount of footage shot on this particular project almost proved too much to handle in the editing. This, together with the erratic slating methods used for synchronizing the sound, foreshadowed many hours of work ahead just to match the sound with what footage was obtained. The film was finished; but even with what might have been adequate preparation, the project nearly collapsed. Woodstock is an exception—an exaggerated instance. Contrast this with the leisurely shooting of Bruce Brown, filming alone with a single Bolex camera. This is not to say that his *Endless Summer* needed no planning. It should point up, however, that the scope and complexity of the subject, by being limited, also limited the chance of failure.

Woodstock's predecessor, *Monterey Pop*, is a similar film in terms of subject; but in the degree of the undertaking it fared much better—and incidentally, it is a more successful film. But *Woodstock* is a monumental attempt to record a monumental event, and because preparation did not match the ambition of the project, the full meaning of the occasion was never captured.

In order to see what goes into making a film that, in its scope and ambition, is much more within the ability and grasp of the majority of beginning filmmakers, let us examine the previously mentioned documentary, *Frogs*, by Charles Salmore. *Frogs* shows that good films can be made with much less money than *Woodstock*; and in some ways, because the scale of the undertaking is smaller, this film may end up being more focused and meaningful than a filmed spectacle of cumbersome physical magnitude.

In an interview with Mr. Salmore, I asked him several key questions relating to the production of his film.

LINDER: How did you get the idea for your film?

SALMORE: One morning, while I was looking at the newspaper, I happened to notice the governor was going to participate in a frog-jumping contest. I thought at first this would make a good political commentary. I'd been definitely looking out for a subject to base a film on. Since I really didn't want to make a political film just then, I thought the subject of frogs had possibility as a children's film—which did interest me—the idea of attacking the whole *non-medical* realm of frogs from a kid's point of view.

LINDER: What did your pre-production work consist of?

SALMORE: I researched the subject thoroughly—everything I could get my hands on that dealt with frogs. I went to all the standard places for leads—to the major public and school libraries in the city—reading all periodicals and books on the subject I thought were relevant. Finally, I plowed through tons of clippings at the local newspaper's "morgue," and covered everything to do with frogs back to the first edition.

The names of two champion frog-jumpers kept popping up, so I contacted them—which took me into still other areas of investigation. Gradually, I began to see that there was a "frog cult," and that some people view them symbolically, with a strong fantasy aspect. From all this material I was gathering I had to sift out what looked like situations that would produce good coverage of the subject. The frog-jumping event was a must, and there were a few other situations that because of the subject's co-operativeness or closeness in miles were chosen. For example, the lady who raises frogs for research, and who looks like a frog, was one; and the guy in San Francisco who hypnotizes them was another. The research took six months of steady work.

All this time, I was looking around for funding, writing letters to foundations—which incidentally didn't produce anything concrete until I was about to call it quits and try to make the film with my own capital. That was when The American Film Institute (with which I was in touch) suggested I contact two foundations which are funding arms for P.B.S. (Public Broadcasting Service), otherwise known as educational television, designed to encourage the independent, creative production of films. One is called the Center for

Creative Cinematography in New Haven, Connecticut, and the other is the Southwest Creative Film Center in Texas. I received a grant application from the latter agency—and proceeded to fill it out in the most minute detail, covering the proposed budget, the film's intention, etc. I was very lucky, and they replied quickly with an approval and a check to go ahead. The amount of the grant was, in all, $5,000, though the film ended up costing $7,000 to make (which included an answer print). From the date the grant was received I had a six-month deadline; three months of that was spent in shooting.

LINDER: How many people assisted you?

SALMORE: The most I had at any one time was nine people—when we covered the frog-jump. I had a cook, a production manager, three cameramen, one sound man, two assistants—and myself, who acted as sound man and director. The least number I had was a cameraman and myself; but let me tell you, it was terrible to work that way. Don't ever do it unless you have to.

LINDER: Did you use anything resembling a schedule or script?

SALMORE: I had a notebook with my appointments for shooting and some notes on things I wanted to be sure to get. [Author's note: please see figure 9.] I did go out and interview some of the people beforehand, just to see what the possibilities would be for shooting, and then I went home and made a lot of notes about details I had picked up on. The practice of looking everything over a day or a week before the filming had the dual advantage of placing the subject at ease, and assisted me in drawing up a rough set of shooting procedures—in sectioning off the project and blocking off what I wanted to cover. In the case of the lady who raises frogs, I knew that I would let her take me on a tour of the frog pens, and then I would sit down and discuss the subject with her. I planned to interweave the voice and images later, in the editing, and it worked out well.

LINDER: What did you think about as you put the film together—about the images and how they related?

SALMORE: I wanted to show people as interesting, fascinating, foolish, ironic—however they happened to appear to me as I saw them. As I looked at the film over and over, I began to see things, relationships I didn't see when I shot the film. Much of the film's intention came out in the editing. I began to see how activities were pointing up human nature—the way people treated the frogs, and so forth. Ultimately, for that reason, the film turned out to be for adults as well as children. It would have been good the way I intended it originally, but now it means a lot more than I thought it would.

LINDER: Do you have any advice for the beginning documentarian?

SALMORE: (1.) Watch documentaries whenever possible. TV is a good place to see them. (2.) Don't antagonize your subjects to get a response—let the subject in on what to expect. Always get legal releases from them, even if they are your own relatives. (3.) Have all your equipment checked out and know it is in good condition before beginning to shoot. Once on location there's usually little opportunity to correct mechanical failures, or obtain more film, lights, or batteries. (4.) Always use versatile assistants—ones who can "grip," run camera, sound, and perform as many filming-related tasks as possible. (5.) And as the director, be sure to establish at the outset that it is *your* film, your vision, and it is you who will make the decisions. If the latter is not done at the start, it is possible that some who are assisting may all too readily volunteer their opinions and ideas, which could be distracting and waste time—and possibly cause you to miss an opportunity to accomplish what you had intended.

An offshot of the social documentary is a film type we see often on television—with animals or fish as its main subject instead of humans. Perhaps it is best exemplified by a number of films under the title *The Undersea World of Jacques Costeau*. What makes this type of film interesting as a social documentary is that lower life forms are used as the main subjects in a way that will elicit an empathetic response from the viewer. I would class many of these films as social documentaries because anthropomorphic qualities are imparted to creatures through interpretations by the narrator, and secondly, because we are shown the events through the eyes of divers, explorers, and scientists who relate to the creatures on an equal footing. The viewer is made to feel that the gap between humans and lower animal forms is not fundamentally that great—especially in the depiction of mating practices, territorial instincts, and the like. Consequently, the viewer is brought into close identity with these subjects. By doing so, he establishes his involvement on a meaningful level, closely comparable to that in a film with humans as the main subject. Added to the viewer's feeling of significance about such a film is the current wave of interest in ecological systems and the awareness of man's dependency on all forms of life for his survival. Certainly, this awareness has contributed the single most important change in our attitude toward films of animals and insects which would hitherto have been relegated to a position of mere curiosity. The nature films produced by Walt Disney were probably the first to arouse the viewer to a recognition of the emotional power such films can have. Although these were not intended as ecology-minded films per se, they nevertheless made us aware of nature's similarity to ourselves—if for no other reason than the fact that here for the first time, we were able to observe the animal world close up and undisturbed by a human presence. Being able to see animals in their natural habitat, to note their close similarity to us, and to see them behave just as they would in the absence of humans become compelling arguments for this type of film as a social documentary. Its inclusion in this genre is predicated upon the degree of meaning the film has to us, and the extent to which we are able to identify with the subjects.

A FILM WITHOUT A SCRIPT: THE INTIMATE DOCUMENTARY

The intimate documentary is a film with a single individual as its subject. It is called *intimate* because, quite often, the approach to it is informal and relaxed, and because there are only a few people involved in its production, frequently including only the filmmaker and the subject.

This kind of documentary is essentially "a film without a script," in that the form, the shape, the direction it will take, and ultimately its meaning, are predicated upon whatever circumstances grow from the filming event itself. In short, a film such as this cannot be scripted because the subject almost always is allowed to, and does, take the filmmaker into spontaneous, unrehearsed areas.

Where the social documentary renders the individual in the context of group interests, the intimate approach aims for an inside look at one person's thoughts and involvements, giving emphasis to his interactions with others only insofar as such an emphasis brings out his unique attitude toward life. In a sense, the less typical a person he is and the more independently he can project his character, the better subject he will make.

In D. A. Pennebaker's *Don't Look Back*, Bob Dylan the man emerges with all the trappings of a venerated artist; but at the same time, he carries with him the baggage of human vulnerability—a certain amount of pettiness, conceit, uncertainty. We see the unapproachable artist and the approachable man; but we wouldn't have, had the camera not been relentlessly and constantly probing. Furthermore, we wouldn't have seen the frailer side to Dylan had he himself not wanted it seen (He had specifically asked Pennebaker not to pull any punches). The need for a cooperative subject in a film of this sort should be obvious.

The subject of Shirley Clarke's *A Portrait of Jason*—a male, negro, homosexual prostitute—sits drinking highballs while talking directly to the camera. What ensues is a marathon dialogue of epic proportions; it sometimes engages the camera (viewer) directly, sometimes Miss Clarke off-camera, and at other times fluctuates between moribund confessions and performing sparkling imitations of famous actresses. Although he makes references to being black, being homosexual, and being a prostitute, these roles never dominate or pigeonhole the man. This film does not attempt to record the details of a male prostitute's life in particular, or even to show the problems of being a negro homosexual. It is intended to document an interesting and unusual sensibility.

The incisive nature of the intimate documentary might give one cause to wonder why people like Dylan and Jason would want to reveal themselves so honestly. Perhaps the reason is that the camera holds the mirror up to the subject in a valuable way, showing him to himself, thus motivating him to begin, and to continue making the film.

The Salesman is an attempt by Al and David Maysles to intimately document the activity of a house-to-house Bible salesman whose "territory" is in the northeastern United States, a lower-middle class Catholic community. The film shows him paying calls on residents and glibly pitching them on his wares. Afterwards, it shows him in a sterile motel room, depressed and candidly expressing disaffection for his work.

Salesman fails to give us as much insight into the character of the man as his complex nature seems to warrant. His hucksterism comes off like petty thievery. Nothing that happens raises the man to the level of human dimension where empathy is possible. His customers, the vulnerable families who go into hock for years to buy his Bibles, are projected by the film as simple dupes; and neither the salesman nor his clients comes across better than plain people with plain problems. *The Salesman* is spread too thin. It tries to cover the ground of both the intimate and the social documentary in one leap.

Making documentaries is a gamble. The filmmaker exposes himself to the indulgences of his subject as well as to his good qualities. To be sure, the Maysles brothers have had their share of bad luck. Their minor masterpiece *Showman* is a case in point. The problem with it is that it can't be commercially exhibited unless its star, Joseph E. Levine, gives back the permission to show the film that he rescinded over a decade ago.

The documentary shows Levine savoring his success as a "number one" film entrepreneur: giving orders to several nervous, diffident aides, and greeting Sophia Loren with a kiss at the airport. (He was a starmaker too.) It pictures him wheeling and dealing in his Spartanly furnished Cannes hotel room, puffing on a cigar and gruff-talking percentages over the phone. It shows him at a reunion with his Boston cronies, reminiscing about the time when he was just a nobody. The film is a good look at a powerful man who, in spite of being soft-hearted, made it to the top. It is too bad that this impressive document, seen only by a few people (at festivals and the like), cannot be enjoyed by the audience it deserves. Even though an agreement was obtained to release the film for exhibition, the subject was able to reverse his decision and prevent the film from being shown. If the subject is powerful enough, like Levine, legal binding is seldom sufficient to protect the filmmaker. Fortunately, this is a hazard not experienced by many documentarians. But there is bound to be some material in an intimate or social documentary that is sensitive and controversial.

In the intimate documentary, the activity of the subject, whether he is a negro male prostitute, a Bible salesman, a great singer, or a powerful film distributor, provides a backdrop and context against which to project his personality. The subject's individuality does not exist apart from the structure of the work and from those pursuits that frame the subject's life. This is perhaps the main reason the intimate documentary is a film without a script. A structure is provided by the subject's own life plan.

The objective in making such a film should be to reveal the subject in the many ways that make him unique and interesting. Therefore, in order to expose him in a natural way, what is filmed should be as spontaneous as possible. The subject should be given free reign in terms of actions and words, for, in a sense, it is he who should guide the film by taking his own direction.

You should, if at all possible, try to work with your subject so that you can *write the film as you make it.* Use the camera to transfer your creative ideas to the film as they occur by thinking of yourself, the camera, and the subject, as one. A script or some kind of plan may be needed when there is an elaborate situation or innumerable events to juggle (as must have existed filming Levine for *Showman*). But the preparation should be thought of as notes, or as a "schedule," rather than as explicit guidelines to be carried out to the letter. A script, don't forget, implies the choreographing and stylizing of the film beforehand.

Your subject is not an actor. And although you cannot, in a strict sense, direct him, situations can be selected in which he can function expressively. Essentially, he directs himself by becoming truly involved in his own activity—whatever it may be. You may, therefore, want him to brief you beforehand on it so that you will know what to expect; you may also want to observe him before filming. After you know what to expect in a general way, then it may be possible to move your subject into more revealing, productive areas where you can select what you want to film.

A good part of making an intimate documentary is that you never know what you will get; it is an adventure. Your subject is full of interesting things to express about himself, about his work, and about others. There is a *flow* to life; and the documentarian can tap it. But what applies to your subject applies equally to yourself while you film. It is not only his life, which develops before the camera, that must be as unimpeded as possible; behind the camera, you must be free to interpret and perceive, and to delight in what is happening.

For many people, it will be good news to know that you can make a film without a script, while for others, the thought of it will be appalling. Although we all feel qualms about how successfully a film will turn out, the way to beat this defeating sensation is to realize that nothing in this kind of a film need be final. In many instances, although certainly not in all, the quality of personal contact with the subject and the informality of the situation will allow additional material to be gathered after the initial shooting if needed. Also, think of it as gathering material for the editing process, which will allow you to cull the brilliant moments from your footage and to throw away what bothers you. Editing allows you to redesign the film if necessary.

chapter 7

Working with the Subject

CHOOSING A SUBJECT
FOR AN INTIMATE DOCUMENTARY

Although most examples I have used to illustrate the documentary and its offshoots are professionally-made films on gauges larger than Super 8mm, this should not preclude their instructive value to the beginning filmmaker. The aesthetic principles in making these films are the same no matter whether you are filming with a Kodak Instamatic or a 35mm Arriflex. However, it would be erroneous to suggest that there is no difference at all between what goes into filming a project like *Showman* and in shooting a smaller undertaking, such as a film portrait of a friend. There are big differences in logistics, time, and expense. What I am suggesting is that once an understanding and mastery of the *form* is achieved, including a knowledge of the many possible filmic approaches, the beginner need only escalate the degree of planning and financing in order to meet the needs of a more demanding film.

I believe that a *simple* start will net greater learning gains for the beginner than a more complicated one that could prove more frustrating than challenging. With this in mind, I recommend that you begin with the least complicated documentary prototype—the intimate documentary. It is a form which, in the main, is simpler (and more immediately rewarding) than news, informational, instructional, or promotional films.

To this end, I suggest that you start where you will feel most inspired. Specifically, the person you choose for a subject should attract you in some way: he should involve you, fascinate, interest, excite, puzzle, or even frighten you. Any of these will do.

Most filmmakers who undertake to make an intimate documentary do so because they are deeply fascinated by someone they know. Jason had long been a friend of Shirley Clarke's before she decided to make her film. The Bible salesman in *Salesman*, as the story goes, had by chance dropped by the Manhattan offices of David and Albert Maysles in order to sell them a Bible. They were so taken by the outgoing character of this man that they practically decided on the spot to do a complete full-length documentary about him.

It is important to remember that an intimate documentary does not have to use a famous or infamous person as a subject. The person can be from any station in life. The only requisite is that he be interesting in some way—or that he is *made interesting* by you, the filmmaker. Those who are just starting out should take the most richly promising route possible.

The arts is an excellent area in which to look for a subject. Almost everyone has a friend who does leather work, makes jewelry, is a potter, or is skilled at refinishing furniture. "Well," you might say, "this is a long way from Joseph E. Levine!"—but not so. The same techniques, the same approaches—indeed, everything you may do on the smaller, more modest scale—can be used to advantage later when the opportunity comes to take on a larger project. Use immediately available subjects on whom to try out your film techniques in order to develop your style. Work first under conditions that will permit you to grow.

If you do not have a friend in the arts who would make a good subject, then another excellent source is a relative or close friend—a husband, wife, child, next-door neighbor, corner grocer—literally anyone who you may find involving, and (very important) who will cooperate. You must find not only a subject, but a *willing* subject. You should find someone who will trust you, someone who won't think you are making the film in order to hold him up to ridicule. If it is a relative or a friend, you will have an easier time gaining his trust than a stranger's.

If you can't think of a willing subject who is an interesting person, you should begin with someone who is interesting *looking*. If the subject consents to let you film him, you may discover interesting personal complexities later in the process. Never lose sight of the intimate documentary as a *discovery* medium—as a way of explaining people's behavior and their activities to yourself.

It could be that—rather than starting with an interesting personality, or an interesting looking person—you will want to begin filming someone's *activity*. Perhaps you have always wondered what went on in a meat packing plant, or better still, you have always wanted to watch the procedure of preparing food in a Chinese kitchen. Almost any skill lends itself to filming—from simple carpentry to upholstering and from gardening to automotive repair. Another, similar way to begin is through a person's occupation—that of dentist, fashion model, saw-sharpener, antique dealer, or postman.

Beginning your film with an activity that is involving to you as well as visually interesting may afford you the opportunity to *find* an interesting person with whom you can make an intimate documentary statement. The activity is fundamentally the *way into the film* for you and for your subject—by involving him in a meaningful action. Finally, the viewer of your film will be more able to relate to it quickly if there is something happening, visually, which he can immediately comprehend.

If, however, you opt for the first procedure—that of locating a person close to you for a subject, such as a friend or relative—then you must *find* an activity for them to become involved in that *they* can relate to naturally and easily. In this case it may be necessary to interview your subjects first to find out what it is *they* are involved in—what activities they enjoy or are skilled at which you may not know about.

For the most part, the reason for having your subject involved in an activity is, above all, so that he will reveal something about himself—his attitude toward what he is doing, why he does what he does, and so on. It should provide a context in which to draw him out.

It is important to remember that your first approach to the documentary must frequently depend heavily upon *visual* images rather than upon sound to convey the sense of your subject. Inasmuch as you probably will not find it easy or creatively convenient, at first, to make a sound track *while filming*, I suggest that you try to say as much as you possibly can about your subject visually; sound can be added later. A person conveys a great deal of feeling about others and about himself through his actions, gestures, and body attitudes—much more than most people would realize. If for no other reason than because you are working in a medium that has an enormous capacity for visual description, you should try first to get as much from your subject visually as you can.

It is good to keep in mind that since you will be relying a great deal on an activity or on the occupation of the subject to animate the film's action and to afford him a vehicle for expression, it is possible, and even probable, that you will tend to *lean* too much on this aspect to prop up your film. This aspect is the informational level—the how-to-do-it part.

The informational part of a documentary is the person's detailed and factual "existence." It is his name, what he does for a living, and what is involved in this pursuit. If you make a documentary that goes into this aspect at length, as an end in itself—such as how egg foo yung is made, or how chairs are upholstered, or how a new generator is installed in a car—then you have made an informational film. The focus is off the man and on his activity.

Frequently, but not always, a documentary film involves some degree of personal challenge to the subject. What is he *trying* to do? If he is trying to sail a boat, what makes it such a challenge? It is possible that your subject may not be challenged enough by his activity to reveal much of his character. Challenge, as an attitude toward the activity, is important because it basically *involves* the subject. When the subject fails to be challenged by what he is doing, the filmmaker should decide to comment on this in itself. Either that, or he should redirect the subject toward an activity that will be more involving for him, and possibly too, more visually involving for the viewer.

DIRECTING THE SUBJECT

Basically, directing a documentary involves either giving your subject something to do or suggesting it. This does not apply as much if your subject is already enmeshed in his normal pursuits, as might be the case when filming an active person like Joseph E. Levine, or where the activity is set or predetermined, as when the subject is working at a craft. On the other hand, the filmmaker should not feel qualms about selecting certain activities for the subject or about making requests of him when it is clear that every procedural aspect of his activity will not contribute substantially to the film's intention, or to revelations of importance.

In the same vein, but concerning the subject's facial gestures while relating to the camera, people generally put on their "best face." The documentarian searches for candor in his subject—a reality which is comprised of as many varying moods as the subject "naturally" projects. He looks for expressiveness in his subject, not bland, stereotyped reactions. It is a person's complexity that the documentarian tries to reveal; thus, if the subject conceals this complexity, the basis for a truthful statement is undermined.

It is important, then, that the filmmaker be able to spot unproductive moments, when the subject slips into standard reactions and moods, and that he takes steps to correct them. One way to get out of a fruitless rut is to confront your subject with the fact that he is not being genuine. However, a tactic of this sort may cure the problem but kill the film in the bargain. It is a gamble; but if your subject has enough confidence in you, directness on your part is likely to yield results.

A more usual way of handling the problem of a subject's playing to the camera—especially when filming children—is to avoid negativism and quietly move on to more involving areas. These are frequently areas where the subject feels most confident. It should be remembered that people generally want to be filmed doing what they know best and what they do best. Again, this is the same tendency to want to appear "good" for the camera. But in this case, confidence with a familiar activity can produce genuine responses from a subject. For instance, if you are filming a child and he prefers playing on the swing to playing in the sandbox, it might not pay to force the situation, even if the sandbox seems to you to have better visual possibilities. The same principle can apply equally to adults.

Negativism, a quality that can arise out of the subject's feeling of insecurity with the filmmaker (or with another subject) or through confrontation with the filmmaker, need not be considered bad per se. What is important is that the filmmaker have control of the situation, so that whatever unpleasantness occurs is intentional and is either allowed to happen or is *administered* to the subject for the purpose of disarming him, or in order to elicit a specific type of response. One of the most memorable moments in D. A. Pennebaker's *Don't Look Back* occurs in Dylan's dressing room when the singer gets testy with a pushy reporter.

By and large, in order to get a natural performance from a subject you may have to psychologically disarm him before filming. A brief discussion with him before you begin is a good method; you should also go over the activity in which he will be engaged. If your subject is a ceramicist who is going to "throw a pot," find out in a general way what the steps will be so that you can anticipate and select angles during shooting. In other words, be aware of the details of your subject's activity. It will not only help to put him at ease, but it will provide you with a mental sketch of the procedures he will be taking.

Finally, do not hesitate to ask him to perform any phase of the activity again if you should feel the need of a different point of view. Many people feel that to break the natural rhythm of the activity, interrupting and restaging the event, would of itself introduce a fictional aspect into an otherwise *pure* documentary event. It should be pointed out, inasmuch as fiction is stylized documentary, that *pure* documentary is pure only in relation to the degree of stylization or the degree of contrivance introduced by the filmmaker. The introduction of some style into the documentary is not only inevitable but desirable when it enhances the chief goal, which is to reveal. Very simply, over-stylization produces fiction.

Usually, though not always, the filmmakers "unfeatured" presence—anonymity—is a quality for which most documentarians would devoutly hope. It would make their job infinitely easier. How to be inconspicuous or "invisible" is a recurring problem. Unfortunately, this is seldom possible. Instead, the documentarian must artificially become "invisible." One way is to cause the subject to become accustomed to your presence. Let him in on what you are going to do; run through the activity a few times; "dry run" the camera—look through it, try various possible angles, but don't shoot any film. Let him get accustomed to the sound of the camera. Dry runs can be performed with or without film in the camera. If the first run is best, and you had film in the camera, you will have the added advantage of choosing from this extra footage when editing time comes. It's best, however, not to let your subject know there's film in the camera (if he thinks there isn't) or it will defeat your purpose. You should take the attitude that you are helping to remove the subject's censors and barriers toward an accurate portrayal of himself.

A *revelation of truth* as expressed in actuality should be the goal. As emphasized earlier, the difference between a fictional and a documentary film account is that the former *creates* truth by setting up a structure which has been carefully, skillfully assembled. (To be sure, the creation of fiction is no mean accomplishment.) On the other hand, the documentarian is a discoverer of latent truth—when and where it exists—and he captures it on film. He is like a miner who finds truth in veins of pure metal. The principal role of the documentarian is to reveal natural human perfections and imperfections. The entire objective in directing a subject should be to lay the groundwork for discovery.

The filmmaker sets the subject in motion within the matrix of his activity; but he also *clothes* the subject in a visual interpretation of the events. The composition of lighted forms and their movement perform as a secondary voice informing the image of the subject. How the subject is presented *is* the subject. Think of the person you are documenting as an *occasion* to make a film—an image, a new subject, and a statement.

EXPLORING THE SUBJECT

After a subject is chosen, it remains for the filmmaker to discover its expressive potential. He needs to know *what there is* to the subject so that he can inflect it for his own purposes.

On the one hand, exploration can begin at the level of gathering information, as Charles Salmore did on the broad subject of frogs in order to prepare for his film. If, like Salmore, you are making a social documentary, then researching the subject is considered a form of exploration. Tracking down leads, talking to your subjects, and visiting proposed shooting sites are standard ways to prepare for this type of film.

On the other hand, in making an intimate documentary, much of the exploratory work may already have been done, particularly if you happen to know the person you are filming as well as Shirley Clarke knew Jason. She knew his repertoire of stories and mannerisms well. Kenneth Anger lived with his documentary subject for a time before making his film on "bikers," *Scorpio Rising*. However a knowledge of the subject is gained beforehand, the filmmaker has to know what he is dealing with before he starts to shoot.

If you are making a film about a potter, visit his studio and observe the process of making ceramics. Most importantly, watch *how* he performs his craft, the special ways he does things. Make notes on any idiosyncrasies he has, or on unusual details regarding his studio. Once, while visiting a potter, I noticed a bean vine growing out of a crack in a wall from which hung a single, bright purple bean pod! I thought to myself: what a fascinating detail—so natural and somehow appropriate. If I had been making a film I certainly would have included it.

What I have been talking about, for the most part, is the *idea* for a film that gets us going—what attracts us, whether it is a shared interest in frogs or a fascination with a person or an activity. In making a travelogue or training film the process is still the same. The subject is apprehended first as a "reason" for making a film about it; the following steps are to gain an acquaintance with it, to decide what approach to take, and to sift out the subject's special, unique features. These I have referred to as *subject interpretive* possibilities—what the subject has to offer in the way of interest and statement.

Exploring the subject can also mean exploring visually with the camera. Viewing three-dimensionally, in the usual way, is vastly different from seeing a "selected view" through a rectangle (the camera) which will, in the end, have to stand on its own as a two-dimensional recorded image. Therefore, in order to give the subject the kind of visual importance it needs—in order to make it cinematic—the filmmaker must interpret the image in the camera. In other words, the subject's innate possibilities for interest must finally be rendered by the camera. Both camera and subject contribute to the creation of the image.

It may be recalled that the *most basic* camera interpretive device is the rectangle itself in which the scene is composed, and through which the subject moves or is moved. (See Part One, "Seeing within the Rectangle.") Being sensitive to it makes a considerable difference as you start to think about visual exploration. You will be doing so *in terms* of the rectangle. There are many ways to view the "rudimentary" filming experience, especially when the camera starts to hum like something alive in your hand, demanding that your imagination and resources produce an image. At that crucial moment, how do you view the subject through the rectangle?

A beginner often produces footage equivalent to the first steps a child takes. He doesn't know where he's going; he is only aware of the marvelous vehicle he is in—his body—and that it's moving. Moving for the sake of moving is the lay filmmaker's first impulse too. And this is good—in fact, unavoidably necessary. Gradually, this phase gives way to more intentional approaches. One way is to regard the rectangular frame as a "butterfly net" that is slapped down over the subject before it gets away. More importance here is placed on "getting the subject" than on "experiencing" it. Another approach is to see the rectangle as a vacuum cleaner that "sucks" the subject into the camera. The emphasis in this case is on moving the camera to and fro, up and down, "getting it all up." These ways of thinking must obviously give way to yet more intentional approaches—to thinking of the rectangle as a discriminating device that selects and emphasizes the subject. This attitude is the correct preparation for the process of visual discovery. As soon as possible, the filmmaker should do his discovering in terms of the rectangle, realizing that what comes into view does so within a circumscribed space. All this is true, of course, only if you deliberately discount that which is external to the immediate view within the space. In other words, the rectangle should not be thought of as a window in a house where one is conscious of there being something beyond the window frame. The camera's frame is more like a frame to a painting: the subject is confined within it, held in an instant of time. But unlike a painting, the subject before the camera is precariously free to "leave" the frame and disappear into the oblivion beyond the frame's edges. One might say, "Well, this is a silly game, pretending that nothing exists beyond the frame's edges, when I know something does." The main reason for pretending that what you see is all that exists is because that is the way the film is seen by the viewer. It is the only way to see what is in the frame *with importance*. Just imagine you are watching a movie as you are filming.

One might ask, what does all this have to do with discovery and exploration? As I have suggested, discoveries are made in terms of the rectangle. Therefore, not being aware of its *dramatic* importance is to be ignorant of the most basic of all discovery tools. Think of the rectangle as like the light from a flashlight, casting its beam in a shape with sharp edges, and you have the concept.

Once we have learned to see within the rectangle, we are ready to see *something* through it. To explore or discover implies that there are visual "appearances" to your subject not yet discovered (or created). It implies that there is more to the subject than we see at first glance.

Although we may have previously "scouted" a ceramicist's studio to see the kind of place it is and to speak to the potter, we are not equipped to see how the studio will look on film until we view some portion of it through the rectangle. When we see the studio with our unaided, total vision, it is difficult to select portions in the same way we do when viewing through a camera.

So we take the camera with us, we walk around with it held to our eyes, surveying the visual possibilities. During this time don't think about the planned structure of your film; be prepared to let things happen.

The first thing I would think of is the light—that is, the available light. (Of course, if there is inadequate available light to film, you will have to use auxiliary lighting, and the process of exploring the subject will have to wait until these are set up.) Always keep in mind that light "sculpts" the image. In moving around the studio, and around the potter, you will discover that everything takes on a different aspect as your viewing direction changes in relation to the direction of the light source. If the light source is coming from the side of the potter as he works at his wheel, then, as you view him from the front, half his face will be lit while the other half will be in shadow. But if you film from the side, from which the light is coming, he will appear fully lit in profile. And as you move to the side of him opposite the window emitting the light, you will find him dramatically silhouetted in "back light," creating a somber feeling.

If you decide to walk around the subject with the camera to your eye, you will find that the potter becomes an *evolving image,* changing continuously as the direction of the light source changes in relation to the camera lens. In performing this exercise, you have discovered two things: (1.) how the subject looks from the three basic views in relation to the light; and (2.) how the subject appears when undergoing subtle, gradual changes in a changing angle and light. There is no way of anticipating the feeling of these images exactly, because there are many variables determined by the immediate circumstances. What the potter looks like—whether tall or short, fat or lean—will influence the feeling of the image. Whether you are filming very close and have included only his head, or only his hands, or only his frame from the waist up, will be decisive. How fast you move will be a factor. And your shooting angle, high or low, will also make a difference. You may, on the other hand, wish to view the subject in disjointed pieces: a close shot of his hands *against* the light; a full shot of his frame *with* the light; and, finally, a shot of his face from the front only half-lit. Instead of using the idea of a continuous, developing image, you may wish to make a montage from these shots after viewing them.

Turning to the studio itself, the objects in the room, the furnishings, and the tools—warrant as much attention as the potter. As you survey these items, think of their capacity to express the man who uses them. Can he be filmed in such a way that objects in the studio can be framed in the foreground? Can you show off some of his work in this way, instead of using the conventional method of filming them separately and cutting them into the film at the end? This way they can be integrated casually, more naturally, into the scene. There are infinite possibilities, but they must be discovered. There is no adequate formalized way to approach documentary filming. The possibilities must be found; then you can decide on a method that uses them. After exploring the subject, how you decide to film and to put the shots together are remaining interpretive acts.

INTERPRETING THE SUBJECT

Interpretation is a method of identifying things perceived; and it is, in one sense, an act of assigning identity. For example, things which ordinarily have good connotations—such as a young woman's breast—might, because of the way it is filmed and thus seen, take on ominous feelings. The way it is lit, its relative size on the screen, and the way the camera moves around it could interpret it as threatening. Of course, the context of the entire film has a great deal to do with the way things are named, perceived, and interpreted.

There really isn't an objective reality in relation to the act of perceiving and communicating. We always see things with a certain bias and subjectivity. Even the documentary, which is thought to be among the most objective forms of expression, in that what is filmed is real, natural, and free of contaminating fictional intent, is never free of interpretation; and in a broad sense, it is seldom free of fictional intent either.

What this amounts to is understanding that we always see with a bias, and that this very bias facilitates communication. Subjectivity in a point of view offers a great simplicity in presenting the subject. Demagogues fully understand and frequently exploit this principle. And so do artists. But where the politico uses one-sidedness to make what he is saying easier to swallow, the artist uses it as "the statement." What the artist has created does not stand for something else. It is what it is. And the way the subject is seen *is* the subject. Therefore, if a woman's breast is filmed in an ominous way, it means that the filmmaker has *seen* the breast that way as he filmed it. It does not necessarily mean that the filmmaker sees all breasts as ominous; but it does mean he saw that one as ominous—in the way the light fell on it and the way it filled the picture frame—and so he moved around it with the camera in an ominous way. (This particular example is taken from personal experience and describes a scene from my film, *The Devil is Dead.*)

When the filmmaker interprets, he *transforms.* Generally, we regard things transformed as being completely changed—Jekyll into Hyde; the ugly toad into a handsome prince. There are, however, degrees of transformation as well as degrees of interpretation. For example, a news event on television can be subtly interpreted through editing; and the same event can be radically interpreted through a *simulation* of it. In fact, the simulation of an event may bear little or no resemblance to what actually happened. Such is the difference between an event transformed slightly through the interpretive act, and one greatly transformed through its fictional reconstruction.

Interpretation is inevitable in the documentary, if only seen through the editing process: that is, what you decide to show as against what you choose to leave out. (You cannot show everything.) As long as this is going to happen, why not inflect your documentary statement intentionally rather than in a haphazard, inadvertent way?

Obviously, if you interpret a murderer as a completely good person you have changed a toad into a prince. This is not to imply that the handsome prince can't have some ugly qualities, and that the toad can't express himself with dignity and grace. In fact, these seeming contradictions are more true than the possible view of a subject as being all one thing—the philanthropist as being all giving, or children as being all innocent.

In interpreting your subject for the documentary it is important that the subject come across with a fair degree of fidelity to what actually exists. In other words, an elderly man filmed to make him look as if he were twenty years younger is not faithful to the way he is generally seen. If, however, the elderly man happens to have a sensitive nose and a mouth free of wrinkles—and if he *also* has dried, coarse, and abused-looking hands—whichever of these two aspects you choose to give most attention to while filming is a valid interpretive choice. It would inflect the meaning, not change it completely. It is largely a matter of leaving the "core sense" of the subject intact and (giving it an appropriate amount of attention) at the same time using visual selection and emphasis to make your own comment. In effect, interpretation is *directing* the meaning. It isn't like showing a sweet, pretty, little girl who has a propensity for misbehavior as being mostly sweet or mostly bratty—and by doing so, misrepresenting the "core sense" of the little girl.

Above, I have referred to interpretation as being accomplished through a judicious use of selection. Another way to interpret is through image size in the rectangle. Very small forms appear curious, interesting, or lyrical; larger forms take on a stronger presence; and *very* large forms tend to be involved with a sense of urgency: They can be highly dramatic and sometimes threatening. Ultra-huge forms or close-ups (where only a part of the form can be shown)—as where a mouth, a finger, or possibly even a pore or a hair fills the screen—provide highly specific details that are very analytic in feeling.

Camera angles will also emphasize certain areas of the subject as opposed to others. A view from the top of the potter's head will surely emphasize the activity of his hands. A view from underneath his hands will emphasize them in relation to forming the clay (but also in relation to his face). A view from his backside at a medium distance might tend to play up the attitude of his body in the way he sits; and a long distance shot will point up his relative positioning in the room.

Movement, itself, can be transforming in both the action of the camera and in the action of the subject. If the camera pans from one point to another, it can have the effect of generating interest in what is arriving in the space, thus dramatizing its importance. And conversely, it de-emphasizes what leaves the space. The same pan can have the effect of a "probing eye" as facets of a given subject are carefully scrutinized and scanned by the camera. But the effects of all movements cannot be adequately described, in that the circumstances and type of subject have much to do with the quality of meaning to the viewer. It is not good to over-formulate your camera movements beforehand, since on-the-spot circumstances are often a better guide to movements you will make at the moment of filming.

Lighting is a major interpretive source in documentary filming. Light is a part of the subject's environment—whether it is a soft natural light coming from an artist's skylight or the stark fluorescent lighting of a factory. A decision to use this available light is an interpretive act. Natural lighting generally has the effect of making things more beautiful than they are. Conversely, high wattage artificial light, especially all-over and undiffused, tends to bring out and to amplify every possible visual banality and flaw your subject may have. Therefore, if you should want to show anxiety and stress in your subject, give him the high wattage treatment. Everyone can recall movies where the criminal is being interrogated under a bright light.

Back light, and especially natural back lighting, can lend a soft, mysterious drama to an otherwise ordinary situation—where, for instance, a person is playing the piano. This lighting silhouettes the figure, delivering a delicate outline of the form. It calls attention to gesture and body movements with less emphasis on detail, so that uninteresting, visual distractions can be minimized while the essential spirit of the person and event can be preserved.

Selection in the editing, image size, camera angle, movement of camera and subject, and lighting are the main interpretive, transforming means available to the documentary filmmaker. Below are described a few others with more specific uses that can be very effective—but in the context of the documentary these must be used carefully.

Reflections in a rain puddle, in a pond, or in a plate glass window transform the subject by compounding it with one or more others, thus creating a kind of visual metaphor. As in a store window, the subject's reflection blends or becomes incorporated with cars, passing people, and with objects in the store behind the glass. Puddles distort the subject's reflection as well.

A superimposition (double exposure) looks like a reflection; but it is more definite and more intentional, and it can be created in the camera (See Part One, "The Body" for details). The superimposition is probably the closest thing to a visual metaphor, in that it is an amalgamation of various subjects which comes together in form and color in such a way that it becomes *one image.* Specific applications of this technique are as numerous as the imagination can conjure. Basically, the image's "economy" is its primary value. Actions and activities can be "compressed," as where a single person is doing a number of things at once that are different facets of the same activity and you want to give an *impression* without dwelling on any one aspect.

Slow and fast motion have the effects of expanding or compressing the time an activity takes. In this sense their functions are analogous to superimposition, but their effects are entirely different. Whereas fast motion is extremely limited in its use (tending to create a comic effect), slow motion is very useful in slowing down sports activities for close examination and analysis. When applied generally, slowed motion tends to generate serious, lyrical, or soulful feelings in the viewer.

Over-exposure will lessen an image's density, making it appear lighter and thinner. Though this is usually an accidental effect, sometimes it is done intentionally. On rare occasions it can be useful in exaggerating lighting conditions that may be harshly bright, or where the heat from the sun is punishing. Such conditions might exist on the beach, the desert, or on snowy mountainous slopes. Over-exposure can produce interesting surrealistic effects, where colors and forms become "washed out" except for deep shadows in people's mouths and eyes. The result is a very thin line around the forms of people—no demarcation between water, sky, and beach—and very pronounced eyes and mouths almost dislocated from their owners' bodies.

Color filters are a way of inflecting the visual interpretation of a scene without changing the subject's form. A deep red filter (with color film) could tend to generate both a sensation of lush visual beauty and, at the same time, one of anxiety. All this depends on the subject, of course. Such a radical change in overall color usually produces an other-worldly effect—not necessarily bizarre, but often strange.

Another interpretive device, framing your subject (filming past something in the foreground), does at least two things. It suggests depth in the picture, and it relates the feeling of the form or forms in the foreground to the main subject. Furthermore, it has the effect of "extending the image" (covered in Part One, Seeing within the Rectangle"), and it adds visual interest through an aesthetically pleasing composition. Typical foreground subjects used for framing are tall grasses, leaves of trees, a chink in a wall, slats in a fence, people's heads, and so forth. Framing is usually done with a wide-angle lens. However, out-of-focus framing—where the foreground material is blurred and reduced to abstract blobs of color—is achieved with the extreme telephoto lens.

Finally, the length of your shots (scenes) can be a very effective interpretive device. Short bursts of film tend to produce a fragmentary effect. The subject is presented in "pieces." This is effective in creating an *impression* where attention to details are not as important as the overall feeling of what is going on. A parade might lend itself well to this technique; so would any mass gathering where there are a lot of faces. This technique is used in the documentary, *Monterey Pop*. Shot fragments also tend to convey a sense of frenzy. But as a descriptive device, fragments can be used to give a number of different views of the same activity—such as a dance—where the viewer may be allowed to "see in the round."

Long scenes, on the other hand, allow *development* of the action by your subject. Here, every detail in progress, as it happens in an orderly way, is featured as important. It is a technique especially well-suited to an event—as in sports—where a moment of critical importance could occur at any time. And the events leading up to this moment are also a part of the total effect.

There are several ways to look at this type of long-running shot. One is from the standpoint of the filmmaker who (like a bird watcher) patiently films in the hope that what he thinks will happen—will happen. Walt Disney Studios expended huge amounts of film on its well-known series of nature documentaries. In this instance, only the "moments of interest" are preserved, while the action leading up to it and the many hours of waiting (all recorded on film) are thrown away.

Another way to view the long-running shot is in terms of viewer-impact. Here, the filmmaker may leave in the footage leading up to the event, the purpose of which is to build tension by making the viewer wait. This is like watching a prize-fight film where most of the action is routine punching around until that critical instant when something important happens. The moment by itself would lack the impact without the total context—the anxious waiting.

Andy Warhol, who has built his reputation on aesthetically redeeming what is banal and ordinary in our everyday lives, has done some interesting creative things with the long-running shot. In his film *Empire*, he stationed a camera so that it pointed out a downtown Manhattan office window at the Empire State Building. The camera is said to have run continuously day and night for twenty-four hours, recording any and all events which occurred in that space of time. The sun came up, the flag was raised on top of the building, airplanes flew by, as did some birds, the weather changed, and so did the sky. Eventually, the flag came down, night fell, lights came on, more planes flew by, lights went out, and dawn came. So little happened over such a long time that everything—however "so what"—became of world-shaking importance. "In the world of the blind, the one-eyed man is king."

In another, similar film, *Sleep*, Warhol filmed a person sleeping for eight hours. Again, the camera ran continuously, never moving from its position. Every twitch the sleeping person made during this time registered on film as an event of considerable importance.

It is an interesting idea, and it certainly is in keeping with film's basic purpose: to record. The simplistic recording of events is as old as cinema itself. However, it is important to remember that the filmmaker has the power to direct attitudes, feelings, and emotions as well. This, in my opinion, is the most complex and challenging use of film.

FILMING WITH GESTURE

As suggested earlier, the pivotal force governing all film imagery is gesture. It rules the effectiveness of what we see. In making the documentary, how we *select* a subject's gestures is of greater importance than generating gesture through filmic devices (camera movement, optical manipulation, and so forth). Since the intention regulating documentary filming has mainly to do with exploring the subject's "circumstances," and "discovering" life examples of importance in a matrix of naturalism and actuality, gestures created filmically must be more restrained than where the subject is shaped more expressionistically in other types of films. The documentarian, in a sense, has one hand tied behind his back, because he must let the film's point of view *grow* out of the material before the camera.

He must learn to recognize subject gesture as it occurs: to recognize its ambiguity and its potential for statement, meaning, and emotional impact. Specifically, any documentary subject has to be involved in activities that show the subject in action. (In some lesser documentaries, the filmmaker has used "talking" as the chief activity—as in films I have seen on Henry Miller and Buckminster Fuller.) Activities provide a focus for the subject's individual approach to problems and situations, illustrating his uniqueness, and allowing him to dramatize his universal qualities. The filmmaker must be ready to react with the camera in order to record these strong subject gestures, and to choose the angles, lighting, image size, camera movement, and so on, which will *contribute* to and enhance the subject's effectiveness. In other words, the filmic devices which are used should complement subject gesture. The documentary particularly requires that interpretation emanate from the subject, and that filmic interpretation follow its cues.

Perhaps a general review of what a gesture is might be helpful. Basically, a gesture governs the flow of the film's action, much like an oscillating electrical current. To put it another way, film gestures are terminal points or units which are like *episodes*, and which provide both the *content* and the *thrust* of the film. Gestures can also be regarded as movements within scenes—or the lack of movements—creating positive and negative spaces. They are like visual phrases. Any time we can regard a movement, a mood, or some form of information as having been circumscribed—begun and terminated in a manner appropriate to the optimum effect and intention of the film—it is a gesture. Gestures are the "happening units" of a film.

The most obvious and familiar of all gestures—movement—can be created by either camera or subject. Whenever the subject—a person, a car, a train, a dog, a cloud, a kite, a wave, a bird—moves, it can be considered a gesture. Most crucial to understand is that every movement has an effective "beginning" and "end." If a wave rolls onto a beach, there is a point at which we are most visually excited—perhaps as it looms large on the verge of breaking. But as the same wave dissipates, our interest wanes. When a seagull takes off from the sand we feel an instant sense of exhilaration; but once in the air, the gull's gesture changes from one of "taking off" to one of "flying." When the take-off has been completed, that gesture is completed and another one begins.

People make a variety of gestures with their heads, hands, and legs and with the trunks of their bodies. They put their hands to their heads to scratch; they turn to look, blink, smile, bend over, get up, walk, run, sit, touch, hit, and caress. Each one of these movements, when thought of in terms of film images, can be viewed as having a beginning and a completion. As the ball player reaches to catch a ball, we follow him with intense interest until he either catches or misses it. If another gesture does not follow on the heels of this event, then the viewer experiences a relaxation of visual tension. The tautness of "attention" dissolves. When the viewer's attention is allowed to wane or is lost, a film can be said to have lost momentum. It is this forward advance, the progression of something happening, that is crucial to the maintenance of viewer interest. However, if the spaces between active gestures are planned and intentioned as a part of the film's rhythm or for punctuation, these non-movements can function as gestures too.

There are "active" gestures where the subject is in motion, and there are active gestures where the camera is doing the moving. Pans, dolly shots, and zooms are the most commonly used active camera gestures.

"Passive" gestures can occur when the subject is either at rest or engaged in a rapid repetitive movement. A still life shot of any sort is passive, as is a child jumping rope. An activity which transpires without any discernible beginning and end—without a clear configurative movement—is passive in film terms, and has to be gauged by *time* rather than by the movement's start or finish. In other words, *how long* it takes the viewer to receive the information and feeling contained in the image is the determining factor.

All images are made up of *structural* elements which are either active or passive. And these are, to one degree or another, imbued with meaning, connotations, and *inference*. In other words, the "sense" we make out of the image, whether in or out of a context, is the inference it carries. Therefore, it can be considered the *inferential* part of the *gesture*.

Turning to our subject, the potter, it can be seen how these ideas operate in a documentary type of film. As you walk into the studio, this time with the camera to your eye, the gestures you perceive are these: The potter is sitting at his wheel, and he has just thrown a formless hunk of clay on it. This gesture is significant as an active, structural image. The sensation of the downward movement of the arm and the attitude conveyed toward the materials is unmistakably a rough, decisive gesture, almost violent. It is a wrestling with the clay, showing that it must be forced and molded with strength. From these gestures, both structural and inferential, we have deciphered an important moment—usable not for its dramatic value alone but because it has furnished an entire point of view for the film! We shall film the potter from the vantage of his physical involvement with the clay. We shall emphasize the "elemental" aspect of his activity. We have, in studying his gestures, hit upon a key to the film's inflection. If we were to continue along this line, we would look for other gestural items to reinforce this idea. We might decide to make use of the dramatic, low key lighting of the studio, mysteriously suggesting a medieval alchemist's workshop. Furthermore, we see how craggy and weather-beaten the potter's face is and how massive, callused, and cracked his hands are. All of this relates to the concept we are hatching—which has to do with the potter's ruggedness, and with his ability to wrest expressiveness from amorphous, earthy materials. We look for still other gestures to support the film's tack. We notice the potter's foot kicking the wheel to make it turn. We film it so that the kicks come toward the camera, emphasizing the gesture's aggressive quality.

On the other hand, we may enter the potter's studio and see it completely differently. We may see gestures which are lyrical and poetic rather than dramatic and forceful. The first thing we notice is that he trickles water on the spinning clay so that he may fashion it better. He cups the formless object in his hands, and as it oozes gently into a shape the excess water and clay run freely, glistening, between his fingers; the spinning wheel is hypnotic and lulling. We notice the poetic quality of the light as it silhouettes his head. We film his foot *from the rear* as he kicks the wheel, so it has a wistful, gently rhythmic motion away from the camera. Here is a place of quiet psychological intensity; the moments appear mystical, in that shapes appear almost effortlessly from the clay. The potter does not struggle, for his command over the materials is precise and calm.

The concept of gesture complements the ideas in the preceding sections on "exploring" and "interpreting" the subject. These are different approaches to the same problem. Gesture is but another way of looking at the process of making a taut, effective statement in film.

chapter 8

Documentary Editing and Sound

EDITING STYLES

In documentary films, one of two fundamental approaches may appear as a dominant style: the heavy use of the long-running developmental shot or the predominate implementation of shorter, disparate shots to form a "montage" mosaic. The former, developmental approach, is *linear* and uses denotational logic; each idea flows as an outgrowth from a preceding one. The latter, montage method, aims for a complex *impression,* circumscribed by many visual points of view, providing an overall coverage. The first method tends to have thrust and drive, and to make a strong impact. The second offers a more generalized feeling about the subject, and it is stronger in connotative *content* and suggestion than the long-running shot.

A Portrait of Jason (See Part Two, "The Intimate Documentary") excellently illustrates the use and effect of the long-running shot. According to the director, Shirley Clarke, the camera was only stopped for the purpose of reloading, and nearly all the footage taken was finally used in the film. The viewer is permitted to see subtle changes in Jason's mood occur as each organic event grows from the one preceding it. As Jason speaks, and one anecdote gives way to another, the workings of his mind are verbally expressed in a *line of narrative.*

Frogs (See Part Two, "The Social Documentary") illustrates the montage method—using fragments of the subject filmed at different locations and at different times. Time and place are intermingled, and there is no clear progress from one event to another. Shots used in this way take on a feeling of equal weight. In the case of Salmore's film, the mosaic he provides is a general impression of the world of frog fanciers, made up of paradox and ambiguity. The viewer is amused at the outwardly silly fanaticism of the frog cultists, and at the same time he is repulsed by their careless disregard for the frogs.

The montage serves the filmmaker best when he must hastily create an impression—and especially so when the idea has the possibility for irony and contradiction. Montage (as well as collage) will allow images which are disparate in time, place, and subject as well as in feeling to be juxtaposed, creating irony, pathos, and ambiguity.

It is important for the editor to understand that the basic difference between a long-running shot and a shorter one is *development*. The longer a shot or a scene in a film is the more developmental it is—in a narrative sense—and the more a *story* can be told with it. In contrast, the shorter shot cannot build in a specific line because there is simply not enough time for it to do so. Therefore, short shots are best suited to the accrual of general feeling, of an impression, created by their brief appearance, which eddies outward, centrifugally, connotatively. Also, when the short shot is used as a "quick cut" it can, by itself, produce excitement and drama.

Although some films, like the ones mentioned here, can be seen to have dominant styles in terms of shot length, many, if not most, documentaries mix the two modes, using them interchangeably. The editor may allow a scene to run longer where its major value is to provide a conclusion or a feeling of impact through development. In *Monterey Pop* (See Part Two, "The Social Documentary") the shots of Jimi Hendrix singing are especially long because the complex series of events leading from his song to the demolition of his guitar are so interrelated that an interference with this "narrative" progression would spoil the impact of his performance. In the same film, while the camera wanders among the crowds of people, individual details of the spectators are handled in short shot montages which allow quick, diverse impressions of the people attending the event.

EDITING FOR CONTINUITY

Continuity allows us to feel that a film sequence is *continuous*—that it has unity. Although continuity is most commonly created through unity of *subject matter,* additional continuity is achieved through well-crafted cutting.

The most frequent breach in the editing of a film is the "jump cut," where a significant piece of the action is missing. If, say, you are filming a person looking at paintings in an art gallery, and while he walks from one painting to another you must stop to change film (or for some other reason), after you resume shooting, if the two shots are joined in the editing it will cause the person to appear to "jump" from one painting to another. The way to avoid this discontinuity of action is to have your subject retraverse the space, and as he walks between the paintings film a close-up of his face. This shot can be used as a "cut-away," which can be inserted between the two original shots, just before the subject is to appear in front of the second painting. A cut-away means to cut away to something else, and it does not necessarily have to be a close-up of the subject. If the subject has a dog on a leash, the cut-away could just as easily be a shot of his dog or a shot of a bystander—or quite possibly a shot of *anything*—as long as it is understood by the viewer to be relevant to the scene in progress. The viewer knows its relevance because he will have seen the subject of the cut-away prior to its use. The cut-away functions best if, as in this case, we have previously noted the dog on the leash, or the bystander, in a medium-long establishing shot early in the scene.

If smooth continuity of the action is desired, where the cut-away is a close-up shot or a different angle of the subject's face, the filmmaker should allow "overlap" when reshooting the scene so that body movement and background can be matched in the editing. When *different* camera angles or image sizes of identical subject movements are joined so that the action does not appear to be interrupted, it is known as "matching the action."

A cut-away can also be made from a "reverse shot" or from a "reaction shot." In the first instance, the filmmaker may choose to film the subject's walk toward the second painting by aiming the camera in its direction and walking toward it. This would enable us to see the experience through the eyes of the subject, called a "subjective view." A reaction shot may or may not be seen through the eyes of the subject. It could, as has been mentioned, be seen from a bystander's point of view, or even from that of the owner of the gallery who is observing the subject study the paintings.

In the masterful little documentary, *Kienholtz on Exhibit*, spectators file past an exhibit of bizarre "environments" made by the artist Kienholtz. Features of the exhibit are shown, intercut with reaction shots of the spectators. There are many reverse shots too—where a spectator may be shown agape at something strange —and then we are given a reverse angle of what he is seeing. Another use of the reverse shot can be found when the subject is performing a task. For example, just the potter's face may be shown as he intently guides his hands to shape the clay—while next a reverse shot of his hands as they work is intercut.

Most of the discussion relating to cut-aways, reverse, and reaction shots is intended to assist in the editing of *continuous action*. These considerations are seldom important when building a montage sequence of distantly related imagery. The beach montage of shots referred to in Part One, "Filming with Gesture," derives its continuity mainly from "cutting on the action," where the tension between the shots is sustained in a sort of relaying effect of the images. Each gesture is cut on the beginning and ending of the movement, and each nonmoving image (or passive gesture) is so economically presented that the film flows evenly. Other techniques that assist in imparting continuity to this kind of montage are the comparing and contrasting of shots in a rhythm of reinforcement and punctuation, using directionality of movement, form and color.

Continuity through cutting on the action and comparing and contrasting images also serves to strengthen the film of longer scene length, one which is built around a single, continuous subject such as the potter and his studio. For instance, the color of the clay, which predominates in the studio, offers subtle, natural continuity; so does the pot form on which he works when compared with other rounded forms in the studio; so do the movements of his hands, his feet, and the wheel. All have screen directions which can be related through manipulation of camera angle and image size. It is by relating these elements through editing, in terms of gesture, that structural continuity develops.

EDITING FOR EMPHASIS

Continuity can be seen as a way to persuade the viewer to suspend his judgment and surrender to the experience of the film. Unity, which continuity provides, conveys feelings of purpose, of rightness, and of context. It helps to create a believable setting, so to speak, in which "things can happen." If the viewer is persuaded through continuity to see the film innocently and uncritically, he will more readily accept the filmmaker's creative decisions to *select* and *emphasize* his material. In addition, the materials with which the filmmaker works are *gestures*. These are his building blocks. It is the selection of these that provide emphasis, inflection, interpretation, and statement.

It has been shown how image size can provide emphasis *in filming*. The close-up creates an immediacy of feeling and it calls attention to detail; the long shot is decidedly not an emphatic gesture in the same way. The long shot's emphasis lies in compositional selection rather than occurring through optical control of composition. It is emphatic by virtue of the arrangement of detail within the frame, particularly where a lone subject stands out in contrast to the surroundings. The close-up is more suitable for use in the documentary because of its dissecting nature, and because it causes the commonplace event to be seen dramatically. The long shot is, for the most part, a fictional narrative device best used where the creation of a delicate mood is the primary objective.

Although the production of the close-up is a feature of the filming process, it is its final selection and its juxtaposition, in the editing, which determines the quality of its effectiveness.

Returning to the potter, we can see that if there are more close-ups of his face than of his hands in motion, the emphasis may tend to fix more on the personality and the character of the man than on a description of his work. On the other hand, if in the editing process we "break down" the image of his hands in motion, we can see how an ultra-close shot of a few fingers grooving the clay can feature the craft process more than if the shot includes the hands, as they sensitively cup the turning object. The latter might point up the quality of the person more than the technical description of his activity. Very important to note here is that the *kinds of shots* which dominate the film tend to swing its emphasis. So that where the potter's cupped hands could possibly be read by the viewer as purely *informative* on a craft level; on the other hand, a *feeling of the man* might possibly emerge if the same shot were juxtaposed to a close-up of his face, from the side—or if the film were replete with images inclining toward a more intimate interpretation.

To summarize: (1.) The structural and inferential content of images (gestures) helps to determine their roles: how they should be used. Some images have clearer, more specific role possibilities than others. The ones which are more ambiguous or more general can suit a variety of purposes, according to how their meaning is inflected by juxtaposition in the film. (2.) The rule system, or the image choices which dominate in the film, as well as their relative positioning, helps to decide the way they are "read," and hence to define their roles.

Although it has been stressed throughout that the structural and inferential aspects of an image are really not dichotomous but rather, that they exist as two obverse sides to a coin and influence each other in the manner of "form and content," it is important for the filmmaker to be able to perceive both aspects as parts of the whole, yet as parts having distinct properties.

You cannot separate the inferential meaning of a flower, say, from its shape and color. Thus, blue flowers strike us differently from red flowers, and tulip shapes are feeling-toned differently from daisies. By the same token, film images project roles, dictated by both their structural and inferential properties, and these in turn can be inflected, emphasized, or even changed through careful placement.

Selection, then, and placement, are means of creating emphasis. But the place at which the image is cut is also a way of determining its impact. Previously, it was stressed that the filmmaker should gather footage with gesture in mind in order to make the editing process more effective. If he has been thinking about the structural considerations of color, form, and movement as well as about the inferential aspects—the image's feeling and connotative properties —then the place where the "action" is cut for emphasis should be simple to choose.

The longer the set of "denotational units" (those which lead naturally from a single action) included, the more a narrative is created through development—and the more specific is the idea conveyed (See the discussion of the child and the slide, Part One, "Active and Passive Gestures"). The *shorter* the set of gestures, the more generalized they become as an image, and thus the more figurative they become. This is true when considering either structural or inferential properties as a basis for an editing decision.

A passive gesture, one that is not moving (or one that is moving rhythmically), is cut according to the length of time it takes to digest its informational and feeling content visually. The longer the cut the more time the viewer has to scrutinize the scene, and the shorter the cut the more unconscious, subliminal, and like a "thought-projection" it becomes. It is also more figurative.

Emphasis is the way your film is inflected—what direction and interpretation it is given. But it also has to do with the smaller syntactical units of the film. Emphasis can be used for punctuating a scene or for dramatizing an especially important moment.

For example, when the potter first throws a hunk of clay on the wheel, the editor may choose to start with a medium long shot to establish the complete action (the man's full figure and the wheel), then to cut abruptly to a close shot of the clay spinning on the wheel, and to follow this by the entrance into the frame of the potter's hands as he cups the clay to shape it. The sudden cut to a close-up provides a full emphatic glimpse of the clay before its forming has begun; and this is followed by the hands dramatically entering the frame to start the metamorphosis.

Now the camera may continue to zoom out (or dolly back) to a medium shot, in order to include the potter's face; and this shot is held, allowing the action to develop, as he uses more and more water to keep the clay pliant and yielding. We may next film the potter from outside the studio through a window, showing the man framed like a painting as he works in the soft natural window light. Following this, we may take a reverse long shot from the interior toward the window, using the light from it to silhouette the man at work. And for emphatic punctuation, we may cut suddenly to a "tight" (close) profile shot of his silhouetted face.

EDITING FOR PACE AND RHYTHM

Although punctuation can be considered as a form of emphasis, it can also help to establish patterns and rhythms. During the preceding description of filming the potter, a rhythm between the long and close shots may be seen taking shape.

Rhythm has to do with repetition and the *systematic* interruption of it. The back and forth movements established between long shot and close-up; between full-light, half-light and back-light; between shots of the man's hands and his face; between high and low angles; between zooms in and out: All of these can be repeated for the sake of variation and emphasis, and the rhythms can be broken for punctuation too.

Let us now examine a syntactical unit which illustrates all of these at once: a speed-up in pace; emphasis; establishment of rhythm; and a compression of time *(and information)*.

In the film about the potter, he has thrown the clay on the wheel and is shaping it toward a completed piece: Let us say it is a bowl. We see him bisque it, glaze it, and fire it in the kiln. And we see him remove it—a finished piece. (The filmmaker should get a close-up of it here for emphasis.)

Now the potter returns to the wheel to make other pieces. He will go through much the same process as he did in making the bowl. In other words, the procedure is fresh in the mind of the viewer and there is little remaining curiosity—except about what pieces he will make next. It may be, however, that the filmmaker (provided that his time and film are in ample supply) will want to film the potter making the several other pieces from start to finish in order to allow the widest latitude in selecting scenes for editing. In this particular film, since we have an idea of how we are going to edit beforehand, we will only shoot the *highlights* of the subsequent pottery procedures, thus compressing them.

In the edited film, after the potter sits down at the wheel a second time, we will show him start the process as usual, by beginning to form the small mass of clay; then, through a time-transitional device such as a cut-away or an out-of-focus dissolve, we will go to a shot of the nearly-shaped piece. (Much *actual* time has elapsed between the first shot and the second.) Immediately following this, we will go to a shot of his throwing another piece of clay on the wheel, shaping it; then we will dissolve (or cut) as before to the nearly-finished third piece, and so on until we have seen, in fast rhythmic succession, a series of compressed events leading to the making of, say, a teapot, a pitcher, a vase, and a plate. We shall skip the bisking process in all the pieces after the first one, because it is a routine procedure we have already seen.

Now we begin a rhythm of briefer events—the glazing process of each piece. As before, we compress the procedure into highlights of the activity, showing just enough at first to establish the necessary technical information, and then dissolving from one successive piece to another, holding for the length of time necessary to illustrate the design and color of each piece before firing. During this sequence, in order to add variety, we might include a few cuts of the potter's intent face as he applies the glazes. The face shots might include profile views, as well as those looking up into his face. Now we see him placing the pieces in the kiln to be fired.

After the firing, when the pieces are removed from the kiln, we might choose to show each piece in close-up, as the potter sets them into camera view. This could be done, first, by a medium establishing shot of his removing one of the fired pieces and placing it on a table. Then the camera could shift to a medium close shot of the table as each piece is placed within the frame of view. Going about it this way, you would have a rhythmic intensity generated by the subject's actions (subject-interpretive) plus a suspense factor (objects entering the picture frame). On the other hand, it might be decided to show off the pieces in another way: by simply cutting to a close-up of each piece, with a close-up of the potter's pleased expression, and finishing with one of his hands (which would be a somewhat poetic camera-interpretive approach).

EDITING FOR JUXTAPOSITION

So far I have said little about the effect created by putting one shot next to another. A cut can have the effect of comparing or contrasting two juxtaposed gestures (images or scenes). The action of the potter's feet kicking the wheel to make it turn may be contrasted to the more serene activity of his hands. For relationships to be drawn between images it is best that they resemble each other as much as possible in size—and if it is an active gesture, that the actions be similar in speed and direction. Relationships between images are also fostered through similar shapes and colors. When analogous properties are perceived as shared by two juxtaposed gestures, then the viewer may be prompted to make other connections as well. In Charles Salmore's *Frogs*, the lady who looks like a frog could have been juxtaposed to an image of a real one—unmistakably establishing a relationship. As it turns out, the goggly eyeglasses the woman wears are perhaps suggestion enough.

Juxtapositional manipulation in the documentary is one of the filmmaker's chief means of inflection and statement. Although it is important to maintain a thread of documentary reality, this reality can be set off and very effectively commented upon by an imaginative placement of shots.

Montage

Any juxtaposition of scenes, images, or gestures in a film can be considered a montage. In other words, if a *continuously running* scene is broken down into segments of action, which are either deleted or rearranged, while additional shots are inserted (of close-ups or of different angles), it could be considered a montage. Montage implies that there is *a degree* of disjuncture between the shots; although time and space have been manipulated in a way that is not normally perceived, that manipulation works to establish an illusion which the viewer accepts as natural.

On a rudimentary level, montage operates in the interest of simple economy. For instance, where it may have been necessary to see the potter go through the entire procedure of making one ceramic piece, it is not necessary to repeat the whole process for all the pieces. Instead, the process is shortened and made elliptic by eliminating elements which are "understood," allowing the filmmaker latitude to point up what he thinks is important, or what will best serve his film's intention. By working with what is understood, the license that the film offers for communication is quite extraordinary. Unless the filmmaker has a special purpose in mind, as did Shirley Clarke in *Jason,* the naive way to make a film is to leave everything in—to be too literal rather than to use film for its suggestive powers. This is where montage comes in. It allows the filmmaker to "piece together" reality—to arrange it in such a way that those things he considers unsuitable to his intention, those things which to him are considered banal or irrelevant, can be eliminated to make way for what he wants to emphasize.

Montage is used principally in the documentary and story film modes. Collage, which is a more condensed form of montage, is discussed in relation to the collage film in Part Four. In the documentary, then, montage juxtaposition is most in evidence wherever the filmmaker needs flexibility—either to shorten or to emphasize elements in a scene. Where it is desirable to include only highlights of a process or a series of events, the filmmaker abbreviates through the use of montage. Economy, in this sense, works hand-in-hand with emphasis . . . for, what is left out—by its effect—features those parts which remain. Montage is, in the truest sense, *constructing* a scene.

But montage works on an even subtler level. For instance, if the potter's first act in creating a ceramic piece is to throw a hunk of clay on the wheel, and next, to begin shaping it with his hands, the action—what we are following with our attention—is programmed, so to speak, by what we anticipate of what we know to be a continuing procedure. In other words, we would watch, albeit restlessly, during every moment the clay is taking form, if the filmmaker were to let us see it. But if, instead, after the clay begins taking shape (the most dramatic moment in the whole process), the film were to shift to a close-up of the potter's face, the filmmaker would have refreshed the viewer's attention, and, at the same time, shifted the emphasis from the technical process to the potter as a person—thereby enriching the scene with a human interest element. Now, when the filmmaker returns us, in the next shot, to the bowl-in-progress, it appears dramatically far along—not as it was before we cut to the potter's face. In fact, some of the bowl-forming process *was* left out. The filmmaker has, through the manipulation of images, compressed time so that the viewer's attention remains sharp. Simultaneously, the feeling for and knowledge of the process is not impaired. By shaping time, as it were, the filmmaker has been able to improve on the ability of the potter's craft to be communicated (in that its boring aspects have been eliminated); and through juxtaposition (in this case, using a cut-away) the experience of observing has been made more personal by directing the viewer's attention to the human element. In this instance, the shifting of shots for emphasis allows the filmmaker to work with *time* as an element of his craft, an element which is as real as the clay is to the potter's craft.

The filmmaker can also distend or *expand* time to create suspense, by using the framework of a continuous event and inter-cutting additional information. Instead of shortening the time it takes to make a ceramic bowl, the filmmaker may choose to make it last longer. Let us imagine that the potter throws his clay upon the wheel and begins shaping it. But this time we are taken via film on a visual junket around the potter's studio, starting perhaps with the potter's face and then moving on to various ceramic pieces he has done in the past, to picturesque lyrical shots of the studio's interior, to the potter's foot as he kicks the wheel. And finally we are returned to a shot of the bowl taking shape—perhaps at the exact spot where we had left it. We will have cut no footage from the bowl-making process, and will have added a good deal of footage from around the studio. The viewer will accept the interlude or interruption because he will have forgotten what stage the bowl was in when we left it. Time, in other words, has been illusionistically stretched, and interest in the bowl-making process has been sustained if not heightened.

EXPRESSIONISTIC EDITING

If the filmmaker is filming a continual, ongoing process, then he not only can insert information directly relevant to the subject, but he can take the viewer on a trip *into the mind of the potter*, or take him into the world of the potter that exists outside the studio. But taking liberties of this sort creates a more imaginative or fanciful type of documentary that is *expressionistic*. It begins to stray from the taut line of naturalism and depart into the area of other realities. The reality inside the potter's head, for example, cannot be verified—it can only be supposed, interpreted, or inferred. It may, nonetheless, be based upon intimate knowledge of the potter—where portraying his idiosyncrasies and psychological make-up is a part of the intention. On the other hand, it may be as simple as wanting to reinforce a mood that is prevalent in the studio.

With the intention of making an expressionistic documentary, the editor will quite possibly juxtapose, to images with the potter, moments drawn from elsewhere, outside the studio. Let us suppose that after we are given the initial shot of the potter throwing his clay on the wheel, the editor inter-cuts images of activities which he relates for continuity on a structural and inferential level: such as a man throwing a dart, a bowler pitching a ball, and an athlete heaving a shotput. Each of these activities can be structurally related because they involve a person throwing an object (and let us suppose they are being thrown in the same "screen direction" and are about the same size in the frame). This sequence can stress the inferential qualities of "skill" and "accuracy"—qualities that the potter must have. Perhaps, as the potter shapes the bowl with his hands, the editor inter-cuts a shot of a mother holding her child's face in her hands, one of a person drinking water with cupped hands from a mountain stream, and a shot of a child shaping a sand castle. Structurally, the images will compare, in that there is a similar use of hands to hold and support. Inferentially, the images connote tenderness, life support, fantasy, and play. They provide the viewer with metaphorical comparisons which can comment upon the potter's activity, and which can deepen its meaning. The same can be done with *contrasting* images. In the documentary, *Glass*, the activities of glass blowers are, inferentially, contrasted with men working in a bottle-manufacturing plant.

The expressionistic form of the documentary allows the filmmaker maximum creative freedom. Staying within the "over-structure" of a basic, continuing activity can provide an umbrella, so to speak, for metaphorical use of imagery, and at the same time, lend it a kind of ready-made continuity. As will be shown in a later discussion of the collage film, disparate images can be structured without some ostensible overriding activity like this to hold them together—in the way, for example, that the potter provided. Continuity in the collage film is governed by another set of rules—one which is created by the filmmaker. He creates his own context, where the documentary requires that he shape an existing context. Both approaches, as will be seen, have their own special communicative possibilities.

It has been demonstrated how juxtapositional use of gestures and images can "graduate" from what can be regarded as a natural realistic approach to one that is more personally expressive. As images get more distant from the basic context of the action, in terms of time, place, subject, and so forth, the more metaphorical and connotative they become, and the less denotative and linear they are. May I suggest that if your main purpose is to convey *information* (the how-to-do-it aspects of your subject), then it would be better to stay close to the contextual imperatives of the subject. Use juxtapositions—but use them subtly and with care. If your objective is to draw forth comment, then a more distant use of juxtapositions might be in order. Analogy and metaphor create new meaning; they elucidate complex, existing meaning. A more linear use of imagery reinforces a line of thought that is set in motion, leading to a conclusion; this technique is more logically developmental.

Many things can emerge from the use of juxtapositions, not the least of which is the generation of new or fresh insight. Think of montage as more than a functional tool: Think of it as a valuable editing device which can provide you with a variety of expressive alternatives.

EDITING FOR THE INTRODUCTION AND ENDING

The ancients have a saying: "Things continue the way they begin." This certainly has profound implications for film, which takes us on an experiental journey through time. A time-oriented medium like film begins somewhere and ends somewhere; and the quality of these termini are crucial to the effect of the work as a whole, whatever the approach or subject. Unfortunately, though, we cannot rely on the wisdom of this ancient saying, insofar as a good start in film automatically implies a good ending. The viewer, however, will anticipate good things from your film if it begins well, and you will have scored a plus if you have him involved at the start.

Therefore, your film should begin in such a way that it both captivates your viewer's interest and establishes the intention of your film. At the very least, the nature of your subject's activity should guide you: This should suggest a natural beginning. However, many novices fail in this department, by *over-establishing* the event or the activity's beginning. Often, a gradual, low key build-up can be avoided by getting right into the activity; once the viewer is involved, use a flashback to the necessary, but less dramatic, informational shot. For instance, in the case of the potter, it might be good to start the film with a close-up shot of the first few exciting moments while the clay is first taking shape, and then either to cut or zoom back to a more descriptive, but less immediate medium shot of the potter in his studio.

As has been previously noted, there are several possible overriding techniques that can be used in the documentary: these should be established at the outset—if not during the first few shots, then soon afterwards. We should know what the *main* subject is: Will it be a social or an intimate documentary; will it be about several people or about one person? How will the film be handled stylistically: a string of long-running shots, or shorter shots in a montage assemblage? Is it to be a more conventional treatment or will it be expressionistic and highly interpretive? And finally, what structural systems are you using? What rule systems? Are you working with movement, form, color, and light as emphatic modes in which to interpret your subject? All of these—from choice of subject to method of presentation—should be established as early in the film as possible. If this is done, it is a good beginning. Once this is done, it is up to the filmmaker-editor, in the interest of continuity, to continue to develop the film's role and rule system to the end.

And it should be a *conclusive* ending, where the factors which are set in motion (the structure of the film with its inferences) are resolved. Just as every activity has a natural start, it has a natural completion. The potter's task is ended when he fires his pieces and we see the finished work; and this is a very natural place for the film to end. Social documentaries may not have quite as clear a cutting-off point as intimate documentaries because the activities and experiences are shared among a number of people. One approach to finding the ending to a social documentary is to ask at what point do the participants in the film realize their goal or gain the satisfaction they are seeking. *Endless Summer* ends when the boys find their "perfect wave." *Monterey Pop* ends when the festival is over.

Important to keep in mind is that the end of any film is the place where the viewer is left to his own thoughts and feelings, where he may assimilate what he has seen and heard. His is the beginning of a new process—that of integrating the film into his person. Before this new process can effectively begin, the viewer *must feel* the film has indeed ended, not just stopped. (For more on editing, see "Filming and Editing for Continuity and Emphasis," Part Three.)

DOCUMENTARY SOUND

Before shooting your film, or at any time during the shooting or editing, ideas for the film's sound may come to you. It is even possible that during the filming and editing you may have been influenced by some sound possibilities you are considering. On the other hand, the sound may be conceived more or less instantaneously, as you conceive the visual image; or, in fact, it may even be an integral part of the image.

For instance, sound and visual image are tightly related in Shirley Clarke's *Jason*, where we see and hear Jason as he speaks. It is clear that Miss Clarke intended her film to be largely subject-interpretive, insofar as the camera remains for the most part anonymous. Jason does the "performing"; and much of the performance is heavily dependent upon what he says and upon how he says it. This is so true that one might even say *Jason* is a "sound-interpretive" film; but whatever it is, Miss Clarke's use of sound is certainly realistic.

Less extreme is Pennebaker's *Don't Look Back*, in which he uses music and voice that are sometimes synchronized and sometimes only adjacent to the images, as a wild track. These two methods of relating sound to image are frequently used in the same film by documentarians.

The wild track (sometimes called a "floating track") is especially practical for the lay filmmaker because it does not pretend to be realistic; it is, instead, a treatment that is more impressionistic (where the sound is anticipated, but wild) and expressionistic (where the sound is unanticipated and unfamiliar). It allows him more freedom to edit as well as the freedom to use unusual, improbable juxtapositions of the sound with image. (The part-realistic, part-expressionistic use of sound is frequently used in many contemporary fiction films.) It is easy to see, therefore, that sound can either be used literally for natural realism or it can be more controlled and shaped for expressive purposes.

A factor which determines the prudence of using one technique as against another seems to lie in how strongly the subject projects himself. For example, Jason is so animated and expressive a subject that to let the sound float freely, out of sync, would very likely detract from his strength, as well as from the film's impact. However, where the subject is less definite about projecting himself, juxtaposing sound indirectly to the images can sometimes be used to "draw out" a subject's meaning.

Returning to the potter, it is easy to see how the available, realistic sounds of his studio might not contribute to a full projection of himself. Even his comments might seem awkward if he were shown trying to talk while concentrating on his work. (This technique is used abominably in television news-gathering.) A film of the potter might better succeed with no on-the-spot sound whatever. The sound could be recorded after the film had been edited, and used as a wild track.

In the documentary *Glass*, a jazz score, which evidently had been composed expressly for the film, is used for the sound track. The mood and rhythm of the music is synchronized with the images in a hand-in-glove way. The music must have been both composed and recorded while viewing the projected film—and then later resynchronized with it in the editing. The effect here is of a sound track tightly related with the visual image, and is similar to that of lip-sync sound. When a given action occurs there is a corresponding sound—like the sound effects of footsteps and doors slamming. The difference here is that the music in *Glass* does not function on a literal sound-effects level. Instead, it is figurative and connotative. For example, as the saxophone sounds a note we see a glass blower in that instant puff out his cheeks, blowing through a long metal pipe. As the bottle-manufacturing machine cranks out bottles, the rhythm of the music imitates, in synchronization, its mechanical maneuvers with humorous beeps and wheezes.

Although it should be noted that all sound, whether synchronized or wild, imparts considerable continuity (almost any movie will hang together with musical accompaniment), tightly realistic sound sync with image does provide *better,* stronger continuity than a wild track. The image will have more *presence.*

But the lay filmmaker who is working in Super 8 may find it frustrating to try to get the kind of perfect synchronization of sound and image found in *Glass.* This can only be done with elaborate and expensive equipment, almost none of which is standardized or generally available. (I am not referring here to the method of recording sound through the camera on the film, or of recording it on a separate tape machine to be laminated to the film later. Both of these methods are inferior or limited in one way or other.)

So, the question of what to do remains for the lay filmmaker without the proper equipment, who wants to create a sound track for his film. It should be stressed that synchronization achieved by running a tape machine and the film together can be quite satisfactory. It won't be as tight as lip-sync sound, but that isn't the most important consideration. In fact, lip-sync, on occasions, will tend to inhibit the filmmaker's freedom and inventiveness. The preciseness and rigidity of the format in lip-sync, plus the compelling quality of its ready-made continuity, are often blocks to subtlety. We can become so enchanted by the magic of seeing people on the screen talk that we become uncritical of what they are saying. The beginner, therefore, at least at first, might find his handcap a profitable one, causing him to place more of the burden for continuity on the structural and inferential relationships of his visual imagery.

In addition, the beginning documentarian is aided in his sound problem simply because he may take greater liberties with the sound track than he realizes. Sound in itself is more abstract than visual imagery, which, on the other hand, is more geared to our anticipatory requirements. Very often, real life is accompanied by sounds that are startlingly inappropriate—many are downright illusionistic. A couple in one apartment may be in a tender embrace, while next door another couple may be vociferously fighting. Through a window children may be heard screaming at play, while inside the building a great research team performs important cancer experiments. All manner of sounds come over the radio while we perform tasks at home and at work. In short, we have become accustomed to absurd and irrelevant sound juxtapositions to daily events, and so we will tend to accept them more readily in film.

The use of sound, then, can be rigid or flexible. It might be important enough to have been the film's inspiration, as one might say was the case in *Monterey Pop*. Sound may become important in the editing process, as it was in *Glass*. Or it might be added as a final step, recorded after the film was shot and used as a wild track, as in the hypothetical film of the potter.

Sound can be exact or approximate synchronization, depending upon how important it is for the image to *produce it,* as in *Jason*. Imaginative use of sound might be needed to interpret a visual image which lacks sufficient subject-interpretive qualities. For example, a street scene in a small town may offer little in the way of visual projection. A situation such as this permits the filmmaker license to interpret what amounts to a "visual generality" through the use of sound. It is good to remember that sound acts as an *indicator*—as a pointer to the intended meaning of the images: It acts to clarify.

In setting out to make a sound track for your documentary, simply remember that it should amplify the film's meaning in some way, and that it can pin down its feeling for the viewer.

A Note on Interview Technique

When you are conducting an interview to be recorded for a sound track, try to use equipment which will produce a fair range of frequencies and tones. Use a *directional* microphone, and record your subject with the mike as near as is possible to his mouth. Use ¼ inch tape, preferably—which can easily be edited—and record in surroundings which are acoustically good: in a room that has a maximum amount of sound-deadening material such as drapes, rugs, pillows, furniture, and so forth. It might be advisable to try recording at night, or at any time when there is little street activity. Provided that there isn't a high wind and that there is an absence of noise, the out-of-doors, in the open air, gives excellent acoustic rendering. Quiet, open countryside is ideal for recording; but such conditions are hard to find.

Before conducting an interview, prepare your questions well beforehand, so that all important points are sure to be covered. Let your subject be discursive and rambling as long as you have the time and the tape—and as long as what he is saying is interesting. Try not to dominate; and for the most part keep your questions general enough that your subject must use his imagination and project himself into them. Not: "Your life is pretty difficult, isn't it?" But instead: "What are some of the difficulties you've been having?" Also remember that besides getting specific information, you should try to get your subject to reveal himself—to be honest and candid.

In most instances, it is best if you edit out your questions from the final tape, so that the subject appears to be discussing his preoccupations naturally and spontaneously. (To help this along, always have your subject either repeat the question before answering, or incorporate its meaning in some way into his answer.) And when you edit the tape, do not feel that you must necessarily present your subject's interview in the order in which it was recorded. Realize that it can be switched around to suit the purposes of the film. You are working not only with juxtapositions of images, but with juxtapositions of sound with image *and of sound with sound* as well. Use these techniques to make a comment. (For tape editing mechanics, refer to Part One, Chapter V, Section 3.)

part III

THE FICTIONAL NARRATIVE

chapter 9

The Fictional Narrative as a Form

INTRODUCTION

The fictional narrative, or "story film," is comparable in some respects to the documentary. Both forms basically derive their material from the grist of everyday existence. The documentary does so through uncovering significance from life examples; the story film shapes these examples for the purpose of *condensing* them into a skillful construction. Moreover, the story film frequently uses documentary reality in various ways to impart veracity and believability to itself. For example, an actor is often type-cast for a part because his natural physical appearance, behavior, and attitude closely conform to the role he will play. Real settings, authentic props, and costumes help to create a "genuine" atmosphere.

Both film forms are narrative, in that they involve the "telling," or relating of life experiences; the difference between them is in the *way* these experiences are told to the viewer. Documentary *exposes* life examples for the viewer to see; the story film determines what they will be beforehand. This is primarily why the story film requires that the *planning phase* be given most attention.

There are exceptions to this, however, where the filmmaker may evolve his film "plan" during all the main phases—scripting, shooting and editing. In a case like this, the film develops more organically than when everything is planned before filming begins. (This is the way a director like Hitchcock prefers to work.) Federico

Fellini and Ingmar Bergman exemplify the freer method of working; but it should be taken into account that they are accustomed to working hand-in-glove with a "stable" of technicians and actors whose idiosyncrasies are well enough known to make a comfortable and successful working relationship.

The story film is often adapted from a short story or novel. The resulting script adaptation is a literary form all to itself—where the story is told through dialogue, directions for the action, and "visualization" for the camera. When a script is translated into film, because it is a different medium, causality in the plot is not as well supported through detail as it may be in the novel. Consequently, films of novels are not as complexly detailed as the literary works from which they are adapted. It is significant, and especially important for the beginning filmmaker to understand, that film be utilized for what it can offer rather than burdening it with the kinds of statements it cannot make effectively. Film is not an "idea" medium, in the sense that it does not permit ideas to be adequately weighed and evaluated by the viewer; film demands quick assimilation of its material because of the ever-present pressure of time. In that alone, film tends to be persuasive, if only in order to force the viewer to accept less than he might normally require for comprehension or *to make judgments*. Film is physical; and its strongest effect upon us is emotional. It is best suited for integration of concepts *in action;* it is a performance with time limits. A story film, therefore, is a performance of life in action—similar to a theatrical performance—yet it is different, in that *movement* and *time* in the latter are less essential and less controlled in the same way. (For more on this idea, see Part One "Motion and Time.") Movement and the utilization of time are the key expressive elements in a story film; dialogue is secondary. For this reason, it is possible to create a plausible, effective story film without lip-synchronized dialogue. A short story film may not need any dialogue. It is important to remember that the most persuasive aspect to film, including the story film, is the documentary quality it has—the life-presence it brings—and the de-emphasis of intellection (or thought), as expressed in Part Two "The Documentary and Its Relatives."

The most important ingredients in a story film are *plot* and *characterization*. Plot is "what happens," and characterization is "who does it." Also, plot is the *rule system* of the film, just as characterization is the *role system*. In a fictional narrative as well as in a documentary, viewers know, more or less, what to expect in the way of the film's action (what it's about) from its rule system—its theme and the way it begins. If, for example, the film is a documentary like *Showman*, featuring Joseph E. Levine, we know we are in for some scenes which will let us see inside a big-time film producer's life. Or, the opening scenes of *The French Connection* tell us it is about "cops" and "criminals," and about the action which is to follow. Generally, the role system in a narrative or documentary tends to dictate the rule system. Who the characters are and what they represent tells us how they will behave (within reasonable limits).

Oiling the Action: Viewer Anticipation

In the fictional narrative as in the documentary, one tenet tends to govern the action: a narrative line—whether uncovered in real life or fictionalized—works toward fulfilling or thwarting viewer *anticipation*. It becomes essential, therefore, for the maker of story films or documentaries to entertain the viewer's anticipation, to either give him what he is led to expect, or to frustrate it. In any case, *some* anticipatory satisfaction must be granted the viewer in the way of conventional treatment before surprises, whatever their nature, are sprung on him.

However, one cannot have a successful motion picture in *any* film genre where the viewer's anticipations are *confused*. The sin which novice filmmakers frequently commit is confusing their own aims with the film's. How often this phrase has been applied to a film: "It's neither fish nor fowl." This colorfully descriptive saying speaks directly to the need for documentaries and narratives to have a singular line of action in terms of plot and characterization. If the line of action is weak or too complex, the viewer's attention will be insufficiently directed. The average viewer brings to the film a considerable amount of preparation and knowledge about its subject. He expects to use it. He anticipates the action on the screen and he either wants satisfaction or he wants to have that satisfaction constructively denied. But if the film frustrates his anticipations, it cannot be because its aims are confusing him. Frustration must come as the result of new knowledge or insight—through the *unanticipated*.

When I refer to frustration of anticipation, I mean that which occurs throughout a film—perhaps periodically, or only at the end—as in the best of mystery films where the "good person" turns out to be the culprit, or as in surrealistic or horror films where unusual turns of plot and characterization occur within a familiar, logical context. Therefore, the film should control the viewer's emotional response; and the only way this can happen is for him to surrender his feelings.

Familiar roles and rules, then, are essential to a successful story; and departures from these can be made (to the enrichment of the film, it should be added) only when the viewer is "with" the film, when he is engrossed in it. The documentary and story film can be thought of as modes which *seduce* the viewer before *inducing* him. Before propagandizing him, before informing him, or before giving him a *new* illustration of life, he must be believing—"sold" on what he is seeing.

Activities and Performers

In conceiving an original story, it may be helpful to begin by thinking in terms of an activity or situation. In reality, this is the same as starting with the *rule system,* because the activity usually dictates the kinds of people who will be *participating,* which in turn should provide easy clues to their characterizations. A "car-wash" situation, for example, by its nature directs the participants—the attendants and customers—to take an attitude toward one another that is more or less predictable and which can be anticipated. Then, a violation or deviation from this expected behavior can provide the film with conflict and drama.

The *role system,* or the interaction between the performers, becomes dependent on the rule system, or the activity. Both the plot and characterization give rise, one to the other, in a mutually generative way. In other words, a person becomes characterized by his actions and by his attitude toward the actions of others. Good story film scripts are usually ones which are based upon *activities* which involve the subjects; this basis is also shared with the documentary.

SOME FICTIONAL NARRATIVE "TYPES"

For the novice filmmaker who is seeking to construct his own film from the ground up—conceiving an idea and writing an original

Normal Lens

Wide-angle Lens

Telephoto Lens

These photos illustrate relative lens distortion between Normal, Wide-angle, and Telephoto Lenses. Note that the normal lens is relatively free of subject distortion, where the wide-angle lens causes the subject's face to elongate with her ears pinned back, and the telephoto lens flattens the subject's face with a sharp reduction in depth.

Normal Lens   Telephoto Lens

These shots show how the picture area in "acceptable sharp focus" diminishes with the use of a longer focal length lens. Note how, in the right picture, the background foliage and the foreground wrought ironwork become fuzzy when a telephoto lens is used.

Basic lighting set-up on which there are countless variations.

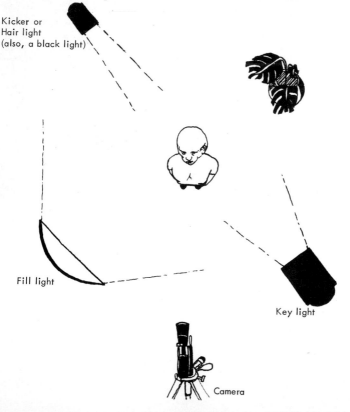

Kicker or
Hair light
(also, a black light)

Fill light

Key light

Camera

Use of levels of the action in *The French Connection*. Action in both the foreground and background makes the image more complex—and more interesting.

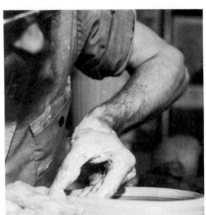

A filmmaker should explore a subject from different angles and under different lighting condition, as seen on both pages.

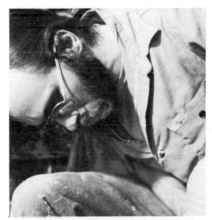

Four separate gestures are shown here, by the child, as he plays on a slide. The filmmaker-editor has the option of selecting all, or only one or two of them to include in his film. On the other hand, he may choose to "sandwich" other images between each gesture of the child—using the child's recurring image as a continuity device.

Teaching a frog self-confidence through sleep-learning; from *Frogs*.

A storyboard for a television commercial. Courtesy of McCann-Erickson for Buick Motor Division.

Note how as the camera position changes, so does the position of the subjects in the frame. For unbroken continuity, subjects should be kept on the same side of the frame, looking in the same direction—unless a transitional device such as a cut-away is used (see text).

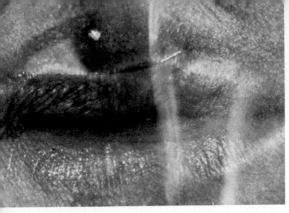

An eye superimposed above a mouth provides an eerie contrast in Carl Linder's *The Devil Is Dead*.

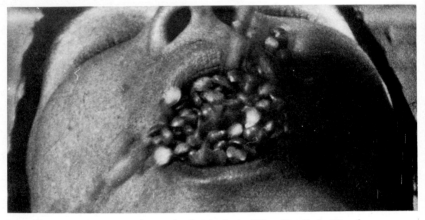

The "Gluttony Scene" from Carl Linder's *The Devil Is Dead*.

The "Castration Scene" from Carl Linder's *The Devil Is Dead*.

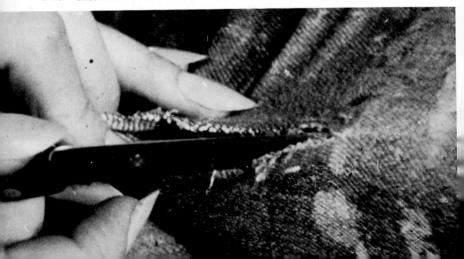

script based upon it—it might be helpful to consider a few broadly categorized film types.

Basic Episodic

The episodic film, like a classic episodic prototype in literature, *Don Quixote*, is built upon a series of segmented activities threaded by the strong motivation, usually of a single individual. I call these "running films." This is because *Breathless* was the first clear film example of episodic film construction I had seen. As you may remember, in Jean-Luc Godard's film, in the opening scene the hero is running breathlessly down a street—and from that moment on throughout the film he runs continuously from one place to another. Along the way, as he runs, he becomes embroiled in a series of minor adventures, and these are given continuity by virtue of his constant search. In many films this "quest" may be as comprehensive and simplistic as a search for happiness. In a similar vein, in Truffaut's *Four Hundred Blows*, the young boy protagonist runs away from home, and finally, away from the reformatory to which he is sent. In another running film, *Easy Rider*, two motorcyclists adventure aimlessly across country on a quest, the nature of which is not clear, even to themselves. But this fact is, in some ways, the point of the film. The running film is one of the easiest-to-control narrative types, mainly because the story usually centers around the in-depth character development of a single individual, seldom around more than two people. In the commercial entertainment-oriented film, the search is usually for something material—such as another person or things of value on the order of jewels, gold, or secret papers—whereas in a more ambitious film the quest is for some lofty intangible such as happiness or truth.

The Situation Film

Another major film type is constructed around a *situation*—usually a place where some people who have a problem live. Because the story is mainly about people interacting with each other, there is often much emphasis placed upon the *qualities* of actions and reactions, and on the sensational, unusual nature of the actions. The situation film, as a rule, is more psychologically involved than the running film; and it is therefore heavy on characterization, on the makeup of the individuals, and on their reasons for behaving the way they do. Alfred Hitchcock's *Psycho* is a good illustration of this film type, and *Sunset Boulevard*, with Gloria Swanson and Eric Von Stroheim, provides an even more striking example. But there are many, many more instances where those who are "holding the fort" (as I like to say) are perfectly sane, well-meaning people. Hitchcock's *The Birds* is a good example of this, where the birds who attack the people seem to be the deranged elements. It could be said that the situation film is fundamentally constructed around the defense of something valuable, whether it is material or intangible, whether family property, or one's own little piece of questionable sanity.

The two broad story lines that I have just described—episodic and situational—are at best only *a way* into the problem of writing or choosing a script. The fact that a running film is built around a single individual, and that the scenes occur episodically as a series of adventures (which are given continuity by the protagonist), should be regarded as an overall structure or as a vehicle from which the inferential meaning of the story emerges as the character's personality becomes defined by his experiences. A consideration of structure prior to making a film allows the filmmaker to place the emphasis of the story appropriately, whether it is to be on character or plot.

Disjointed Narrative

During an earlier discussion of the expressionistic documentary, it could be seen how *scene length,* as a simple structural consideration, can affect meaning. In other words, it was pointed out that short scenes tend to give impressions rather than to convey explicit details leading to conclusions. Longer scenes, on the other hand, permit more linear development because the action has more time to develop.

The disjointed narrative characteristically has short scenes and is usually less developmental of plot and character than a film of longer scene length. *Last Year at Marienbad, 8½,* and *The Trip* are some main feature-length films that use the type of scene fragmentation to which I am referring. Scene disjointedness is occasioned by the themes of the films, which in these instances have to do with illustrating mental processes and with remembrances, dreams, fantasies, and hallucinations.

Disjointing the narrative can be a viable poetic approach to the story film and is especially suited to a short film format. (Long films using this technique *throughout* tend to tax the viewer's attention.) Disjuncture of scenes allows much more to be said in a briefer time, mainly because the actions arc implicit, less detailed, more elliptical. A film constructed in this way, one that cuts narrative corners, so to speak, overlaps the domain of poetry. When scenes are out of order and the story is presented impressionistically (or expressionistically), the image as metaphor comes into play. This juxtapositional use of scenes generates meaning between them as between the lines of a poem; characters and actions become generalized and figurative.

The short 16mm films of Bruce Baillie typify this way of working. They are running films, poetically impressionistic stories built around a single character, a persona who represents the filmmaker and who is the corporal embodiment of his thoughts.

But the structure of films such as these says much about their inferential meaning too—the themes and subjects. Disjointed narratives are largely imitative of thought processes. Thus dreams are well-suited to this form. And because disjuncture of scenes can also have the effect of raising our level of apprehension, it is a good method of presenting tales that are suspenseful, fantastic, or strange. The horror film has traditionally employed disjuncture of time and place for shock value. At a time when many short narrative films are more and more about fears, compulsions, and fantasies, this fragmented, poetic approach may well be worth the beginning filmmaker's attention as a possible way to express personal sentiments and to say something about his state of mind.

Also, the disjuncture of images and gestures can perform as a montage, offering the viewer an impression or "overview" of a feeling instead of presenting a line of action. If the theme of a film is *fear,* and the scenes illustrating it are short vignettes of this emotion held together by the mood but not necessarily unified in a conjunctive, linear fashion, then the overview of fear becomes the modus operandi for the film.

Surrealistic Narrative

Another poetic mode, the surrealistic narrative, is one in which
the disjuncture of context occurs *within the frame,* rather than one
that dislocates the film's linear progression. Surrealism in film, as in
other media, is created through the control and arrangement of
subjects. Roman Polanski's early short film, *The Fat and the Lean,* an
allegory of a "slave-master" relationship, plays its scenes out-of-
doors instead of in-doors where they would occur more naturally. A
thin, half-starved-looking dreamer serves his loutish, fat, insensitive
master, feeding, shaving, and clothing him while he sits in an old
wicker chair in a yard full of high weeds. The dislocation of these
activities within an outwardly logical context heightens their feeling
of "reality" through improbable contrasts to such an extent that
they become exaggeratedly real (although they remain believable).
Surrealism evokes uneasiness. It ruptures the natural order, suggests
unpredictable things, and opens the way to thematic directions
dealing with unfathomable mysteries, psychological compulsions
and obsessions, and witchcraft—those things which relate to a
controlling or destructive power over others.

Although Polanski's *The Fat and the Lean* is a short film, it can be
seen that most, if not all, of his feature-length films are strongly
allegorical—almost like morality plays. But where he uses almost
no surrealistic techniques in *Knife in the Water, Repulsion* and
Rosemary's Baby are more on the order of surrealistic allegories.

Federico Fellini mixes surrealism with disjointed narrative
technique in *8½,* and this is one reason why this film comes across as
more carnival-like than as a true narrative. Surrealism requires the
foundation of conventional logic—at its base—and this cannot take
hold when impressionistic-expressionistic techniques are employed
at the same time. In contrast, Fellini's *Satyricon* is more fully realized
in its use of surrealism, but once again this film (which is one long
allegory) is defeated by the lack of believability to start with. I feel
that, overall, this is Fellini's failing in all his films. His basic premise
is already too fantastic to allow the viewer to get involved and begin
to care. It is only when surrealism can take hold in the imagination
that it will work. And this can only be accomplished when (1.) the
theme of the narrative will permit the bizarre and the unusual, and
when (2.) departures into the fantastic grow *effortlessly* and *rightly* out

of a structure that is basically reasonable—and one that plays upon our *familiar* anticipations.

But surrealism is used to depict states of mind too—hidden or implied—where the subject of the film reveals his thoughts through behavior, choice of activity, or attitude.

[This sometimes occurs in the documentary film; but because of the necessity to hew closely to real events in the process of uncovering that which will provide ·creative emphasis for the filmmaker—surrealistic techniques are used sparingly and with subtlety.

A student filmmaker made a film portrait of her daughter, and in it is a sequence where a sculptor, who has just finished bronze-casting a tiny figurine in the daughter's likeness, chips gently at the girl's lips with a tiny hammer. Although this process is not an unusual phase in the finishing of cast figurines, when it is emphasized (through a close-up as it was here) in the context of a film such as this it becomes surreal. Thus a standard procedure can become a symbolic gesture.]

Luis Buñuel is a filmmaker historically associated with surrealism who initially gained his reputation with the short film, *Un Chien Andalou* (An Andalusian Dog), a procession of weird, and even of a few horrifying, images. There is a feeling of naturalness in the blasé way bizarre events occur in the film. This aspect seems to be at the heart of truly successful surrealism. The nonchalance, the obliviousness, and the candor of the attitude adds poignancy and irony.

Surrealism is a strongly symbolic language, and because it is, it relates the viewer to his own deep unconsciousness where psychologists have theorized that vague racial memories, archetypal stirrings, and dark libidinous urges are lurking. This is to imply that however personal the imagery may seem, it can still communicate with the viewer on the more general, unconscious level.

Le Sang d'un Poète (The Blood of a Poet), by Jean Cocteau, justifies its surrealistic imagery by framing it in the context of a poet's mental adventures. It should be noted that this film is built around the encounters of a single person and that it is constructed in episodes.

It begins with a scene of a poet in his garret who has just discovered to his amazement that there is a mouth whispering to him from the palm of his hand. At first he is distraught at his apparent affliction and tries to drown the mouth by sticking his hand in a glass of water. When this fails, he rubs his bare chest and allows the mouth to kiss his body. Realism is carried to such an extent that the mouth is seen leaving a trail of glistening saliva across his skin. With his magic hand the poet touches a classical-looking sculpture of a man that comes to life; afterwards, he dives through a mirror, which momentarily turns into shimmering water, only to solidify again once he has passed through it. As in other films of this type, although the in-frame context contains out-of-place happenings, the lack of fanfare with which they occur helps to sustain believability.

The surrealistic story film is perhaps the most creative of the fictional narrative forms; it generates new relationships which give rise to new meaning. Where most story films rely upon the audience's familiarity with customary roles and rules, the surrealistic film works with the familiar only to gain our attention and confidence, using it as a pretext to jar the viewer with poetic, in-frame juxtapositions.

The surrealistic film is a form which has been popular with filmmakers at various times—mostly in Europe prior to World War II—and it is significant that this period roughly paralleled the ascendency of psychoanalytic therapy. Now, after several decades, during which the world's consciousness has been on external matters, for the most part political, the widespread experimentation with "mind-expanding" drugs, among other things, has renewed interest in what might be termed *the fantastical.* The horror film is becoming popular again. This is a thematic mode that permits extravagant use of a disjointed in-frame context in which emphasis is placed upon the mystery surrounding arbitrary destructive events, dreaded monsters, and so forth which we suddenly discover in our everyday midsts.

Although certain changes in our lives have prepared the way for a greater acceptance of the surrealistic film, there is also much impetus coming from those people who, were it not for film, would be using the written medium to create poetry. I say were it not for film because the advent of 8mm, and now Super 8mm, has literally put a camera in the hands of anyone who wants to make films. Technology or economics are no longer barriers to the film artist who chooses to film poetry rather than (or in addition to) writing it. The camera has indeed become as commonplace as the pencil or typewriter. The surrealistic film is, of all the modes, perhaps closest to the written poem. Surrealistic imagery is even quite *literary,* in that it is at once strongly symbolic and narrative. As will be seen in a later section on the collage film, there is another way to create poetry—one which is fundamentally *non-literary*.

chapter 10

Pre-production—
The Planning Stage

IDEA SOURCES FOR STORY FILMS

Most people who read this will be making *short,* fictional narratives, at least before trying one that is full-blown, feature-length. Therefore in this section I will list some ways in which material can be found for adaptation into a short film. (Presumably, those doing longer films will not need coaching.)

Somehow, almost everyone who has thought of making movies has had the urge to make a story film; and almost everyone has had the painful experience of wondering where the story will come from. Interestingly, most story films do not take their first form in the script stage. Even when script writers write, they start, usually, with a basic idea written down, just as any story is written. When written by a script writer, the idea frequently comes into being as a synopsis. That is to say, the basic *action* (chacterization and plot) is conceived in perhaps no more than the space of half a typewritten page. Gradually, this story line becomes filled out, "clothed" in the details which will make it complete and richly engrossing.

Although story lines can be suggested by news items in the papers, heard over the radio, or seen on television, it takes a fairly practiced, professional writer to expand a story from so little. An Indian reservation which is being threatened by a big strip-mining company may provide an idea for a "situation film"; or the women's liberation movement may suggest a "running film" about a young girl seeking an equal footing with men.

But these are springboards at best. There is an easier way to go about it than starting from "scratch." An entire story line and its outcome is often provided in narrative poems or narrative song lyrics. The poems of Charles Bukowski are rich in mini-plots and characterization, as are those of William Carlos Williams, Dylan Thomas, and Hart Crane, to name a few. Contemporary balladeers Bob Dylan, John Donovan, and Joanie Mitchell not only suggest story lines in their songs, but also produce a mood through the music which the filmmaker can use as assistance in interpreting the lyrics. Songs like this can also provide ready-made soundtracks.

Finally, an even more complete source—the short story—can be found in abundance, if not in the library, then in many current magazines. (The film *Brother Orchid*, a classic of the late 1930s with Humphrey Bogart and Edward G. Robinson, was adapted from a magazine short story.) Short story writers like John Steinbeck, Katherine Mansfield, Edgar Allan Poe, Hemingway, Kafka, and Chekhov offer fertile material for film adaptations.

But the short narrative film need not be as *complete* a story as one might think. A film can be a vignette, a fragment of a story, or, very simply, the embodiment of a mood. Some films I've seen come across like "gags" or humorous little interludes. Here are some outlines of a few I remember.

A housewife is setting the dinner table, preparing for guests to arrive. She goes into the kitchen, obviously tired, and sits on a stool. There is a cake beside her in a white bakery box. She looks wistfully at the box, then timidly lifts the lid for a little peek. Then she opens the lid all the way, sticks her finger inside for a bit of the icing, and licks her finger with childlike glee. She looks around to see if anybody is watching, takes the cake out and puts it on her lap, and this time takes a big wad of frosting in her fingers and stuffs it in her mouth, rolling her eyes, licking her fingers, and smacking her lips while the frosting now has made its way down her chin. She rubs it over her face and smears it on her neck. Now she's bathing in the icing and eating it at the same time. She opens her blouse and (you guessed it) begins to rub her chest and breasts, with the icing in hedonistic ecstasy. We now cut to the dinner table filled with guests as our heroine hostess enters the room with *the cake* on a serving platter, fully intact. She turns to the camera, smiles impishly, and winks.

In another film the scene is a backyard on a sunny afternoon. A husband and wife are seen in lawn chairs talking—or at least the wife is talking. The camera takes up the husband's point of view as we now see the mouth and lips of the wife moving incessantly. Now the camera moves ever so slightly to the side, back to the wife talking, and then wanders skyward, coming down to rest on the daughter sunning herself in a bikini on the lawn; then it moves to another corner of the yard, where the dog plays with a cat. Now the camera returns, albeit reluctantly, to the wife's tireless yammering. What makes this film so humorously effective is the reality of the camera movements in imitating the mental wanderings of the captive, bored husband.

Ideas for films like these frequently come from dreams, places, or personal experiences which may have left an indelible impression. In fact, any autobiographical material is fair game for a story idea; and because the filmmaker is personally involved, sometimes these make the best films.

Story ideas can come out of documentary situations, too. What might start out as an intimate exploration into the life and activities of someone may suggest fictional directions which would help clothe a tighter, more stylized version. As has already been noted, news items can trigger thoughts leading to a story line. Similarly, events happening to you in the natural course of a day (like the "cake orgy" film) also make good nuclei for stories, provided that you are attuned to their possibilities as story material.

WRITING A STEP OUTLINE OR TREATMENT

In movie jargon, an *outline* is virtually the same as a *treatment*. One way to think of it is as a "script synopsis," where only the essential story material of the script is included. If it is to be a half-hour film, the outline might run to twenty-five pages, and then again, it might be sufficient to have twelve to fifteen pages. An outline for a very short, slice-of-life vignette may be no longer than three to five pages.

The principal function of the outline is to rough out the story so that an idea of the line of action and of the characters can be put into a concise form. This enables the gist of the story to be communicated to those people involved in making the film whose suggestions may be needed in developing the outline into a script—usually aimed for a commercial market of some sort. Such people include, of course, the script writer himself: He must see if the line of action is sound enough to proceed, or if it needs revision.

Others, especially those people who may be financing the film, such as backers and producers, will need to know what the story is "about" to see if they will want to devote their time, energy, and money to the project. In other words, anyone who must give his approval to the concept of the film before it is "finalized" in script form will want to see the outline. When the outline is pondered by the script writer and others, changes are inevitably made which of necessity are dictated by talent, time, or money. Sometimes the changes are made in order to sharpen and tighten the story itself so it will make more sense, or have more impact. Other changes might be made to accommodate the particular personalities of the performers, the available locations, and so forth. The outline enables major changes to be made at the outset, so that the basic structure of the story will be sound before a full-blown script is undertaken. Customarily, major changes are made in the outline stage rather than later.

An outline is usually written in the third person. "He, she, it, or they did so and so." The entire story is told in this manner, usually in brief paragraphs, and the ideas are not expanded upon in detail. There is an effort toward brevity and conciseness when writing an outline, plus a concentration on the *action* as it develops from one point in time to the next, without elaboration. The opening sentences of an outline might go something like this:

> Fade in on a hot-rod roaring along a desert road in the late afternoon dusk. Another car pulls out from a side road in front of the speeding car, and there is a grinding crash of tangled metal, and moans. Suddenly, all is still but the peaceful sound of crickets. A woman is on the phone to the police, and we learn that she is the mother of the teenager who was driving the hot-rod. She explains that her boy, Billie, had left angrily after having an argument with his father. In a police car, officers are arriving at the scene of the accident. They pull to a screeching halt, with the headlights of their patrol car cutting through the smoke drifting from the flipped-over, burnt-out ruin of Billie's hot-rod.

Outlines for extremely short films, such as 60-second and 30-second advertisement "spots" for television, are usually referred to as treatments. A treatment is nothing more than a briefer, scanter, more "bare bones" representation of the action, where little more than a sentence or two, at most, is needed to outline each shot or scene. Inasmuch as this type of film is often an advertisement, an industry rule-of-thumb suggests that an average of three seconds be allotted for every shot description. A 60-second film would, therefore, have an average of twenty different angles and scenes.

But not all short films need treatments (indeed, not all films need a script). However, some film forms do require a treatment. In this grouping—along with advertising films—can be placed most commercial animated films, as well as short, narrative vignettes, three to five minutes in length. I think it can be seen that short films—with the exception of the expressionistic variety, covered in Part Four—do need more exacting planning than longer films.

Short films of the expressionistic variety allow the artist's intuitive sense to serve in lieu of a treatment or outline. As far as many collagists are concerned, much of what is accomplished by a treatment in other types of films is performed for him in the editing process. In other words, the film collagist looks at his available footage and makes his most crucial decisions while engaged in editing. This is an "organic" way of working as opposed to crafting a treatment before the filming begins. (More about the collagist and his way of working later.)

WRITING A SHOOTING SCRIPT

Unless you are making a very short film, you will want to expand your outline into a full-blown shooting script. If it's a half-hour story film—from a twenty-five page outline to about seventy-five pages of script. If a 90-minute film, sometimes the outline will be almost as long as the shooting script—100 to 140 pages. Here, the difference between the outline and the script is mainly a matter of form, where dialogue is inserted to replace exposition, and where the writer may feel some camera directions should be included to aid the director. Also, a final shooting script differs from the outline and early drafts of the script in that each scene will have been assigned a number.

Let us now briefly review the procedure leading to the shooting script.

The writer gets his initial idea from a variety of sources. These may include news items, personal experiences he has had, books he has read, people he has known. The sources for story ideas are almost endless, and are limited only by the imagination of the writer himself. But, as has been noted, to develop a story from such a scant beginning requires a consummate writer indeed. He must clothe his people with characterization, and he must be able to justify the plot in terms of the characters' probable motivation. It is the characters, after all, who move the plot along.

The novice filmmaker who is finding it difficult enough to learn the exigencies of filming may want to bypass having to learn to become a writer first. If his chief concern is making films, he may prefer to find what is called a "property," or a written story that has been published (that he must obtain the rights to if the film is to be sold), or a story that is in the public domain and free of legal tangles.

The next step is to boil the story down into a synopsis or outline, delineating the action without embellishments. Once the outline is done, there remains the task of recreating the story *in terms of a film.* That is to say, the action must be seen as a series of meaningful scenes—as a visual experience primarily, and augmented by dialogue—resulting in a shooting script from which the director will work.

The difference between a literary story and a film story is mainly in the time allotted to the reader and the viewer to assimilate nuances. The written story allows an infinite amount of time for the reader to grasp extreme subtleties, and the reader's mind can perform miraculous transitions from mood to mood, place to place, and time to time. The reader is inhibited only by his ability, or lack of it, to expand upon and ruminate on the story within the limits of the text. His imagination is a magic carpet.

On the other hand, the maker of films must guide and direct the viewer on this journey of the imagination. The film medium takes the reins of control away from the viewer, because there is not enough time, as images appear and leave, for the viewer to take a substantial tack on what is assaulting his visual and auditory senses. Therefore, he must trust that the filmmaker will make the necessary logical and emotional connections for him, and so there will be little for him to decide during the viewing experience.

I have belabored the film versus the literary experience simply to show that the shooting script (although in a written medium) remains but a "program" of the film to be made from it. Rarely are shooting scripts interesting or engrossing as literary works in themselves. Let's face it: A shooting script is a means to an end—and that end is a "moving" filmic experience. The *visualiza-tion*, then, of a literary work, a short story, or a novel, is a craft much to itself, requiring a script-writer who is able to take a literary piece and re-fashion it in filmic terms. What are those terms?

It is well known, especially in Hollywood, that a fledgling script-writer will frequently abandon his literary adjectives learned so well as a novelist or playwright for more "filmic" expressions such as "pan," "dolly," "close-up," "long shot," and so forth. He will include these in his script like a beginning cook who doesn't know the meaning of moderation in seasoning. One well-seasoned Hollywood script-writer told me that in his first scenario (script) he put in something like 178 shot directions in a 20-minute film. Of course, he found out later that decisions like those are made, for the most part, in the directing of the film—and a good many more are made during the editing process.

The mysterious thing that the script-writer chiefly does is to build "construction." To quote my Hollywood writer friend, "In film I've come to realize that the outline is worth fifty percent . . . it is as important as a screen play [shooting script]. I think that the reason some writers are paid fortunes—the really good ones—is not for their witty dialogue. They are paid for their construction ability. When I say construction, I mean building a story right down to the finest detail . . . within scenes, within scenes, and so forth. I know this because producers rewrite your stuff to death! When they call me back I ask 'What did you want me for! you must have hated my stuff, you changed so much of it.' 'Hated it!,' they say, 'we thought it was fantastic!' Somehow, I know they are telling the truth . . . but that's when I ask myself, 'What did they want with *me*? What were they after?' It took me a long time to find out. What they really wanted was *construction*. The pace, the rhythm, the whole fabric—dialogue, yes, but that is not what the producers are really after."

Even though *construction* may be most sought after in an outline or shooting script, it may be an unclear idea to the novice filmmaker. In a practical way it might be helpful to show what could happen to a paragraph when expanded from the outline into a shooting script. Let's use the previous outline example where Billie has wrecked his hot-rod.

FADE IN:

1. EXT. AREA BY CALIFORNIA DESERT HIGHWAY—LATE AFTER-
   NOON DUSK. AERIAL VIEW OF LATE FIFTIES MODEL CAR AS IT
   SPEEDS ALONG. We hear loud rock 'n' roll music on car radio.

2. TIGHT IN side view of car as it roars past, music louder.
3. INT. CAR, the driver, Billie's POV out windshield, as he sings with car radio.

BILLIE
(singing)

I just wanna see if you can bring me back, to
see if I lack, what you need . . .
Oh, you'll never know my special knack
Until you get me back baby . . .
until you get me back.

4. TIGHT SIDE VIEW of Billie's face, and hold, as he continues to hum with music, and turns face toward camera, looking out car's side window at something in passing.
5. ANGLE on rusting hulk of wrecked car beside highway, Billie's POV.
6. INT. CAR, POV out windshield as car pulls out from side street in front of Billie's car.
7. TOP VIEW of Billie's car swerving and skidding toward other car.
8. EXT. CAR of other driver through his windshield at his horrified face.
9. LOW CLOSE ANGLE of cars in grinding crash.

It should be noted that the two sentences of exposition in the general outline are expanded to no less than nine individual scenes in the shooting script version. It is in the detail, I believe, that the biggest difference between these two forms can be most graphically illustrated. It is true that not all outline material will warrant expansion to such a degree; but since this is the opening few minutes of the film, which are extremely tense and dramatic, much care, even more than usual, is given to the crafting of scenes which make up this *montage*. (Montage is the construction of action and story through a discrete series of related shots, as opposed to a single, long-running shot, or through narration or dialogue.)

Also worth noting is that even though directions for camera are included by the script-writer, it remains ultimately for the director of the film to decide just what type, and how many, shots he will use. In effect, the script-writer can suggest camera angles, and so

forth, but in the final judgment the director does not usually feel
bound by them.

In addition, it is traditional that even though the script may be
changed by the director—some scenes deleted and others added—
the original *scene numbers* are *never* changed. Scene 7 (above) may be
crossed out by the director, but no other scene will be called Scene
7. However, if a scene is added between Scenes 6 and 8, then this
will most probably become Scene 6.1 or Scene 6-A—and a scene
added after that would become Scene 6.2 or Scene 6-B, and so on.
In other words, the original numbers given to a shooting script are
never changed. This custom has evolved out of the pragmatic need
to keep the lines of communication open between all of the people
working on the film—from wardrobe to set designers, to actors, to
the camera and sound technicians. In the commercial film industry
all script changes are made at the same time by running-off (Xerox
or mimeo) various colored sheets to represent various stages of the
rewrite by the producers or the director; and these are carefully
issued to all people holding copies of the script so that the changes
will be uniformly made at the same time.

The tug-of-war between the script-writer, producers, and directors is an on-going family squabble over whose judgment must or
should ultimately prevail. The writer's "case" is that a well-crafted
film script should not be tampered with to any great extent, without
his consent or knowledge, by those making the film. His argument is
that much thought has been given to each and every event, every
corridor and passageway of the plot, and that to ignore certain
needs of the story which make it plausible, is to ignore those details
in characterization, and so forth, for which the writer is paid to
concern himself. On the other hand, the producers and director
may feel that the writer has not taken enough things into
consideration to make the film well-paced and have impact; and so
it is felt that changes must be made in order to make the film a
realistic project. The writer works in his ivory tower but we (the
director and producers) are the ones who must cope with realities;
and therefore we must have license to make whatever changes are
necessary. In truth, both sides have a valid case; and both can be
validly accused of getting "carried away" with the concerns of their
own bailiwicks—and not infrequently to the detriment of the film's
success.

The best solution, I believe, is to have a good, continuing,
working relationship between those who write the film and those

who make the film, as the film is being made. Unfortunately, this is a rather wishful ideal, except where making the film is more a labor of love than a commercial labor.

But those who make films for the joy of it will more or less naturally acquire a close working relationship with the key parties concerned. Often where a film is made for creative, expressive purposes, the writer, director, and producer all wear the same hat.

It is my intention here to grant the reader a taste of what happens while seeing the script-writing process through from inception of the idea, to outline, to script. It can be seen that different types of story films require different approaches. Much is decided by the length of a film, by its intention—whether commercial or otherwise—and by the needs and desires of those concerned. There is no set way of approaching the script-writing process—only ways.

STORYBOARDING KEY SCENES

What is a storyboard, and why is it important? A storyboard is very much like a comic strip and even looks like one (see insert). It is a series of pictures representing key scenes of a film in the order the scenes appear. But more than that, the storyboard "frames" contain important information, such as the size of the subject or subjects (whether a close, medium, or long shot), the placement of subjects in relation to each other (composition), and the positioning of the camera (whether high, low, or level). If it is a "dressed-up" storyboard, it may even contain additional details, such as props, color and style of wearing apparel, expressions on the faces, and even dialogue or narration.

A storyboard is used whenever an exacting relationship is required between subject and camera—usually for a period of seconds or minutes. Storyboards are always used in the making of short animated films, in advertising films, and in brief segments of longer, feature-length films where subject-camera relationships are extremely critical to plot or impact. Also, a storyboard is needed whenever a tight construction of scenes is important to the informational content—such as in training, educational, and industrial films—and in mystery films. Alfred Hitchcock has been known to sketch camera-subject relationships for many of his scenes. He gives these sketches to his director of photography, making the line of communication between the director and camera quite ideal. It should be noted, in this respect, that Hitchcock is an exception rather than the rule among directors. On the whole, the use of storyboards is confined to a rather narrow spectrum of filmmaking. It is a tool which aids in *precision*. Yet, kinds of storyboards vary anywhere from the comic strip variety to a series of quick line sketches on a note pad. Some take the form of elaborate water color renderings, worthy of exhibition in an art gallery. But the purpose is always the same: to let the filmmaker know what important scenes are going to look like beforehand, thus giving him an extra bit of control.

There are two main kinds of storyboards, and though both accomplish the same basic aims, one is a bit more flexible than the other. The most common type is the comic strip format—where there are several rows of frames on a single, large piece of paper or poster board. The filmmaker, in visualizing the key scenes of his film, will fill in the frames with drawings of his characters, subject size, camera position, and so forth. The drawings might be simple, child-like stick figures, or they might be filled out and fully formed, à la Leonardo Da Vinci. Either approach achieves about the same end.

Then there is a storyboard made up of either 3×5, 4×5, or 5×7 inch file cards—one card to represent each scene. These can be placed in rows on a large backing (like a small blackboard), and can be held in place by strips of clear plastic, forming a slot into which the bottom edge of the cards can be placed, thus enabling them to be pulled out and switched around. This method allows the filmmaker to jockey his scenes around for greater visual and emotional impact, trying different combinations, and eventually coming up with the best one. There is no doubt that this kind of flexibility is extremely useful when there are, say, twenty key scenes in a 60-second spot advertisement, where the best possible combination is of crucial importance.

It may be recalled that the story treatment is fundamentally like a storyboard, except that it is *written* instead of pictorial. Often the concept of the story is worked out first in treatment form before going on to the storyboard. The two can work together.

PREPARING A BUDGET—FOR THE PROFESSIONAL FILM

In planning the details of a story film, and some other types of films, the preparation of a budget as a forecast of production costs should be figured with precision. A budget can tell you how much you *need* to spend in relation to how much you *can* spend.

There are two fundamental ways to approach making out a budget. The most ideal way is to figure out how much the film will cost and hope that you get all the money you need. The other way is to have a lump sum, a predetermined amount to work with, and to tailor your budget to fit the amount allowable. More often than not, the filmmaker is given the task of "bringing the film in" on a fixed sum. And more often than not that sum is below the ideal.

Here is a list of a few things that tend to drive up production costs. The foremost villain is the *quantity* of film needed for the production. The amount of film expended in shooting is determined by several factors. The total film to be shot is budgeted in terms of "shooting ratio." If the shooting ratio is three to one (3:1), then the budget will call for enough film to allow for, say, 3,000 feet of film to be shot for every 1,000 feet actually used in the finished, edited film. No shooting ratio is the same for all films. Not only do different types of films require different shooting ratios (documentaries can run as much as 20:1 or 50:1), but another factor can be the difficulty of the scenes to be shot—and how exacting they must be.

For example, scenes that require different maneuvers and stunts may have to be shot again and again before a satisfactory "take" is obtained. Film takes can be spoiled by unprepared actors or poor acting. Any scene included in a script that is fraught with possible unforeseen fluffs will increase the shooting ratio. However, these troublesome scenes can possibly be altered or even eliminated by simply changing the story around.

Often overlooked is that the laboratory cost increases down the line as the shooting ratio increases. Every foot of film shot must be developed; and, customarily, a work print is made at the same time. The work print enables the filmmaker to screen his day's shooting (called "dailies") and leave the original untouched, only to be handled later during the final editing process. To dramatize how much the cost is multiplied: a 100 foot roll of 16mm color film may cost $8.00 for the raw stock alone (which gives about $2\frac{1}{2}$ minutes in running time at sound speed); developing this roll of film may cost $6.00; and a work print may cost $8.00. By the time you are finished, $2\frac{1}{2}$ minutes of film has ballooned from an initial expenditure of $8.00 to $22.00. Almost three times as much.

Something which could bring down a shooting ratio is increasing the amount of shooting time, allowing greater care to be taken setting up shots. In some instances it works, but it is more than likely that it will pose an even costlier item on the budget—the number of days needed to complete shooting. The more time spent shooting, the more the salaried people and rented equipment are tied up. Hired actors are frequently paid on a daily basis, although some are paid a fixed sum for the duration of the production, whether the shooting takes ten days or fifteen days. Equipment, on the other hand, is almost always rented on a weekly basis (much cheaper than renting by the day). If the production runs ten days instead of seven—the cost could end up in terms of the low weekly rate for seven of the days, plus the expensive day rate for the remaining three days. Consequently, one of the first things to determine in a good budget is the number of shooting days. This, in turn, sets the amounts for particular items detailed in the budget.

If the production crew—cameraman, soundman, and others who are helping—are getting remuneration for their work, their total cost can be figured on the basis of how many people you really need. There are jobs a willing cameraman and sound technician can perform when not running camera or sound. Although in commercial industry films the unions have deemed it taboo to expect, or even to ask, members of the crew to perform tasks undesignated by their craft, there are many films made where union practices are not strictly observed. There is a degree of flexibility in this area, and although a good many technicians will not work for less than union scale wages, they will often perform additional tasks if the requests are within reason. On an extremely low budget film, allowances by the production crew are frequently made to fit the realities of the circumstances.

In most instances where the production is intended to satisfy the personal, expressive needs of the filmmaker rather than being another commercial product, production crew and actors will often *volunteer* their services gratis, just to be able to work on a film with more to its intention than to entertain and make money. Such an arrangement could lower the total budget considerably.

But even a production with the most lofty intentions will have inevitable costs such as equipment rental. Most filmmakers find it economically cumbersome to own their equipment. The overhead is simply too great to bear. Equipment is not used 365 days a year. In fact, it may only be used a few months out of the year. The rest of the time, equipment depreciates in value without the benefit of its use. Also, as equipment ages it tends to become technically obsolete. Moreover, insurance on equipment breakage, loss, and theft makes ownership truly prohibitive on a year-round basis. The only alternative is to rent equipment—an additional item for inclusion in the budget. Yet here, as before, sometimes corners can be cut, without any sacrifice of quality, by planning judiciously. It may be that the amount of equipment, lights, tripods, and so forth can be reduced. It might be cheaper to rent a piece of equipment for one day or two days than for a week (at the weekly rate). This means planning for the *exact* day you will need the item, and hoping it's available when you go down to rent it. Such nit-picking can be troublesome, but it can pay off in the end.

An even less flexible area than equipment, as far as cost is concerned, is raw stock and processing. Of course, the amount of film to be shot is determined by the shooting ratio (allowable by the peculiar needs of the film and the money available). The film stock is usually purchased at a fixed price (Kodak publishes its price list), although sometimes film can be purchased through labs at a discount—or better still, there are "marts" where surplus film finds its way after productions are completed. (Filmmakers rarely use up *all* the film allotted for a production.) As far as film processing is concerned, it is such a competitive matter that most laboratories have their prices pretty much in line with each other. There are cut-rate labs, but just be sure the quality isn't cut-rate as well.

There are certain steps in making films (16mm in particular) in post-production that might be classed as luxuries. There is a set ritual in perfecting a final commercial film product, such as getting just the right color balance in the final print, the right image density, and the right fades, dissolves, special effects, "wipes," and so forth. These professional extra "goodies" sort of put the fun back into the filmmaking process after the film is shot and edited. In other words, there are things you can "order" the lab to do for you (the way you might order chives and sour cream with a baked potato, in place of using butter). This ritual includes what is known as A & B rolling (splitting the film original into two reels with black leader between the scenes on each roll). The purpose is to eliminate splice flashes and to facilitate optical effects. Other considerations in the professional editing of a film include having sound transferred from ¼″ magnetic tape to a sprocketed magnetic tape commensurate with the gauge film being used. In turn, this reel of sound is also split into several reels—of dialogue, music, effects, and so forth—in order to facilitate "mixing." When the reel of original (negative) film, plus the mixed sound reel, is sent to the lab, they are instructed to make a *timed composite print* (called a *first trial print*). After further corrections are determined, a first, and even a second, *answer print* may be required before a satisfactory version of the film is obtained. After a good print is perfected, an *internegative* is made, from which are made numerous *release prints*. All of the aforementioned parts of the post-production ritual form part of the cost which must be met.

However, parts of this process can be eliminated or bypassed. You may not be constrained to A & B roll your film, in which case you save on the cost of black leader (as well as saving time). Your sound transfer and mixing can be as simple or complicated as you need to make it. The number of optical effects performed by the lab can be reduced or even eliminated. The first and second answer print stage might be totally eliminated—along with the internegative (if you only need a few prints for yourself, they can be "struck" from the original). In other words, once you have been involved in this ritual a few times, you will find that certain of the standard procedures can be modified or eliminated altogether. Your decision will affect the entries you make on the budget sheet—and the final total.

In the post-production, editing process, there is more equipment which must be rented, such as a moviola, viewer, splicer, rewinds, and so forth. The number of days in post-production will necessarily affect your budget figures.

Other types of budget items to be considered are: transportation and meals for production crew and cast, props and costumes, and phone calls. Every cost should be accounted for in the budget if it is to be realistic and accurate. Additional information on budgets can be found in some of the magazine articles listed in Appendix B.

SCHEDULING THE FILMING AND BREAKING DOWN THE SHOTS

There is still some organizing to be done after writing the script and making out the budget. It involves having a *time-table*. This details when and where the shooting events are to take place.

If some of the filming is to be done on location, time must be allotted for facilities to be secured, an apartment to be rented, a campground to be reserved. The time of year will determine the probability of good or bad weather. And of course, casting, procurement of props, and rehearsals must yet be done. A target date to start shooting must be determined.

Even though your script or treatment will have the scenes numbered, rarely, if ever, are scenes of a film shot *in sequence.* Usually, all the interiors at a given location are shot at the same time, and likewise for all the exteriors. All the scenes involving a certain actor may be shot at the same time, and so on. In other words, you must sit down with the script and scan it in order to obtain the best, most economical arrangement of shots for every shooting day. Once the schedule has been worked out, then all those who are in the production will know when their services will be needed—and most important, a lot of time, effort (and possibly money) will be conserved.

CASTING FOR CHARACTER TYPES

Whether the film is documentary in "form" or a story film, the camera is always recording an event taking place in front of the lens. One could say that film is, first and foremost, a documentary medium. Perhaps because of this fact, and also because of the distance between the viewer and events taking place within a rectangular screen, the two-dimensionality of the image, and the control, in general, over what is seen, we require that the "subjects" of a film be especially convincing.

In casting for a story film, the director should be sure that the performers he chooses are especially well suited to their parts. An actor's looks and manner must correspond to what is commonly called in the film trade as a "type." Fortunately or unfortunately, it is a truism that many people possess certain characteristics in looks and behavior which can be identified with an occupation; and in many instances, what is visible that a person projects can be associated with attitudes he has toward other people.

All people project "vibrations" more or less consistent with certain moods, such as ebullience, sadness, seriousness, and so forth. And there is a small percentage of people whose personalities are "styled," who are sort of streamlined versions, and who have strong self-images along role-playing lines. It is for this, latter, exaggerated type that the story filmmaker should be on the lookout when casting his film.

The most outstanding, visible features of a person are his physique, his facial structure, and the color of his skin. Simply put, if a script calls for the part of an oriental, it would be illogical to cast a Caucasian or a Black in the role. By the same token, a more subtle choice must be made when casting according to occupation. How does a storekeeper look? (Would he look like Percy Kilbride?) How does a doctor look? A secretary, construction worker, artist? In making decisions of this sort, perhaps the first place to turn is to a film that has used a certain type successfully. If we go to a Bogart film for examples of a gangster, policeman, crooked lawyer, drunken doctor, or mistress, it may give us some ideas. However, there is a pitfall inherent in this approach: namely that character types tend to change with the times. Today's gangster or gun moll may look and act differently from those of thirty years ago. Morticians, prostitutes, airline pilots, gamblers, jockeys, delivery boys, students, housewives, and so forth: All can be said to have characteristics that seem "appropriate" to their occupations. But mind you, it is important to avoid the possible misconception that pronounced characteristics are frequent, or that they are found in abundance among those with readily labeled occupations in real life. Here, we are not talking about real life, we are talking about a *stylization* of real life, about a "cartoon" representation of people as expressed by the exaggerated features they project.

One of the great masters of type-casting is Federico Fellini. It is not surprising that before he became a film director he had been a cartoonist for Italian newspapers. Inasmuch as the cartoonist captures the essence of what a person projects—especially in looks and physical attitude—this experience equipped Fellini with a unique casting ability. It is well known that casting for Fellini films is a long and thorough process, and that it has paid off in extremely convincing character portrayals.

On the whole, it is better to use a non-actor whose looks and behavior fit a part than an experienced, even talented, actor whose appearance and manner are not quite right. In Hollywood films we see miscasting all the time. The reason is that actors are under contract and must be used in films—sometimes in any film—simply to justify their salaries. And, we often see miscasting in student productions, where pressure is on the student filmmaker to use his friends and those immediately around him.

In short, the needs of film are different from those of the theater. The chief difference lies in the necessity of film to establish quickly the *presence* of the character. This need for expediency can best be satisfied if the actor projects with himself totally: in looks, mannerisms, and body attitudes. This quasi-realism, not as much needed in the theater, is probably one of film's unique requirements. Even though the story may be make-believe, the film medium must present it realistically and convincingly—if indeed realism is the objective.

REHEARSING THE SCENES

It goes without saying that shooting a film does not begin without first seeing how the action is going to look: where the actors will move (blocking), and what lighting set-ups will be needed.

Although everything that takes place on a set, "on camera," is technically the province of the director, he cannot possibly be involved in every intricacy. Therefore, a few assistants who are familiar with the script can be invaluable in helping to rough out some of the following details.

Movements by the actors, as well as by the camera on the set, can work for or against the practical necessities of shooting or the aesthetic intention of the film. In other words, what may be practically feasible may not be aesthetically desirable, and vice versa. Actors cannot roam willy-nilly about the set while on camera because they are not (film-wise) moving in the three-dimensional space of a set; instead, they are confined within the two-dimensional limits of a rectangular frame as viewed through the camera. The first step, then, is to "choreograph" the scene in such a way that if it is necessary for the actors to move out-of-frame, the camera can be properly cued to follow the action by using a pan, zoom-out, or close-up. Consequently, a rehearsal is needed to prepare the actors for the limit and direction of their movements, as well as to familiarize the cameraman with the movements he will make. During these rehearsals, it is a common practice to use chalk marks on the floor in order to show the actors precisely where they are to begin their movements and exactly where they are to end up. The camera operator, in turn, is following the notations made on his copy of the script—as to pans, zooms, and the like.

So far, I have mentioned that one of the most obvious needs for rehearsals is to coordinate the movements of the actors and camera. Yet another big reason for rehearsals is to obtain the appropriate inflection, emphasis, or mood from the performance of the actors. In some cases veteran actors will have a repertoire of moods to draw from, complete with gestures and facial expressions. This is particularly true in the case of actors who perform commercially for television and some films. However, where inexperienced actors are used, it may be up to the director to help focus them on specific interpretations of the dramatic action. As the saying goes, the director must "pull the performance out of them." Several rehearsals may be needed to accomplish such an optimum dramatic climate.

Less obvious is the need for rehearsals to check out props to see if they work, or to be certain that they have been assembled and properly placed. Do chairs break away as they are supposed to? Do telephones ring, and guns fire?

Finally, of no less importance is the number and positioning of lights. Although lights can be set up, and diagrams of their positions can be made during blocking rehearsals, frequently separate lighting rehearsals are needed. Lights are hot, and as a rule they are turned off when not absolutely needed—for the comfort of the actors and crew as well as for economic reasons. It should be kept in mind that as an actor moves (or as the camera moves) within a given lighting set-up, the quality, intensity, and mood of the light changes. Therefore, radically extreme movements by camera or actors require new lighting set-ups in order to preserve lighting continuity when the scenes are joined together in the editing.

chapter 11

Production

LIGHTING FOR THE STORY FILM

A chief difference between lighting for a story film and lighting for a documentary film is the filmmaker's greater control over the former. In the story film there is little reason for accepting less than what is needed to accomplish the job effectively from the standpoint of technical competence and creativity. In reality, the aspect most often beyond the control of the filmmaker is money. Even here, he has the choice to make a film without sufficient funds—and skimp—or to wait until such time as there is enough money. And lighting equipment, however crucial and important it is to filming, is not the most expensive item on the budget.

A rule of thumb is: It is better to have too much light than not enough. A lack of adequate light can produce several serious drawbacks in filming. Perhaps the most important consideration is depth of field (the total amount of acceptable sharp focus in a scene). In most, although not in all, instances a great amount of depth of field is desirable. This is only achievable with a lot of light, or with a film having a high ASA rating (coupled with the use of a wide-angle lens). Of the two choices, a high level of illumination is preferable. (Films with high ASA ratings are likely to produce graininess and reduce sharpness of image.) A large amount of depth of field—referred to as deep focus—will allow the actors to move toward and away from the camera without dropping out of focus while the camera is set for a *single* distance setting.

On the other hand, if *shallow focus* is desirable, the light level should be reduced to minimal intensity, and a telephoto lens should be used. Shallow focus is implemented to blur the background or foreground of a scene, or to focus attention on a subject in the background or foreground. By turning the distance setting, a hitherto unnoticed subject in the background or foreground can be caused to "pop" into focus, while visually dissolving into a blur what had been previously seen. This trick use of depth of field can be a highly effective creative tool.

As explained in Part One, a major determinant of depth of field is the lens aperture opening. The smaller the opening, the greater the depth of field (hence the larger will be the f/stop number). F/11 yields deeper focus than f/5.6. In general, those working to maintain commercial standards in the film industry try to arrange their lighting set-ups to allow an aperture setting of around f/11. In fact, this might be considered the key f/stop number, because it affords the greatest depth of field without causing a degradation of the image (which tends to occur at greater f/stops, especially around f/22). In summary, for most filming purposes, high intensity lighting is preferable.

Under studio conditions, it must first be decided from what direction the *main* source of illumination will come. In story filming this decision is usually influenced by the realistic light source that is "understood" by the viewer to exist. If the subject is standing by a window, then other lights (to boost illumination) will have to be "in line" with the direction of the window light. A principal source of illumination such as this is called the *key light*. It could be anything from a lamp in a room or an overhead chandelier to the headlights of a car or candlelight. The cinematographer relies upon his key light to give him the camera's f/stop setting. The other lights—those used as fill for the shadows, lights to set off the subject from the background, hair lights, and catch lights for the eyes—are placed in such a way that they balance the key light aesthetically in terms of contrast and overall mood. The key light, in other words, always provides the basic guide for the use of other lights. Lighting decisions are mainly determined by experience as well as by the personal preference of the cinematographer. More on the order of routine considerations are: Is there enough light for depth of field? And is there enough detail in the shadows—provided by the ratio between key light and fill light?

When filming out of doors, there are modifications to the previously mentioned guidelines. First, bright sunlight is intense and harsh. The intensity of illumination can provide for deep focus and is an asset, but it will also create nearly impenetrable, harshly delineated shadows. To offset this, the filmmaker must use reflectors to bounce the light into the shadows for "fill," and a scrim made of nylon or silk (or other screening material) must be held between the subject and the sun to diffuse shadow lines and the sun's rays. (For more detail on lighting accessories, see Part One.)

If the exposure meter can tell the cinematographer how to achieve the correct level of key light intensity, then the *contrast glass* (a monocle-like affair he peers through and usually wears around his neck for convenience) tells him how to correct the lighting ratio between highlights and shadows. The contrast glass more accurately represents the difference between light and shadow (as it will appear on film) than the judgment of the unaided eye. For color filming the ratio between light and shadow should not, under most conditions, exceed 3:1. Or to illustrate it more graphically: If, say, 3,000 watts of light is used for the key light, not less than 1,000 watts should be used to fill in the shadows. (This holds true, of course, only if the lights are the same distance from the subject.) If the ratio is increased, the highlights may be "washed out" and detail in the shadows may be lost.

Because film (more so than still photography) is especially suited to the arousal, building, and culminating of emotions and to the manipulation of emotions in a time-framed continuum, the tools of crafting these emotions are especially prized and utilized. Chief among these is lighting. Lighting has long been acknowledged as a major mood-setter—matched only, perhaps, by *sound,* and *gesture.* Light not only generates the image on the film—and literally makes it possible—but the use of light (lighting) dictates *how* the image is made. Lighting might be considered the *conveyor* of the image, the way voice intonation conveys words.

When film was still the stepchild of theater, during the first three decades after the turn of the century, it was very voguish to use the knowledge and expertise learned in the theater. Lon Chaney's films in particular are a good example of this. The range of human emotions—terror, horror, fear, caution, suspicion, shrewdness, comfort, well-being, over-confidence, foolishness, playfulness, childishness, sentimentality, lovingness, disappointment, anger, rage, passion, recklessness, daring, despair, and hopelessness—were regarded as stock-in-trade ingredients to be "cooked up" in every scene, like a ragout.

Lon Chaney, "the man of a thousand faces"—and a thousand

emotions to go with them—required a range of lighting situations to complement and enhance each emotional situation. Out of those early years the film industry was endowed with a valuable legacy from the theater; and the cinematographers carried their raft of secrets with them like sought-after gourmet chefs. The skills, the touches, the flourishes of lighting became an obscure art, the know-how of which was handed down from father to son, in the manner of the medieval trade guilds. Even the names of various lights took on the aura of rare spices or magical incantations: "baby" (spotlight), "baby tenors," "baby juniors," "baby seniors," "baby-baby's," "scoops" (lights that can be hung from suspended bar-grids or horizontal poles across a studio overhead), "big eyes" (solar spotlights used out of doors), "softlights" (used to break down harsh shadows), "molepars" (made by Mole-Richardson, Co. especially to intensify light needed for high-speed photography), "nooklites" (especially designed to fit in small, narrow crevices where lights are difficult to conceal, or where a space is limited), "broads" (designed to light large areas intensely and evenly). Along with the types of lights is a panoply of hardware including brackets, clamps, stands, hangers, cups, stirrups, plates, sleds, grips, spuds, and adaptors. To change the quality of the light emitted from the source there are devices to cover a light such as cloth "cookies," "cutters," "flags," and "scrims." On top of that, there are more accessories to attach to the fronts of lights like "barn doors" (to keep the light from spilling over into unwanted areas), "scrims," and "diffuser disks" (to soften the light), "conversion filters" (to alter and correct light color temperature and color balance). There are "single silks," "dots and targets," "color/diffuser frames," "baskets," "snoots," "boxes, holders, and covers," "high stacks," "lens guards," "matts," "hot and cold lenses," "lens guards," "irises," "shutters," and last but by no means least, "gaffer tape" (an extremely strong tape used to attach lights to walls, posts, and so forth).

I strongly advise the beginning filmmaker *not* to memorize the above list, unless for the purpose of amazing and baffling your friends. I *do* emphatically suggest that you obtain a complete up-to-date catalogue of lights for sale by one of the light companies such as Mole-Richardson, Colortran, or Lowell. Gradually build up a reference library of catalogues and other materials to furnish these terms and related information as you have need to use it.

While it is true that in generating mood and emotion you will want to know the tools of the trade, it should be emphasized that an overdependency on equipment is often a substitute for inventiveness. By the same token, lighting *hardware* can be classed as a convenience and a luxury—nonessential to creating mood in many cases. As the film *industry* grew in wealth and magnitude, so did its "needs," as well as the people to help fill those needs. Small specialized industries have grown up over the years to support the ever-increasing needs of a film and television empire that seems to be enlarging daily. With such phenomenal growth, it is not difficult to see how these supporting industries, together with their skilled workers, are, in a sense, self-perpetuating. Along with the need to insure their continued existence, these peripheral service groups have perpetuated what I indelicately call "myths." These myths involve renting the filmmaker a whole toolbox full of tools when all he may need is a screwdriver. Whole lighting trucks are rented filled with lighting equipment. Sound trucks are rented filled with sound equipment, and so on. When film budgets soar into the millions of dollars, why not go first class?

Facetiousness aside, let me say simply that an amazing amount can be done in a creative and practical way with a few well-placed lights and some planning. Instead of getting armed with every device to generate, modify, and modulate light known to man—first find out what you really need.

To those who truly seek a basic understanding of the principles of lighting, I recommend they try an almost foolishly simple exercise. Take one strong light and move it up, down, and around a single subject—a person—closely enough that the directionality of shadows shows clear changes as the direction of the light source changes. This is the most rudimentary of lighting experiments, and doubtlessly not the last you may try. If you bear in mind that the basic mood is established by the strongest source of light, your main job is to remember the moods created by a handful of lighting positions. The other lights—the catch lights, hair lights, background lights, and fill lights—are mainly supplementary to the key light. It is the position of the key light that is the "key" for the mood. Not only should it be a mood-setter, but it should flow from a direction that is probable and realistic, such as from a lamp or window, understood to be the "realistic source" of illumination by the viewer.

Generally, if a key light comes from below a subject's face it creates a sinister, eerie feeling; if to the side, it can generate artful and sensitive shadows known as modeling: These are poetic and gentle, suitable for love scenes. And if the light emanates from above the face, it serves to minimize shadows altogether, although not entirely eliminating them: good for a sober, factual mood, and most frequently used in training films, documentaries, television talk shows, and so forth. A key light on a level with the face, and aimed into it, will generate flatness and starkness. The details are washed out, two-dimensional. This is one reason why a light mounted on a camera, although convenient, is to be avoided.

So far, I have mentioned positioning of lights as relating to moods. Now I shall say something about how the *quantity* of light can be important in that regard. Light quantity has to do with the amount of light falling on the subject. A light meter, whether separate from or built into the camera, is used to measure the light illuminating the subject. It measures the light in *footcandles*. The more footcandles of light that bounce off the subject, the more brightly lit we can say the subject is. But photographers don't refer to footcandles of illumination because it is easier to translate their meaning into f/stops. In most cases he tries to arrange the number and positioning of the lights to register around f/11 on the meter. Another way a photographer-cinematographer may refer to the amount of light he has on a set is in terms of "watts of light." The term watts is used most effectively when the lighting set-up is stabilized. If he says he has "3,000 watts of light," it means something as long as the distance from lights to subject does not change.

The relative "brightness" of a scene has to do with the difference in intensity between the key light and the fill light. If the difference is small, or none exists, and there is a fairly even illumination of the scene, then it is considered high key lighting—reinforcing to factual or comic moods. However, when light and shadow are in sharp contrast, resulting in pools of light and dark areas, it is called low key lighting—a good setting for mystery, high drama, or fear.

Finally, the *quality* of light, whether "soft" or "hard," has a good deal to do with mood. Light is softened by some method of diffusion, such as passing through a fine mesh called a scrim and made of screening material—a cheese cloth or piece of nylon fabric. Frosted glass will act as a diffuser. Whatever the material, it has the effect of softening the lines created by shadows. It creates a somewhat velvety mood. It is often used for love scenes and sequences involving babies—and to soften the wrinkles in an older person's face. Light from the sun is usually softened with scrims as a matter of standard practice.

"Hard light," on the other hand, has been used to emphasize realism, or to portray life in a harsh, unglamorous way. It is produced by using undiffused sunlight, or by using studio lights placed quite close to the subject.

Whatever the choice of lighting mood, it is important to preserve it from shot to shot in the same scene. This is called maintaining "lighting continuity." When an editor juxtaposes shots from the same scene, the quality of lighting (intensity, directionality, and diffusion) must match. An error in lighting continuity can easily be made when close-ups of reactions and other details are shot out of sequence or from varying angles to the master shot. As the position of the actors or camera angle changes (inadvertently or purposely), so does the lighting change.

FILMING AND EDITING
FOR CONTINUITY AND EMPHASIS

Although continuity is the name of the game, generally, in every phase of filmmaking, there are specific areas in putting together the total mosaic of the film that require extra attention.

First on the list of continuity devices is camera angle. When the director looks over a script he develops a feeling for the angles he wants in order to emphasize feeling or to change the visual pace. The standard angles are the long shot (sometimes referred to as the "master" shot), the medium shot, and the close-up. If there is enough time and money, the director will canvass a scene with all three shots, just to "cover" in the event that while polishing the film's intention in the editing, flexibility can be given to character emphasis and to dramatic moments which may need building up or toning down.

A master shot, also sometimes called an establishing shot, is a camera angle wide enough to obtain all of the essential ingredients of a scene   the characters, props, and features of the locale. Once the viewer is given this visual data, the film can begin to build upon details generated by medium shots and close-ups. However, any significant change in the scene, or introduction of a new character, may necessitate returning to the master (in the editing) for the benefit of the viewer's orientation. Long shots are also used for aesthetic reasons (see Part One, "Seeing within the Rectangle").

A long shot is used most frequently in a film set in the out-of-doors. Here, it is natural to have an expansive, broad view. This is in sharp contrast to the intimacy the viewer anticipates in a closed-room set, where new characters enter through a door, and where a medium shot may suffice to broaden the angle of view.

The medium shot, where the subjects are shown from "head to toe," is what I call a factual shot. It is best used to sustain the prevailing feeling and relationships—unlike the close-up, which pin-points emotional changes as they occur. The medium shot is objectively descriptive.

The close-up has come into wider use in the last few decades with the advent of a smaller frame size for viewing—notably with Super 8, and with the smallness of television screens. The smaller the image size, in a sense, the more appropriate the close-up, in that it has the effect of reaching out and bringing the viewer in. But the close-up has a host of uses, giving the filmmaker greater versatility of expression. The large subject size it offers creates immediacy of feeling, and it also captures the viewer's attention to "grandstand" or point up a poignant moment. It is a punctuating device. And, of course, close-ups call the viewer's attention to details.

Another standard item the director knows he may need, and therefore should always provide for, is the *cut-away*. The cut-away is known in filmmaking as an "escape hatch"—or more academically, as a transitional device. The cut-away helps the editor out of situations where he knows the viewer will require a shot to ease what might otherwise be an abrupt transition. It is especially useful whenever the camera is recording a continuous action which is interrupted, either for the purpose of shortening the "time" involved, or in order to lengthen time. Shortening or compressing the time of an activity is usually done to eliminate unnecessary details. For example, a business executive gets into his car and drives to work. Certain key steps in the action are important to creating the "sense" of his driving to work—such as a single medium long shot of his getting in the car, starting it, and pulling out of the garage. The following shot could picture him driving on a freeway, but briefly. The next time we see him he is coming through the door of his office and saying hello to the receptionist. When the two shots are cut back to back, the time between his leaving for work and suddenly coming into his office would seem absurdly short to the viewer. So, to make the action plausible, a transitional cut-away is in order. The most logical cut-away is to a different line of "parallel action" in progress. The cut-away could be to the man's wife as she dresses the children for school. It could be any shot understood by the viewer to be relevant in some way to the general line of the action. It could even be a shot of something in the office, such as a person waiting for an appointment to see the soon-to-arrive executive.

A lengthened, or expanded, version of a sequence is usually done to generate suspense or a feeling of expectancy. In other words, the total action—from the time the executive leaves the house till he enters his office—could be drawn out. Here, once again cut-aways assist in overcoming the time differential, but in this case, without the cut-away it would seem absurdly long.

Let us assume that the reason for drawing out the action is that the executive's mistress has unexpectedly come to his office. She is the visitor who waits. Now, the cut-away to the wife dressing the children takes on an unusual poignancy. We might even put in cuts of the office staff peering around corners to get a glimpse of the nefarious visitor. These cuts are intermingled perhaps with interior car shots of the carefree executive as he drives to work, tapping his fingers to bouncy music coming from the car radio. The expression on his face is totally unsuspecting of the surprise waiting for him at the office. In this way, extending the action with cut-aways and different angles of the main action can contribute to a heightening of suspense.

The term cut-away refers to cutting away from the main line of action to a related subject or action. In a sense, cutting away can refer to intercutting another line of action in progress, simultaneous to the main action. In editing this is called *parallel cutting*. It involves two actions going on at the same time, which at some point intersect or come together as a culmination of a suspenseful buildup.

To make this apply to the executive, we would develop the line of action involving his wife a bit more. For example, we could have her dressing the children, and suddenly discovering that her husband has possession of a dry cleaning ticket she had planned to use during her daily errands. She decides (indicated perhaps through "interior monologue") to make some sandwiches and surprise her husband for an impromptu picnic in the park, and to pick up the dry cleaning check at the same time. Now we see her bustling around in the kitchen, humming to herself, unsuspecting of the unpleasant surprise that awaits her. In the meantime (as we learn through intercutting) the husband has arrived at work, met his visitor, and ushered her into his office. In the ensuing discussion with his girlfriend it is decided to have her return to the office later—so that they can have lunch together. At lunch time his wife arrives at the office just as he is coming out the door with his girlfriend—his hand on her waist. He introduces the woman to his wife as a business associate—and gives his wife the dry cleaning check. Annoyed and hurt, she goes away to do her errands. This, then, is the intercutting of two parallel actions with the intersecting "payoff," or result. Continuity is increased through the complexity of the two interwoven actions.

But continuity is also buttressed through "cues" that the filmmaker thoughtfully includes. These are other devices, such as the use of the *reaction shot* and *subjective camera*. The wife knows that the mistress is not a business executive because we are allowed to see *what she sees* as her husband and the girlfriend make their exit into the hallway from the office suite. We get a close-up of his hand on the girl's waist. And quickly, we get a reaction shot of the disturbed wife's face—a reaction shot of the husband—and one of the mistress's face. The shaken husband quickly tries to explain. The wife senses something wrong. The mistress is sullen and condescending to the wife. We can see how the skillful intercutting of subjective and reaction shots are timed in a way that builds to a crescendo of feeling. Although timing in the editing is important, the director must be on his toes to anticipate the montage of shots that is possible for later editing. If he is aware of what may be needed in the editing, he will make certain that there are enough shots of different kinds with which the editor can work. If necessary, the director will run the actors through the action again and again until he gets all the camera angles he needs.

Timing has a lot to do with continuity, in that good timing provides for a smooth flow in what could otherwise result in a cumbersome rendering of a complex scene. It is up to the director to provide the editor with enough camera angles; and if he exceeds the needed length of a shot there is no harm done.

The editor, on the other hand, must be sensitive to the length of the shot he includes, because too much could deflate the tension, and too little could be insufficient to register with the viewer. (A general discussion of where to cut a shot is found in Part One, "Shooting Your Film.") In brief, shots depicting action are best *cut on the action,* meaning that the editor cuts as the action progresses and before it ends. Shots depicting nonmovement (static shots) are cut immediately after the feeling and information of the shot has been transmitted to the viewer.

A continuous action must be filmed in such a way that in the editing it *appears* continuous. When filming a segment of action as a master shot there is little worry about continuity of movement if only the master shot is used. But this is not generally the case. A person opening a door and entering a room provides us with a classic example. It is not practically possible to get a master shot of the entire sequence. The only way to get one would be to film both sides of the door at the same time, so that as the person turned the knob and entered we could see him on both sides of the wall. This, of course, is only permissible in surrealistic films—where the camera might be stationed at the top of a "break-away" wall, filming downward. In a simple realistic narrative, however, the director must first show the person with his hand on the doorknob opening the door in one shot, and then show the person entering the room in another shot. In filming the second shot the director has the actor "run through" the action a second time, so that he will have a slight overlap from the first shot—vis-à-vis the position of the door and the actor. When the editor gets the film, he is able, through this overlapping of the action, to match the movements of the door and the actor in such a way that a fluidity of movement is preserved. If the action isn't matched acceptably, the result is a *jump cut,* where the position of the hands and body appear to jump.

Filming overlapping movements and matching them in the editing is as standard to filmmaking as flour is to baking. In contemporary filmmaking, however, where, increasingly, suggestion and impression substitute for a literal representation of the action, both directors and editors are less hamstrung by the need to match the action than in former times. But there are occasions when suggestion and impression will not suffice. Where the viewer must be appraised of the precise visual details necessary to the plot—as in a James Bond type of film—differing camera angles must be planned and edited with the care given to a fine mosaic.

Another device comparable to matching the action is observing the *eye line,* or, to put it another way, observing the need to keep the characters in the same relative position in the frame when changing the position of the camera. If two people are talking, and person "A" is in frame left and person "B" is in frame right, then "A" must always appear to the left and "B" must always appear to the right no matter what position the camera assumes. (See insert.) The exception to this is: if the camera simultaneously films as it moves *around* "A" and "B" so that the viewer has been adjusted to "B" switching to frame left and "A" to frame right. If "A" and "B" have not been filmed with this consideration in mind, then they will jump back and forth from one side of the frame to the other. This breach of continuity not only leaves the viewer confused, it leaves him with a bad case of "mental" tennis neck. (For more on continuity see "Editing Styles," Part Two.)

SOME THINGS YOU SHOULD KNOW
ABOUT STORY FILM SOUND

It is not the intention of this book to provide a technical guide to professional sound recording, editing, and mixing. There are already some excellent books on this subject (see "Suggested Reading," Appendix B). But in the context of the story film, there are some rudimentary things the beginning filmmaker may find useful to know and to consider.

For the most part the story film has come to be associated in our minds with lip-sync dialogue. It is true that many films, especially those made in the last forty years, would not have been able to sustain the kind of psychological intricacy found in, say, detective films without lip-sync sound. Neither would we have had a plethora of narrative "musicals," nor certain kinds of films that are very "talky," like those of Jean Luc Godard. Yet there are a host of films that I suspect would not lose much if subtitles were used instead of spoken words—like those of Ingmar Bergman and Michelangelo Antonioni—where their work is quite adequately sustained visually.

The question is, why bring up such a point if indeed all professionally done films today rely substantially on lip-sync—and if it has become an indispensable convention? The answer is, there are a lot of films made today, by nonprofessionals, by students, or others working independently; and these filmmakers, for one reason or another, are simply not able to meet the demands of equipment, time, and money placed on them by sound synchronization. In fact, there are many story filmmakers who, by using methods other than lip-sync, might actually improve the quality of the story, especially where the films are less than a half hour in length.

What, then, are some of the alternatives to lip-sync sound? First, it is possible to have spoken dialogue in a film, but to have it used adjacent to the image as a sort of interior monologue. These "thought ramblings" can be extremely effective in conveying plot progression and setting mood. Once the filmmaker has established this as his method of operation, the viewer will accept it, and will not miss lip-sync sound.

Un-synched sound is known as "wild sound" or a "wild track." Other types of wild tracks use music or random sound effects. A typical kind of random sound effects track might be the sound of a radio as someone moves about in a room, together with sounds of children playing, and cars going by, and planes overhead. In all these instances the viewer cannot see the source of the sound, and therefore he does not expect to see sound synchronized to specific visual events.

When sound is used in an indirect way like this it tends to take on a *generalized* quality, guiding the viewer into wider areas of the imagination than even lip-sync will permit. The use of wild sound is more than a stop-gap measure, more than a second best solution. If approached constructively, wild sound can serve the maker of short story films especially, often in a more appropriate way than lip-sync sound.

It may be useful at this point to review some hints on recording. (More on sound is offered in Part One, "Introduction to Sound," and in Part Two, "Documentary Sound.") In recording sound, whether live or by jacking in to another tape machine or record player, it is best to use a reel-to-reel $\frac{1}{4}$ inch tape machine. This way a high quality recording can be obtained, and the tape can be easily edited. Later, after the tape is edited, it can be transferred to a cassette cartridge, if desired.

Regarding microphones, the filmmaker should know the two basic types and their uses. For recording speech and eliminating unwanted peripheral noises, it is best to use a unidirectional mike held six to eight inches from the mouth. This type of mike has a "reception pattern" directly in front of it and excludes (or receives poorly) all other sounds to the sides of the mike and to the rear. In some unidirectional mikes this is called a "cardioid"—or heart-shaped—pattern of reception.

The other type of mike, called omnidirectional, might be used to capture a variety of sounds at one time. It is ideal for recording street noises, and such things as clinking dishes or the chatter of patrons in a restaurant. As suggested by its name, the omnidirectional mike has nearly equal reception from all sides.

Once the sound is on tape, the filmmaker has the choice of at least three ways to "play" it with his images. The first method—used professionally—involves synching the sound with the image. Once it has been synched (through methods too complicated to describe here), it is usually applied to the film in the form of an optical sound track. The second method is to record the sound on a tape machine, edit it, and then, either apply it to the film in the form of a magnetic track or as an optical track—after "rough synching" the sound with the image on a synchronizer. The third method is to record "wild sound," edit it, and play it separately on a tape machine simultaneously as the film is being projected. The latter method has been used extremely effectively by beginning students. Often, the film's start and finish have been accurately synched with the sound tape to within a five-second discrepancy. Even moments within a film where an image was to fall with a given sound were remarkably close, practically on cue. Admittedly, playing sound separately with the film is not ideal. However, if one is working in Super 8, it is encouraging to know that a certain amount of success can be achieved with such a loose method. This is especially true inasmuch as sound synchronization in this gauge film is not within the reach of most people at this time.

My own films do not use lip-synched sound. I use wild sound, and it is somewhat "aligned" later by having the taped, edited sound transferred to magnetic sprocketed tape and matched end-for-end in a synchronizer. I then have the sprocketed, synchronized sound tape made into an optical negative track, which is used with the negative "picture" to make a "composite print." A composite print is where the sound and picture are brought together on one piece of film, with the sound image running down the side of the print. My own way of working is discussed in more detail in Part Four.

part IV

THE EXPRESSIONISTIC FILM

chapter 12

Making an Image:
Making a language

WHAT IS MEANT BY EXPRESSIONISTIC?

Expressionism is a term first linked to various artists in the 1920s, most notably in painting and in the graphic arts. Their objective was to distort reality, or representations of nature, in order to convey personally expressive statements. Along with the expressionistic painters came the first expressionistic filmmakers, mostly working in Germany. These included Slavko Vorkopich and Robert Florey, and the most remembered film of the early part of this movement is probably *The Cabinet of Dr. Caligari.*

But many of the films now classified by historian-critics as expressionistic appear, for the most part, to be academically designated. The true spirit of expressionism is seen in many, many films, especially those made by little-known independents working in 16mm during the first two decades after World War II. They are the so-called "Underground Filmmakers," some of whom are still quietly making films and distributing them nationally. Filmmakers like Stan Brakhage, Kenneth Anger, and Jack Smith owed nothing to the establishment. They could afford to make and live with their little films as they made them (for better or worse), and to invest them with personal statements close to their individual sensibilities. Having known many of these filmmakers, I can safely say that they made their films when they felt like it and that they didn't care much about what the "public" thought. The money for making their films came from a variety of sources—from indulgent wives, foundation grants, patrons—in some cases just from "scrounging." They did whatever most artists do to get money to live and work. They made their films because *they wanted to,* and they made them *the way* they wanted.

However, expressionistic can mean more than just having it your own way. And it does mean more than a kind of undisciplined visual caterwauling in film (although I have nothing in particular against that either). Freedom of expression is certainly a part of it, and it involves experimentation, the willingness to try something new, to change things to suit yourself. But it encompasses self-awareness as well, and the awareness of what is being committed to film. It involves an understanding of the form, the medium of film, so that when a personal statement is made or discovered it can be strengthened and reinforced through learning about what you have done. It is having the persistence to stick with this departure from "nature" until it takes on the firmness of a new reality.

The filmmaker today who undertakes to make expressionistic films will probably be working in Super 8. Or he may even be working with video instead of film. Sixteen millimeter film is no longer cheap to buy and have processed—what with inflation, and declining natural resources (from which film is made). The intimacy of Super 8 is ideal for the expressionistic filmmaker of today. It will not hamstring him with burdensome financial considerations. The size and weight of the camera and the ease with which the film can be projected point to a new generation of Super 8 film poets and artists.

It is with this in mind that I offer the ideas in the last part of this book.

MAKING AN IMAGE: MAKING A LANGUAGE
(Shaping and Communicating a New Language)

We see everything in terms of images, or units of sense: we either perceive the order in things, or we give them an order. An image could be described as an orderly perception. Its arrangement gives a definition that allows us to remember it. It is simply that we can see the order in some things more readily than in others.

For example, some birdcalls are broadcast at a cyclic frequency beyond our ability to hear their sounds; also, many birds' sounds that we *are* able to hear are so rapidly executed and complex we cannot get the complete melodic system as it is broadcast. What we do receive is a generalization of the melodic system, and we register the feeling of its gesture. In other words, we have an "idea" of what it sounds like. To us, however, that *is* the birdcall, even if it is not the call as it is sung. The version of the birdcall we get is one we can perhaps remember, or even reproduce: This version is the image.

It is the same with visual images. They are sent from the subject, as well as produced by the camera; and our eyes receive these "broadcasts." Since every visual perception is more or less inaccurate as a total apprehension of the subject anyway, we see only a *representation* of what actually is. We can remember a few faces in a crowd, but we can't see, much less remember, every face. What faces we do manage to see become, for us, the image of the crowd.

When we film a subject, we are making an image—in that the image we see is held and preserved on film. The choice to film a subject from a given view results in an image of it that we have selected.

If we can preserve images as we see them, we can also project these images, which in turn become statements—no longer emanating from the original subject, but from ourselves. It is like broadcasting a memory world of what things were at a given moment in time. But more important—what is projected as a statement, also becomes an image vocabulary for the filmmaker. It is a way of speaking to others.

To understand this principle fully is to have freed yourself from the need to imitate everyday reality. What is "literal" is the most safe, unchallenging view of the world in terms of personal expression. As the director of *The Godfather* and *The Conversation*, Francis Ford Coppola, succinctly put it: "I don't think any film I have made even comes close to what I have in my heart."

One way to avoid the literal approach is not to become a slave to your subject matter. In other words, if you are filming a beautiful baby or your favorite pet, rendering the subject as it is usually seen is quite different from using that moment, that baby or that pet as an *occasion* to make filmed images—as opposed to making an image for the occasion.

So often when we get the camera in our hands we feel a sense of power—which is normal. But most of the time the power is more imagined than real—like carrying an unloaded gun, or an unloaded camera, or an unloaded mind—because when we aim the camera at something, we feel we are making an image when really we are "registering" an image, generating facsimiles. Only an *interpretive* image is new.

It is not interpretive to film children as sweet and innocent, as toddling and charmingly awkward; skid row bums as pitiful and deserving of sympathy, or else lazy and good-for-nothing; and sunsets as being nostalgic and lovely. But children can be elegantly sinister, as in Goya's painting *Infante*, or hedonistic as in Hieronymus Bosch's *The Garden of Earthly Delights*; and bums can be marvelously articulate, while some are undoubtedly happy with their own down-and-out social structure. Sunsets can be cold and blue instead of warm and cozy orange.

If the subject is seen by you, and recorded as a different and unique image, it is like placing your stamp on it, an insignia that is like a fingerprint or voiceprint. The filmed image becomes like a "sightprint."

The point is that a filmed image can be more than a copy of reality—it can be a reality itself. Once it is realized that your filmed record does not necessarily have to relate to what is commonly understood as reality, then you can proceed to make images *into a reality,* and hence make a language. You will, in effect, be doing what painters, sculptors, dancers, and writers do all the time. However, film is such a compellingly documentary medium that, unlike paints, clay, and words, which are "suggestive" mediums, even serious filmmakers are often sidetracked from exploring its highly suggestive possibilities.

THE PERSONAL APPROACH

Generally, most creative artists take it for granted that their materials must be shaped by their hands and imaginations. But the creative filmmaker is faced with the special problem of lending his interpretation to materials—the subjects he films—which are *already* formed. In a manner of speaking, they are intractable, in a creative sense, because they persuade us to view them as they *are*, realistically, to accept their established, time-honored meanings. Unlike the filmmaker, when the painter uses a subject, he is expected to choose his method of rendering, whether it be representational (faithful in a realistic sense) or abstract. Film is not generally thought of as a personal means of expression, like painting. Probably for this reason, those who have wanted to work with a more literal representation of reality have gravitated to the mediums of still photography and motion pictures rather than painting or sculpture; and this is still true today. To be sure, much that is beautifully inventive can come from this way of working. However, as more and more people are making films, and as the medium of filmmaking is maturing and developing, people are trying to find more ways to expand its ability to say more and mean more. Inevitably, the solution to pushing back the frontiers of expression in filmmaking lies in working with unconventional approaches to the medium by seeking means of expression, as well as subjects, which have not in the past been deemed appropriate to film. The conventional, expressive usage is the lingua franca that is used in most filmmaking: in story films, documentaries, educational and training films, and so forth. Filmmaking conventions are like those in writing—news articles and popular novels—the rules of which are taught in schools, and are to be found in dictionaries and books on American English usage.

Similarly, there are schools which teach the conventions of filmmaking, and there are books which perform the same function. This book shares the same goals, but with an important exception. It stresses ways to bypass conventional filmmaking rules in order to facilitate the personally expressive statement.

But first, here are some examples of conventional filmmaking, some reasons why they are conventional, and some reflections upon what this kind of approach accomplishes.

The detective, gangster film is certainly a well established form. If the subject of such a film is playing a Bogart-type tough guy, the role insists on a strict interpretation of the character's total image. Everything the actor does must be consistent with its familiar key feature (tough guy); an image like this is difficult to change and resistant to shaping into a fresh, new statement. The narrative form, with its conventional roles and rules, opposes radically different interpretations. It is chiefly a fulfillment-of-expectation experience, and does not derive its main strength from the improbable and the new, as does the more personal, experimental approach.

The personal filmmaker rearranges reality, "creates new worlds." To accomplish this, he transforms his images so that they are pliable materials, like paints and clay. Once transformed, the subjects and images in an altered and reordered state give feedback to the filmmaker, further suggesting ways to emphasize and strengthen his personal conception.

The conventional filmmaker, on the other hand, is concerned with the expression of emotions in film as if they were apples and pears, or cherry and chocolate syrup at the soda fountain. In a real sense they are—to the movie studios and TV networks. These emotions can be clearly defined and accurately, mechanistically evoked in the viewer. The experiences we have while watching a commercial or a story film product are Pavlovian responses triggered by a predictable arrangement of images. What we feel about the characters or the outcome of the story has little if anything to do with us as individuals; but it definitely has to do with us collectively. Such "an experience of emotions" might have its place: We do enjoy a stroll in the woods or a tasty meal. We don't expect to be surprised by these experiences, because in this case we are looking for fulfillment. We don't look for them to be of a different quality; but we have come, rightly or wrongly, to expect them to be better than ever and more intense.

Playing upon conventional emotions, the filmmaker constructs his film to conform to a plan, a script (and in many cases a formula), that outlines the roles of the characters and the plot-rules under which they operate. The script is minutely scrutinized for material that can be shaped in the editing room which will make the audience joyful and sad in the proper places, once the film is finished.

It follows that if the aim is to elicit the same emotion from the greatest number of people, then the experience which produces the emotion must be familiar, based in reality. Francis Ford Coppola, who typifies this way of working, once said, remarking on *The Godfather*'s success, "Imagine having millions and millions of people all over the world sit in a room and totally surrender their brains to you for two hours."

These experiences as images on the screen could be called "hard-core reality," even ordinary reality. Many conventional films, such as Biblical Epics, purport to deal with experiences of a more "majestic reality"; but even these cannot escape the quality of ordinary reality. How often have we heard one of the Twelve Apostles speak with a Brooklyn accent?

The conventional film has got to be recognizable and familiar. In the film *They Shoot Horses, Don't They?*, the setting is an old-fashioned ballroom in an amusement park atmosphere. The characters involved are hucksters and down-and-outers. The point of the story is "the futility of existence," from the standpoint of the slave as well as the master. The intention of the film is to create a sense of extreme, unmitigated futility redeemed (in the film) only by death, a mercy killing. Futility is a familiar emotion. What brings it on is constant frustration. A bunch of "losers" trying to win a dance marathon turns out to be a great vehicle for this simple, powerful emotion. But the film, in spite of its use of a formula, is successful for what it attempts (unlike the pawns in its plot). Another film dealing with the same theme, but even better done, is *Treasure of the Sierra Madre*. And a more recent example of "dramatized futility" is the excellent made-for-TV movie, *Duel*, about a driver of a car who is ruthlessly pursued by a driver of a heavy-rig truck, where this particular emotion is spiced with fear.

In any of these films, the actions and events which turn on our emotional systems are true-to-life experiences. There is never a question about how the viewer is expected to feel; it is all predetermined.

An example of an European director who depicts ordinary reality in a very extraordinary way is Federico Fellini whose films are truly "dream cinema." It is as if he and the whole human consciousness were asleep, playing out a concoction of nightmarish and ribald fantasies; this quality is found especially in his *8½* and *Satyricon*. Considering that his films are intended for a wide audience, his images (especially in these films) are very personal. Note that by comparison to another, purer genre of cine-poetic filmmakers, exemplified by Cocteau and Buñuel, Fellini's personal inflections don't seem so extreme. But more than this, he reaches into a kind of socio-archetypal consciousness for his images: They are rather like ancient Greek masks, epitomizing the entire spectrum of emotions at a glance. His haunting faces are of this world, yet they belong to other worlds, too.

Fellini's work is a big step in the direction *away* from the deft manipulation of ordinary reality that characterizes the film work of a good craftsman like Francis Ford Coppola.

His films represent a step toward the creation of a personal, visual language. Fellini's films are hybridizations. His method of working is removed, in that he transforms his characters through costume, make-up, and, often, through unusual settings. But what does he transform his characters into? He alters the familiarity of his characters in appearance (and location) so that he can make a *freer* statement about people, and thus about himself. This freer statement has a particular quality: It is the way *he* sees his fellow man (hence himself), rather than playing out how his fellow man sees his fellow man. In searching for motivation, he works from the inside out, instead of (as the conventional filmmaker does) from the outside in.

From his previous experience as a cartoonist, Fellini is probably aware of the principle: "Exaggerate a thing enough and it will become something else." In other words, the thing will change: A metamorphosis, or transformation, will take place. But in spite of the weirdness in his films, Fellini still has his characters relate to each other in conventional ways; the transformation is not a complete one. We learn that this is an intentional tack, and that he is very much aware of the need for the story film to have at least a modicum of conventionality. In his films the ordinary reality occurs mainly on a psychological level, especially in types of conflict. This is what allows fairly general audiences to relate to his films; thus he gets his "vision" to a large number of people.

That conventional emotions are turned on by the filmmaker's manipulation of ordinary reality is easy to see; but what happens when ordinary reality is treated in an extraordinary way? Fellini's films result in a kind of personal expression; they are "tinged with personal expression." But because what is seen in his films is not so improbable as to cause us to have seen the world in a *vastly* different way, it is clearly a matter of degree. His method of working is a true personal expression but doesn't go all the way. (I have previously mentioned that the story film requires a regimented treatment; I trust that these remarks about Fellini's films or about any other films will not be taken as value judgments.)

To create a truly personal film, conventional subjects—those subjects which inhabit ordinary reality—have to be treated with irreverence. In my own experience I see the personal film as demanding the most intense, honest communication with myself possible. I become totally reliant on and trusting of my own impulses. In this type of film, my main interest is *not* in reaching large audiences. (Later in this part I discuss in detail how I approach filmmaking.)

Making a personal film means more than being involved, because it is very possible to be involved in making a conventional film. It means being engaged in freeing the subject from its anticipated meanings. Becoming free of conventionality in filmmaking requires trying to see personally, exercising a need. It is in the PROCESS of seeing personally that this need is worked out by trying to see things *differently*.

The desire to make a film that says something different to viewers is a shared motivation among the fine arts painter, sculptor, writer, musician, and dancer. It starts with the desire to try something new. The motivation may arise out of boredom, out of a restless desire to shape things to suit yourself, or from a need to delight yourself—to play games with yourself, amuse yourself. The need for amusement alone is enough to stimulate a person to move in the direction of personal expression.

Process connotes an activity of some sort, an engagement with something around you—as the sociologists say, an "interaction." The need for personal expression exists as a form of *energy*, rather than as it is popularly conceived, as a "vision" or "statement." The latter is a mistakenly romanticized version of what drives the artist, and others, to express themselves personally.

If I were asked to define personal expression I would say, from my experience, that *it is the shaping of this energy (need)*. It is a human (and animal) instinct. The energy manifests itself when there is a need for self-reliance; it is close to areas of awareness and self-preservation. It is like a territorial claim, an assertion of identity; but instead of shaping this energy into a violent act of aggression, it is formed into a creation that is aesthetically assertive.

Although personal expression is a game most often played alone, it is not a lonely game. It gives the player a sense of continuity within himself, as well as with elements that make up the outside world. But better than that, I think, is the fact that the filmmaker can regard *everything*, or anything, as his resource material. The field of possibilities is limited only by his imagination.

Several years in the teaching profession have led me to believe that personal expression can be cultivated, given the willingness to participate and learn on the part of the filmmaker. I have also found that it is always beneficial to the "expressor" in some way or other, if not always *creatively* productive. It doesn't result every time in something beautiful or amazing. Producing something of lasting value to yourself and others is like "hitting the jackpot." The gambling analogy is a good one because to film from a personal interpretive vantage does involve a willingness to take a "risk," another way of characterizing the game of personal expression.

Assuming you want to be personally expressive in film, and you have the need, but you don't know what to say—at least you know you want to make a film that is YOURS. You want to record things as you see them, not as they are seen by everyone. It is likely that, if you haven't ever filmed anything as you see it (as opposed to "social seeing"), chances are you haven't any idea of what you want to see (aim your camera at) or of how you want to see it (a method of approaching your subject filmically).

In other words, if you don't know how to begin you have to find out through experimentation. The best way, I've found, is to try a lot of different things which will convert what is experienced as ordinary reality into a transformed state. The key word is *experiencing* what it is like to see things differently.

METHODS OF TRANSFORMATION

Who hasn't played with a pair of corrective glasses belonging to a friend and seen familiar shapes distorted or bent out of shape. Or who has not been amused in a house of mirrors, or watched trees become elastic in a pond's surface reflections? THIS is seeing things differently. This is the beginning process, too, of seeing things personally. Seeing differently is the start of seeing as you want to—and of shaping what you see. This is what I meant earlier when *process* was mentioned as an integral part of seeing personally. Once you have discovered the "asocial" way of seeing you have been catapulted into the world of personal vision. You have, in a sense, been put into a different orbit, one quite apart from the everyday, the ordinary. We have heard about what drugs can do to induce a state of transcendental visual excitation artificially; but unlike drug effects, filming is an *integral*, not an artificial, experience: *It is capable of being recorded.* It is an experience that can be "replayed," as it were—one that can be revealed to others. It is, in a sense, a language.

Let us look at a few primary ways to put your imagination in orbit. These methods are, above all, available to anyone through the simple use of what can be found in the home, on the street, or in the country. The only special thing you need is a camera, and the willingness to explore, to experiment, *to find* your personally expressive energy.

I call these "ways" *methods of transformation*. There is no set order, so let's take them as they come to mind.

REFLECTIONS

Perhaps the most available, frequently encountered type of visual distortion is the reflection. We see them in puddles, pools, and mirrors, in shaped chromium surfaces like electric irons and car bumpers; we see them in fenders of cars and their shiny painted shapes; we see them in plate glass windows—in any surfaces which are glossy and reflective. But when we see this phenomenon we pay little attention to it ordinarily. We see it and let it go at that. Many people tend to be condescending of that which is unusual; while some are respectful, others may want to turn away with a certain feeling of uneasiness, prompted by fears of the unknown, of something not fully understood; and still others may think of the unusual as comical. However we experience these reflections it amounts to something we can appreciate ourselves, alone. But what if you could film these experiences and share them with others? Filming in a certain way, at a certain time, may quite possibly be a one-of-a-kind experience, a unique image. Through the camera you would be able to show others what you had found. But more than that, you can use this very reflection as a language-like component (to be covered more completely in a later section). You can construct meaning with it, beyond its value as a curiosity.

The rule is: *If you can see it you can film it.* The reason many people don't notice reflections is probably because they are looking at the object itself and rejecting the reflection on its surface. There seems to be something in our psychological make-up that resists the obliterating effect of reflections in objects; very probably this is a primitive reaction. Forms themselves are visually modified by their reflections. The French would call it *trompe-l'œil*, tricking the eye.

Let's look at it this way. Objects—all objects—can be used to make visual images on film. The images which are created and which are afforded by the objects can resemble them exactly, or the image created can be virtually unidentifiable as the initial object. If this sounds like double talk, simply envision a full-length *representational* photograph of a person you know. The photo represents the person, or "stands for" the person. Now imagine a close-up photograph of the person's hair, which may resemble a forest of curved sticks growing on the moon. The close-up shot of the hair is not intended to represent the person, even though the person was the source, or the subject, from which the image of the hair was extracted. On the other hand, the representational photograph is intended to preserve what we think of as the "identity" of the person in the picture. It indeed "looks like" him. We even have a convention of saying that such and such a photo is a good "likeness," or not such a good likeness. On the other hand, the image of the person's hair could be anybody's hair—if indeed you can determine that the image you are looking at *is* hair. Whatever the image derived from the hair tells us, it does not tell us the identity of the person. It may, however, tell us other things. If it is a motion picture film of the hair, what it means will have a great deal to do with how it is used—what it will be placed next to. (This is covered at length in a later section, "The Film as Subject.")

The point here is that the subject (the person) has served as an occasion for images with different purposes. One purpose could be to convey a sense of the person's identity; the second extracts "an image" from the person. And this is a crucial point: Subjects can have an infinite number of possibilities for the creation of images. (I say, *can have*, because not all do; and the latter are what I call "intractable subjects.")

The medium of film allows us to change the world we perceive, to use it to proliferate images of endless variety. At the risk of over-extravagantly praising this possibility, the medium of film has allowed us, literally, to enlarge the world visually and thus to expand our consciousness through transformation. We are not only able to speak with new images, we are able to say *new* things, and to have experiences never before experienced.

Reflections offer an extension of the visual possibilities of objects. These visual extensions certainly do little to help the representational identity of the objects—when it is their functional identity we are interested in. What, for instance, could we call the identity of a rubber band? To hold things together? If it is as general as that, our image of the rubber band must change somewhat as it is put to various uses. In short, the character of the rubber band is determined by its function. When it is not in use, the rubber band is a rather lifeless, contemptible object.

Subjects are something like rubber bands until we use them. At least, this is a desirable frame of mind to have if you want to make a language. It is easy to learn to document an ordinary image, but in order to document a new image, you must either discover or create it.

In the case of reflected images, much can be discovered and

created too. One can create reflected images by taking a device—for instance a concave or convex mirror—to a spot where you can position an object in the mirror (thus transforming it) in order to film it.

The close-up technique, previously mentioned, where hair was the subject, can also be both created and discovered. You can, through close exploration of any subject, discover exciting new images. This happens *as* you view through the camera. In filming, you can't possibly know what you are going to register on film before you actually see it through the lens. That is why the image waits to be discovered.

PRISMS

It is a common experience for many people to have fun looking through the bottom of their glasses while drinking; or else they may have mused over the strangely distorted scene projected through a bottle on the table cloth—an image that is not only shaped by the contour of the bottle but colored by its liquid. You can film this. And, to take this idea a step further, you can hold a glass to the lens of the camera and film through it as if it were another component of the lens you are using. You can turn it in front of the lens—which will alter the image—or you can move from one subject to another. The glass or bottle are but a few devices at your disposal. There are also cut-glass ornaments from old chandeliers; and there are glass prisms (used as paper weights), glass table tops, and glass base lamps.

A note of caution: When you are filming reflections in hubcaps or electric irons, or when you are using glass tumblers or a bottle, play at the game of not letting the device you are using be seen. Don't let the viewer know what you have used, not because it is such an important secret, but because you don't want to disillusion the viewer. Your main interest should be in creating the image, in shaping it—and not in revealing or displaying your "means." Think of yourself as a magician. Don't let us see the edges of the drinking glass or the rim of the hubcap. We are interested in the images the hubcap produces, not the hubcap itself.

CLOSE-UPS

The effect of the close-up as an image-producing and transforming vehicle cannot be overrated. It is one of the most magnificent of your tools, and you should use it often and with unabashed delight. The closer the world gets to us (or us to it), the more it changes. An insect seen from a distance is just another bug. But when seeing it close-up through the wonder of macro-photography, the ordinary taken-for-granted bug becomes ominous in grandiose detail: its particulars are fascinating yet horrendous. One has only to turn on the television to see a replay of *The Hellstrom Chronicle* or the "nature series," like *Survival*, to appreciate how a bug's legs can resemble huge brushes covered with bristly hairs or how its antennae may suggest a Martian electronic being. The textures and particulars of the close-up world can be made available to us, in this century— when before, with our unaided vision, we had been prisoners of the generalized, functionalized nature of objects—slaves to the commonplace, to the always, ever-seen world. Although we have been limited to that kind of "visual fugue" since the dawn of man, exciting worlds are now revealed to us—both those under the sea and in outer space.

What you see with a close-up lens (because only you are seeing it) is personal and yours alone; when you record it on film you externalize it, you prepare it for public reception. This is why, as you view the vast, near privacy of your world while at the same time recording it, you no longer have to resort to telling someone of your visual experience. Your visual excursion can now be seen by others very much as you first saw it.

Methods of transformation represent a tinkering with the ordinary visual world. Thus, through reflections, we can have warped and stretched trees; we can distend and compress their linear perspectives by "shooting" into supple sheets of mirrored plastic (and other curved shiny surfaces) much the way Stan Brakhage did in *Prelude: Dog Star Man*. (For more on *Prelude*, read further along in this Part.) In addition, we have bent and multiplied our subjects with prisms; and we have "reached" our eyes into the Lilliputian world of insects through close-up lenses.

Color the Scene

Further, we can transform the subject by changing its color and the color of its setting. By placing a piece of tinted translucent material in front of the lens while filming—any kind of colored glass will do—the color of the material will be imparted to the scene. Many items normally found around the house will suffice, such as drinking glasses, glass bottles, paperweights, or sunglasses. Clear plastics used in children's toys and in appliances, or just a small booklet of "gel samples" will do; the latter are especially handy because the booklet is compact and offers a wide range of color choices. Even colored liquids, like wine or Kool Aid, can be used to film through. Contrast filters used in black and white photography are quite useful too. By coloring the scene through the use of these materials, your filming can generate unusual moods and emphases of feeling.

By changing the color of some familiar, perhaps lifeless, scene, you can give it character. The beach, for example, can actually be a visually dull place (except possibly for the relief offered by people). The student films I have seen of the beach often turn out to be less interesting than those made in the back yard, where at least there are trees, flowers, and other provisions for the eye. People, sand, sky, and water at the beach are dumped on the viewer in such gross quantities—and with such repetitiveness of movement—that as a subject for personal interpretation, there seems little left to discover —that is, provided it is filmed normally, without the use of a transformational technique. The easiest way to alter a beach scene for expressive purposes is to film it through a filter or some other, similar materials like those named in the preceding paragraph. Other situations where the scenery is monotonous—such as the desert, the open sea, even wide expanses of mountains—respond well to a change in what we think of as their usual coloring.

LIGHT TRANSFORMS

Yet another transformational device is the manipulation of light itself. When filmed in the late afternoon, the "wide expanses of sameness" just mentioned are beautifully transformed in a light which paints everything in an exquisite orange with dramatic shadows; and when filmed against the sun, we see silhouettes. Beautiful photography seems to be created most effortlessly in the late afternoon.

The "soft light" which filters into a room through a window tends to paint a velvet mood—quiet, fine like a mist settling over the subject. Here, the subject's face is gently, sensitively modeled in a soulful kind of illumination. Such lighting heightens intensity, and it is the preferred light for subtle transformations in documentary technique where naturalness is the aim.

The color of a light source can be controlled by using colored bulbs, or by putting filter "gels" over the light itself (as they do in a theater). Beginning filmmakers often ask about the difference between the color generated on the film this way as opposed to coloring the subject with filters held to the lens. First of all, colored light creates "pools of color," so that it is possible to have a person in the right hand part of the picture frame illuminated by a red light, and one on the left hand illuminated by a blue light. But if you should use a filter over the lens, the color of the filter will dominate as one color for *all* that is in the frame.

Light should be thought of as a creator of forms without which there would be no shape (and much less color) recorded on the film. Light is to the filmmaker as the chisel is to the sculptor, paint to the painter, or lumber to the builder. It quite literally determines the intensity and delineation of the forms you see. Understanding this, what we think of as an exaggeration occurs when the subject is incompletely lit, or else lit in an exaggerated fashion, such as having the light source coming from below, or else having it wipe out the features of the subject as the result of being too close. One good way to test the properties of lighting is to start with a single source of light and try filming the face of your subject (with a constantly running camera) by moving the light slowly from side to side, up and down, then, close up and far away. With this exercise, you should get an idea of the full range of possible lighting angles; and at the same time, you should discover other ways to transform the subject.

If light can be regarded as a major transformational tool, then movement and time are equal in importance and usefulness to the personally expressive filmmaker.

MOVEMENT

Although much has already been said on movement, some added comments on this important subject seem appropriate here.

The camera can be thought of as an extension of the body. As an extension of the eye, it sees where the normal, unaided vision cannot function, ultra close-up, and at long distances. It is also an extension of the hand, arm, trunk of the body, and the legs. Although you may view through the camera, it is the body appendages which direct the view. *What* is seen is also *how* it is seen.

As the camera moves, so does the eye; as the body moves, so does the eye.

When the camera performs as subject, it is really the impulses of the filmmaker, guiding the camera, that we sense. Every person has physical rhythms, motions, and gestures which are peculiar to himself and which reflect his body tone and state of mind. These are conveyed in movements while filming and are transferred to the film. The slightest movement of the camera can reveal something of the filmmaker's state of mind. We can imagine how difficult it is to hold the camera still while filming on the morning after a late-night party. Those little shakes reveal a physical instability, and, perhaps, an equally precarious spirit. When we film under tension or stress, this too will transfer to the image. When filming a terrible or embarrassing event, for example, the camera may shy slightly to the right or left. I knew a woman once who had just come back from a trip to Japan, and while trying to film the interesting sights, people, and their manner of dress, found herself very distracted by the frenetic activity and bustle. Her camera darted from one thing to another. Upon seeing her film, I was able to sense her frustration and distraction; her movements revealed her state of mind.

How many people have experimented by filming the ground as they walked? Every hesitation, every pause to examine is recorded, so that when the film of these actions is projected, there is a re-experiencing of movement; but perhaps it is even more significant to note that the movement is related to the selection of the items to be seen, and is an integral part of how they are seen.

The camera records movement, but it also records what is seen *in terms* of movement. In a sense, the movement plus the subject being filmed become wedded—joined, as it were, to create a joint subject. An excellent example of this technique is Jud Yalkut's film *Down by the Riverside* (a filmed recording of an art show exhibit at the Riverside Gallery in New York City).

But how are the subject and camera movement wedded to produce a conjoined subject, a transformed subject? One must first accept the premise that the way a subject is seen is part and parcel of the subject proper. For example, a train when filmed moving toward you is a different train, figuratively, than when it is filmed moving away from you. The gestures of the two train examples are quite different, and they mean different things to us, evoking different sets of feelings. When the train is moving parallel (from one side of the screen to the other) to us, the camera can perform in one of several ways in relation to the train. Here are a few: The camera can be aimed perpendicular to the axis of the moving train so that the effect is "happening to be there at the same time the train was coming," or "waiting in anticipation for the coming train."

Also, the camera could either move into the direction of the on-coming train in visual confrontation or it could move in the direction the train is going, giving us the feeling of being left behind. Movement in relation to the subject by the camera contributes to a certain mood. Although this could be considered transforming, to an extent, the subject itself does not become a vastly different image. In other words, a train is a train, even though we may relate to it in different ways.

We might justifiably ask, what is a truly transformed image? Is there a standard way to view a train? Of course not. There is only a generalized train. The train must first be *seen*. It must be interpreted before it becomes a particular train. Its particularization is the beginning of its transformation. To single something out as a subject is like a first step on the transformational scale; and when we move in relation to a subject we take a bigger step.

Camera motion in and of itself implies importance to the viewer; it implies that something is being related to—as when we turn to see that which has entered our field of attention. In a like manner the camera turns to see; but it also chooses, confronts, explores, lingers, and shies away; it is relentless; it is timid and it withdraws, it, in short, is you. It is you, the viewer through the camera, and you, the viewer of the projected film. Both are the same. The actions and motions of the filmmaker are perceived by the viewer as his actions and motions.

Motion can transform the subject—not only slightly, but so radically that there is no vestige of the form or color of the original. To dramatize this point: If you will adjust your camera to anywhere from four to two frames per second, and pan quickly while filming, in big sweeps, the resulting images on the screen will be streaks of colored light—not cars, people, sun, or moon—but streaks of light. It is while considering this phenomenon that it is possible to see how a subject is merely made up of light, color, and motion—both ultimately and on the most substantial level. It was always that way; except that now we are able to see the components of all filmed subjects as if they had been submitted to a chemical analysis revealing their molecular structure. Here, there is no "subject" as such—no person, no car—only what we can interpret from the abstractions we see. A moot and philosophical question is: Are these streaks of light still to be considered people? Furthermore, are identifiable images of people and other subjects to be considered as what they are, as opposed to being seen as forms made up of colored light? To entertain these questions is, I feel, a way of probing deeper into the capability of the film medium for broader statements of perhaps a different nature. I think that such questioning helps to open up the idea of what film is, and what it can be.

As demonstrated, movement can utterly transform a familiar subject into an image composed of nothing but abstract streaks of light. Although it is a bit Flash Gordon-ish to suggest one can "zap" a thing into something else by manipulation of the camera, you can concretely change the "record" of the world by making your own record through movement. (We can see how Stan Brakhage did this in his *Anticipation of the Night*, where much of the film uses the "streaking" technique just described.)

Consider that by filming at faster than normal speed you can slow down the subject and generate lyricism or pathos, a sense of the serious or the profound. By making the camera go at a slower than normal speed, you can generate farce, comedy, lightness of spirit.

Through *time lapse* photography you can "arrest" time, and by doing so speed it up. You can compress hours, days, weeks, or months into *seconds*. Is this not transforming the familiar, real subject through motion? (Also not to be overlooked is that stop motion is also a transformation of the subject through time, to be discussed next.)

The relevance of this observation to the personally expressive filmmaker lies in his understanding that filmed movement is always interpretive, thus transformational. The degree of transformation (the degree of abstraction) depends on how radically the interpretive means are employed. If the interpretive means is extreme, as in the "streaks of light" example, then we can say that the filmed image becomes the *new* subject. This leads to the creation of a completely new subject—one generated by the filmmaker—and one that is the product of *his own* expressive impulses, to do with as he chooses.

TIME

You can also transform a subject by changing the film time involved. To alter time in this way, start from the obvious: that, first of all, film runs through the camera at so many frames per second. This represents a "unit of time," a slice of time. When both the filming and projection speeds are identical, what is filmed is a realistic representation of events during the space of time the film has measured. To put it more graphically, just think of fifteen feet of Super 8mm film as representing a sixty-second unit of time when the film is projected at eighteen frames per second. It can be regarded as being like a single sweep of a clock's second hand, representing sixty seconds. We could, therefore, almost tell time by how many feet of film is being projected. I say almost, because there is always a slight variation in projection speeds of projectors—in the same way that some clocks run fast and some run slow.

Now, assuming that the camera and projector we are using will run accurately at, say, eighteen frames per second, we can further assume that whatever the camera has "seen," or photographed, in the space of fifteen feet (one minute) did in fact occur during the space of that minute. This, then, constitutes a record of *actual* time, or what is called "real time."

On the other hand, if we shoot fifteen feet of Super 8mm film at fifty-four frames per second, and project it at, say, eighteen frames per second, it will take us three minutes to view what has actually transpired in one minute. By this method we can literally "stretch" time. And, in the same way, we can "compress" time by shooting the film at any speed *less* than eighteen frames per second and projecting it at eighteen frames per second. This altering of our illusion of time is referred to as "screen time." It has been transformed, made elastic, and serves the imaginative life of the viewer in a way that functional, actual time does not.

For purposes of creating a collage within the film frame, two different subjects which were filmed at different times can be superimposed. For example, a car which has turned over, and is burning, does not have to occur at the same time as an image superimposed over it of a child laughing. But because these two events are *seen* simultaneously (as in an earlier illustration), they have the implication of *happening* simultaneously.

The foregoing is an illustration of time disjuncture within the film frame creating the illusion of simultaneity. The same feeling can be established by intercutting lengths of disjointed shots with each other in a linear fashion, making a kind of collage. The child laughing can be separated into any number of segments between which any number of events can be placed; when these events are viewed together, they will convey the illusion of occurring at the same time.

SPATIAL CONTEXT

Another way to view transformation is through altering the "normal context" of a subject by placing it in an unfamiliar one. A normal or ordinary context is a situation, a set of circumstances, or even just a setting, in which we are accustomed to associating certain objects, animals, or people with their attendant attitudes and behavioral characteristics. For instance, a usual setting might be a city street; and people would be dressed in city clothes, moving about as we would expect people to move. In addition, the buildings, cars, and activities would be appropriate to the setting of the city. All of these elements go to make up a normal context.

Now let us take one of these elements from the context of the city—say an automobile—and let's place it, instead of on a city street, driving on the surface of the ocean. Impossible? It may be impossible, in that the image violates reality, but it is not impossible as a symbolic, figurative statement for poetic or expressionistic purposes. The "how" of creating this image is through superimpositional technique (detailed in Part One). The important thing here is that few people have experimented with the possibilities of expressing thoughts and feelings in this manner. (I have used superimposition as a form of cine-poetic expression extensively in my own films, which I discuss later.)

In order to transform subjects for the purpose of personal expression, the inflexibility of the past and ordinary means of film expression that have come to dominate our thinking and our communication with others have to be put aside. Once it was thought that wild and extravagant images like the one I just described were exclusively the province of the painter or the sculptor. There was even a time, not far in the past, when these "freed" artists were fairly ridiculed, even persecuted, for attempting to create an image as outrageous as the one I casually mention above. It should be noted that at this writing over half the world, including the Soviet Union and China, is busy repressing artists who would seek to depict reality in other than realistic terms. This is not so much a comment on politics and government as it shows how very conservative thinking remains on the subject of social realism versus personal expression, at least 100 years after personal artistic expression became a widely accepted way of working—beginning with the poets Rimbaud and Verlaine, the painters van Gogh and Munch, the sculptors Brancusi and Barlach, and the filmmaker Méliès.

To return to the discussion of how things can be transformed through an alteration of spacial contexts, it is important to realize that new contexts provide new meanings, in the same way that old and familiar contexts reinforce old meanings. The application of either old or new contexts should be determined by your intention, whether it is to spin an old yarn well, or tell a new one which you have made up.

In a later section, context is described in relation to both *montage* and *collage* as being an assemblage of related or else unrelated images. When using context as a transforming tool, the subjects or images making up the contexts to be juxtaposed must be unrelated in an important way in order to generate new meaning.

It has been discussed how we perceive contexts in terms of either *setting* or *sequence*. What we perceive inside the contextual frame is the setting context, or what is often referred to as the *in-frame* context. Sequential, or *linear*, context is provided by a closely occurring series of images which are accepted as "belonging together," and which are therefore related. Should any of the sequential images appear as unfamiliar in the context we are experiencing, then our "persistence of expectation" and "our persistence of attention" are momentarily interrupted. Whether we are able to resume our attention and expectation depends very largely upon the nature of the relationships we are experiencing, and upon whether we can "adjust" to them or not. If we succeed in making the adjustment, new meaning is created in our minds. If we don't succeed, then only anxiety, apprehension, inattention, and lack of meaning will result. The goal in using contextual transformation should be to create new meaning while permitting it to become effective and integrated by the viewer as experience.

Of the two—setting (in-frame) context and sequential (linear) context—it is definitely harder to alter the elements of a familiar setting and have it accepted by the viewer than it is to introduce unfamiliar images occurring in a familiar sequence. Why this is, exactly, I don't know. It may be that what happens over a period of time (in sequence) is more flexible in regard to expectation than what we perceive as an immediate experience within the frame.

When items from one setting context are placed in another, a surrealistic feeling is created. But, as emphasized above, it is harder to assimilate the experience of a car parked in a living room or superimposed over a living room than it is to see a car in a *sequence* sandwiched between images of a living room.

We will accept the car parked in the living room as comedy—but it is comedy of the absurd. New meaning is not created, even though old meaning is ridiculed. In true surrealism, the car must careen off the street and plow through the wall of a house and then be seen "at rest" in the living room. In this instance, although we are experiencing a radical setting context alteration, we are able to justify it through the story and "how it comes about." In other words, surrealism is quite closely related to the literary mode, to the idea of the conventional story. As noted in Part III, "Surrealistic Narrative," surrealism is perhaps the only way a conventional story can generate new meaning. It is for this reason that those who attempt film surrealism find that they must work with story material that permits the absurd to be seen as other than comedy. Jean Cocteau, therefore, chose as one of his vehicles the fairy tale, *Beauty and the Beast*; Stanley Kubrick uses both prehistoric and futuristic settings for his *Space Odyssey*; and in *Satyricon*, Fellini plays out its grotesque episodes against the backdrop of ancient Rome's fertile decadence. In each of these instances, the viewer is psychologically prepared by the nature of the story setting to see the context altered in an *unfamiliar* way. The stories themselves give rise to the expectation of fantastic events and bizarre happenings.

In *Beauty and the Beast*, the castle to which the ugly transformed Prince has been exiled is virtually alive with surrealistic paraphernalia. Human arms reaching through walls hold flaming torches to provide light in dim corridors, while chalk-white Grecian statues pose unflinchingly as only their eyes follow Beauty through the castle. What might be thought of as disparities in any other setting, here, are at the most surprising—though not improbable.

But incongruent images may not be so easily assimilated, even when the setting will permit surrealistic license. Such, I believe, is the case in *Space Odyssey* with the controversial "monolith," a perfectly smooth, rectangular stone monument discovered, in the early scenes of the film, by ape men. The stone slab is clearly a symbol for a "supreme consciousness"; and yet it appears in the film with little preparation, and again later, on the moon, and, finally, at the end of the film. There is something painfully lacking: Perhaps the disparity in continuity is too great, and the improbability too boisterous. Whatever the precise reason, the monolith symbol does not gain total audience acceptance.

On the other hand, Fellini's *Satyricon* is more like Cocteau's *Beauty and the Beast* in that fantastic images are almost a commonplace. The setting is festering Rome as we witness the universal psyche agonizing and writhing like a partly exploded, oozing brain. We see terrible uncontrolled dreams folding in upon each other, compounding ugliness with something far worse. It is a cannibalism of the unconscious—consuming reason, compassion, and finally, even pleasure. It is a setting of such a devilish nature that anything of a surrealistic nature could happen, and does.

If the setting context constitutes what goes on within the picture frame (a frame of motion picture film), then sequential context is what goes on from one frame to the next (outside the frame); it is, in effect, the *juxtaposition of setting contexts.* When each of the setting contexts is related to the other through a common subject, a situational setting, or events contiguous in time (as described later in *Making a Collage Film*), this juxtaposition of setting contexts constitutes a montage. But when the setting contexts (picture frames) are not joined in at least one of these ways, and there appears to be a large disparity between the succession of images, you have a collage.

What all this boils down to is that what image we choose to put next to another in the making of a collage decidedly influences the way in which each of the images in succession is interpreted. The use of this method unquestionably works toward transformation of the image; it is another of the transforming tools.

To show how images can be used in a variety of different sequential contexts, I am reminded of a film I once saw taken at a race track, and of one particular image: an old man standing with his crumpled racing sheet—a real trooper—with his mouth open, as if transfixed. It looked as if his mouth could have caught flies in it, standing agape like that for such a long time without moving a muscle. Obviously this fellow was watching the race, and I guess he had his last two dollars bet on a horse. It was really an expression of incredulity . . . an expression, one of amazement and the other of disbelief. It was an ambiguous expression; and if we didn't know where he was, he might have been anywhere. In other words, a filmmaker could create an interesting effect by putting this chap in, say, the context of a "peace demonstration" (through juxtaposition) where he appears to be listening to a person giving a haranguing speech. This takes a man out of the context of a race track and puts him at a peace rally, but why not? His is a perfect expression of attention, and one charmingly characterized by the set of his mouth, and his age. In utilizing his expression when making a collage film, it could be thought of as a word or a phrase. Let us think of this phrase in a different context now.

Think of this old man sandwiched between images of a two-year-old child playing in a sandbox. You would have an entirely different effect: We might suppose that the man is reminiscing about his childhood, or maybe we interpret that he is "like" the child playing in the sandbox (if you "feature" the racing sheet), or perhaps you might intend for us to *read* him as simply watching a child at play. You could even convey the impression that what he is watching is really *his fantasy*. You can work with the image of the old man in many different ways.

It is important, however, that we *free the image*. Some images already have a certain ambiguity about them—like our man at the racetrack—where you might not know exactly where he is (perhaps because the shot began medium close and came in very close on his head). For all we know he might be "waiting for Godot," because we don't see the racing sheet any more, nor are we able to see where he's standing. Until he was put into a context he was merely a person in a void. He could have been placed in any number of contexts because he had been "freed" as an image. Yet, had he been standing there with racing forms in his hand, and the letters on the forms said "Alameda Racetrack," then this would be a fixed image in the mind of the viewer. Also, if the man's expression happened to be rigidly related to this specific event, you couldn't make it malleable. You are restricted to using him as "a guy at the racetrack," and that's all. And when such restriction of an image occurs, this begins to take on the quality of the narrative film. However, by freeing the subject through transformation (in this case a closeup), we can use various contexts to make an image say anything we wish.

COSTUME

Transformation can be achieved through costume—which can include dress, wearing apparel, hair style, and even facial structure. I am simply suggesting that you become aware of these qualities, not necessarily that you make a special, conscious effort to change the appearance of your subject.

Through costume, perhaps, is the most effortless and natural way to effect transformation. Because of this, it is an especially suitable method for documentary or narrative films, where stylistic intrusions such as filters, prisms, double exposure, and other distorting methods would be distracting. A slight adjustment in the clothes of a person, or in their hair, can be very expressive either of your point of view or theirs. For thousands of years, clothes have been used as a method of identification, pin-pointing the wearer's attitude, occupation, or intention. And most notably, costume has been used for centuries as a method of transformation on the stage.

Transformation can also occur through the use of faces. Fellini is known to cast almost all his films by face. His searches for interesting faces are legendary in Rome: When he is ready to cast for a film, he will put ads in all the papers. People flock from every corner of Italy, from neighboring countries, and even from America to have their faces scrutinized, to be in a Fellini film. Why? Because, in actuality, faces, like clothes, are masks. In the film *Sunset Boulevard*, remarking on the expressions film actors had in the twenties, Gloria Swanson said "In *those* days we had *faces*." And indeed, in that film, hers is a remarkable face. Taut and gaunt, goddess-like, statuesque, and evil.

In reviewing the points discussed, if you plan to use a number of different images which are vastly different in "areas of experience" —such as a parade, a person swimming, and a freeway accident— all in the same film, you will have to find some way of releasing these images from the necessity of their being referred to in a particular *time* or *place* through transformation. Once you have done that, the images will amalgamate with each other. You do this by removing them from their usual, ordinary contexts. You can change an image's context through the use of close-ups, filters, reflectors, and so forth—all the methods of transformation I have discussed— and also through editing.

By simply putting a small piece of a scene in your film you can even transform it through gesture—by highlighting the gestural—by extracting it and using only the essence of the scene. (See Part One, Chapter IV, Section 2.) The viewer is able to see the outward act, and to be exposed to the feeling without knowing the "why" behind the gesture as supplied by the gesture's context of ordinary reality. With the isolated gesture at your disposal, you are able to inflect it any way you wish and make it say what you want it to. You can virtually take any piece of ordinary film (which has not been previously transformed by any of the devices discussed) and most effectively transform it through editing.

Making a collage film through editing is rather like making a junk sculpture—as if you were rummaging through a junk yard and found a piece of generator with an interesting shape. If you chose to put an entire generator in the sculpture, instead of a single piece, there would be a tendency for the observer to say to himself "Oh, there's a generator!" The idea here is: You don't want people to think about the old identity of the subject you are using in your film; you want them to see your film as a thing in itself, as articulated by your own visually expressive language.

chapter 13

Making a Collage Film

THE DIFFERENCE BETWEEN COLLAGE AND MONTAGE

The concepts of montage and collage are closely enough related to create some confusion about how they function—and they do function differently. Where montage is a patchwork of images *that are related,* collage is the juxtapositioning of images *that are disparate and unrelated.* Collage is a more extreme degree of montage—as far as the logical relationship of shots is concerned.

The shots in a montage are held together by a common subject—common to either theme, people, place, or time. The viewer, in seeing this collection of shots, is aware of the "sense umbrella" the common subject provides. He will accept the montage images as reinforcing each other, rather than as challenging him to make connections between them.

There are several typical types of montage. One we are hardly aware of, and which is basic to most documentary and story filmmaking, is telling a story with a series of "contiguous" pictures. It's very much like a comic strip where a single line of action is broken up into fragments comprised of different camera angles, cut-aways, and the omission of irrelevant details. In a basic sense this is a montage. Today, the patchwork quality of the shot arrangement seems perfectly natural to us. Yet there was a time when filmmakers felt constrained to film action with long, continuous-running shots. More or less, the effort was to document everything and to include it in the edited film, attempting to approximate the way we see a stage play. Even into the 1930s the long-running scene was popular.

Other types of montage include subjects involving place. Such a film might be titled *Santa Monica on a Sunday Afternoon*, *Mexico Today*, or *Cities in the Desert*. In these instances, the kinds of shots used can vary widely in content while retaining continuity as a whole. In another montage type, time serves as the continuity device. Such films might be titled *Germany, 1938*, *The Roaring Twenties*, or *The Day John Kennedy Died*. People with experiences in common can tie a film together too, as in *The Liberated Woman*, *The Vanishing Indian*, or *Swamp Dwellers in Cajun Country*.

The concepts of montage and collage are by no means opposite— any more than male and female are opposite. They simply contribute to creativity in different ways. Montage constructs the "sense" of an activity without actually showing all the details. In montage, "stage continuity" is eliminated in favor of building intensity, and furthering the action, through a careful *selection* of shots. Only the important aspects of the action are shown; and these are arranged for maximum emotional impact. Montage allows the viewer to accept an arrangement of shots with *a degree* of sense distance between them; the shots are held together by a common subject—as to person, place, time, or theme.

If one were to use montage in filming a dancer, it would be like moving around the subject, taking short bursts of film, without making an attempt to show how one movement leads to another. Here, the filmmaker is not after a thorough document, but an impression of the dance. He illustrates it through a selection of details and dramatic gestures which will be reconstructed in the editing. As a montagist he feels no obligation to render *every* movement. Being able to do this is one thing that distinguishes the home movie-maker from the more accomplished filmmaker.

To the collagist, on the other hand, only *one shot* of the dancer may be necessary to his film. He might juxtapose only a single shot of the dancer with, say, a shot of a construction worker carrying and assembling materials. The worker's functional movements viewed next to the dancer's grace may appear, at first, to be awkward in contrast, yet a comparison might suggest grace and sensitivity in the worker's movements, while illustrating at the same time the functional quality of the dancer's movements. Such a switch can be an enriching point of view, even though it is unconventional. The dancer and the construction worker are seen in a new light. The decision to use these images in juxtaposition is the collagist's. Rather than abiding by the expectations of a more conventional logic, he creates and designs his own context for the film. In effect, he creates his own subject, his own logical system.

What is really being discussed here are *forms* of exposition—the two most important means, or basic structures, in making a film statement. Montage unfolds an idea, the general premise of which is understood and accepted. It draws heavily upon what we know from our shared experience with the subject matter. Collage, however, puts things together in a new way, so that often the viewer is surprised by what he sees. He cannot, as he is used to doing, relate as strongly to his experiential memory. Collage is, in fact, a fresh, if not new, experience. By using images in an unfamiliar context, collage tends to generate *new meanings* from new relationships. However, the ways of experiencing these meanings and relationships exist mainly within the contextual structure of the collage film itself. Such is the case illustrating the laborer and the dancer where *similar movements*—stepping, reaching, lifting, and so forth—form a bond between the two vastly different subjects. Their gestures become *means* for the viewer to tie the subjects together meaningfully. Through "gesture," their juxtapositions become meaningful. Since there is no ordinary logical justification for these images to appear side by side, justification must be provided. Although the peculiar kind of sense that emerges from this type of juxtaposition is unfamiliar, it nevertheless *becomes* familiar. It becomes important to the viewer because the film itself provides the context rather than drawing from one outside the film, as happens in montage.

But what are some of these unusual, unfamiliar relationships that have been suggested? Nearly everyone who reads this will have, at one time or another, made a collage—a composite from pictures cut out of magazines. If in a magazine you should happen to find a large overall picture of a pastoral scene—a pasture with cows and a barn in the distance—and in this pasture you very neatly place another magazine cut-out of a bed, you will have created a rudimentary collage. The bed has been placed in an unfamiliar context. Now let us suppose you find a magazine cut-out of a cow and place her in a bed (a human's bed) which you have sitting in the pasture. It is as if to say: "A bed is like a human's pasture," or "a pasture is like a cow's bed."

One of the greatest pictorial collagists of the 1920s is Max Ernst, who is a master at creating "environments" from assemblages of antiquated magazine illustrations. Today, the film counterpart of Ernst might be someone like Larry Jordan, particularly one of his early films called *Hamfat Asar*. (Jordan's films, as with many others mentioned in this Part can be rented from the Canyon Cinema Co-op, Rm. 220, Industrial Center Bldg., Sausalito, Ca. 94965—or, the Filmmakers Co-op, 175 Lexington Ave., N.Y., N.Y. 10016.) It must be noted that both of these artists are collagists in the pure or traditional sense, who mainly use old illustrations from medical and phrenology journals, and from early engravings of the Rodolph Bresdin variety.

Now let us examine in detail a hypothetical series of collage images. If you juxtapose a shot of a bulldozer pushing down the walls of a house (a wrecking operation) with a shot of a squirrel eating a nut, and follow this with a shot of a person hitting a golf ball, you have the beginnings of a collage film. Each of the individual scenes seems to be out of context. But if each of these "items" were to be placed in the same subject context through narration, the sound track might inform us that the bulldozer is clearing land for a golf course where squirrels and humans can play. This little montage would no doubt make an effective TV commercial for a land developer.

If the above sequence were a collage film, and there were no narration, what would hold these shots together? The bulldozer, the squirrel, and the golfer are performing *analogous* activities. Their gestures are comparable (if you see it that way). Although the activities may not look alike at first, each gesture is "banging against something" and could be said to represent forms of *impact*. The bulldozer is impacting with a wall, the squirrel's teeth with a nut, and the golf club with a ball. Although these can be thought of as comparable *structural* relationships, they have contrasting *inferential* relationships. One image shows the process of destruction, another that of obtaining nourishment, and another is an image of recreation. In each instance we are shown another inferential side to the general structural gesture of "impact." By this token its meaning is deepened through *ambiguity* (discussed in detail in a later section). In still another way it tells us something about each of the activities (or gestures) as they mutually "inform" each other. Taken totally, they constitute a kind of paradigm of related movements.

Each shot informs the other in a cross-pollinating fashion. Swapping, relaying, interchanging: Each shot borrows meaning from the other.

So far, I have mainly discussed collage as it occurs when juxtaposing disparate shots in linear succession. Now I would like to go into a way to create collage *within the picture frame*, through superimposition. This technique is often referred to as double exposure, because it involves "laying" one image over another through multiple exposures—twice, sometimes three times. As a filmic technique, it is fairly common to see multiple exposures in commercial story films—and even in certain television "series" where the theme involves the "unknown" or the "occult."

Superimpositions are most often created in the laboratory rather than in the camera. Few cameras are equipped to make them, but some, notably models of the Bolex, give very good results. Super 8 has been excluded because of the limited wind-back facility of the cartridge. But those filmmakers shooting in Regular 8mm and in 16mm should have little problem making superimpositions in the camera.

The effect of multiple exposure is a little like viewing a person's body through a transparent raincoat. You can see the person's form underneath, yet the raincoat clearly retains its own form. Each maintains an independent existence, and at the same time, each contributes mutually to the meaning and function of the other. Although the raincoat is, in effect, superimposed on the person's body, the latter acts to *fill in* the raincoat. Superimposed images appear to fill in as well as *lay over*.

The effect of superimposition in a conventional film is on the order of a poetic simile. Let us imagine a huge face superimposed over ocean waves. If this hypothetical image were being used in a story film, what comes before and what comes after it might suggest that the person to whom the face belongs is lost at sea, or that his thoughts are like the sea, or that he has a great love of the sea. Yet if the same image were used in a collage film, the face and the ocean would be seen as more integrated. Unlike the former illustration where the face was "like" the sea, here the face becomes a *part of* the sea and waves—and, in turn, the ocean is seen as a part of the face. A formal transformation is created. The ocean and the face are inextricably wedded as one. They cannot be separated or pulled apart the way you would be able to separate a few frames of ocean from some frames of face. The images in a superimposition are not mechanically juxtaposed; they have been blended together to create a new entity.

Where one image is over another, the dominant one—usually the larger of the two—is the one which is "characterized" by the other. For instance, if the face appearing over the waves were small, then it would tend to give a quality or character to the ocean. The ocean would be the principal subject, and the face would act as a kind of modifier. Likewise, should the face take up most of the picture frame, and the ocean be seen as subordinate, the face would be characterized by the water and waves.

Multiple exposure also can be used to create the illusion of a different, unique image. In other words, the two overlays in a composite superimposition go to make up one image. This is the way we view the embellishments on a coat of arms or an insignia. Each part becomes relegated to the whole, creating an "emblematic" effect.

Imagine an eye superimposed above a mouth with nothing else in the frame other than a surrounding matrix of skin. Although it is highly unusual to see these two facial features in this exact relationship, they nevertheless do amalgamate and integrate, as shown in a still from my film *The Devil Is Dead* (see insert). They blend together as if made that way naturally. The illusion is created by the fact that both are facial features, and the skin background makes the forms blend together.

If used skillfully, superimpositions can put you in the business of creating new forms by being able to borrow parts of people (as well as of other things) and integrate them. Superimpositions generate an other-worldly presence of dreams and fantasy.

GATHERING MATERIAL

The first step in making a collage film is the gathering of material, assembling images to place in a meaningful sequence. To many people it may sound like a funny way to go about making a film, because most filmmaking is thought to be done first as a script, after which a search begins to find ways to realize the script visually. This is certainly the way story films and some documentaries are made. But the collage film is different from these forms. The initial step in making a collage film is deciding what to film. Next is filming it. And last is deciding how it is to go together.

Think of yourself as a "found objects sculptor" who likes to comb beaches and dig through junkyards for odd objects and pieces of things. You choose this or that because it is *interesting*, and perhaps more important, because it is *suggestive* of something. You may not know what the parts suggest until you get them all heaped on the floor of your garage—until you are able to sit down and ponder what you have and begin to see similarities, relationships between the forms. You hold some of the pieces next to each other, and they seem to relate, suggesting other interesting relationships. Finally, you begin putting the pieces together. A form made from the pieces begins to take a single large shape. It begins to have a single gesture. We feel that although many disparate pieces make it up, it has unity and statement.

But the nagging question persists. *What do you film?* I have found that, at first, it is easier to use an *occasion* to garner images. For most people this isn't difficult. An occasion could be a birthday, a parade, a trip to the country, an outdoor barbecue, washing the dog, fireworks on the Fourth of July, or swimming at the beach. An occasion is a reason for being there. But it is something else too. An occasion is an event. Sometimes it is naturally visually interesting and sometimes not. A parade or a trip to the country might have stunning visual possibilities, but washing the dog or cooking a meal may not be so promising. There are ways, though, to transform the most visually banal event—as described in an earlier section on "Transformation."

The good thing about making a collage film is that you can use practically any images you happen to have. You can utilize existing footage, whether it was taken last summer or whether it happened as the result of trying the exercises at the back of this book. In whatever way you might have come by the footage, it is usable. Even if someone gave it to you, it is usable. The collage film is especially important in that footage taken for completely other reasons can be utilized to make statements of aesthetic value.

THE FILM AS SUBJECT: ROLES AND RULES, GESTURE, AND AMBIGUITY

As has been suggested, making a collage film is a little like writing poetry. And like a poem, this type of film uses a special kind of logic: It comes close to what could be called "metaphorical."

I would like to suggest, too, that collage filmmaking is a good way to gain a basis for all other filmmaking—just as writing poetry teaches the value of words, their properties, and their exciting possibilities. One only has to go over some names of great novelists and playwrights to bear this out. James Joyce, Ernest Hemingway, Tennessee Williams, and William Shakespeare—in most cases they were poetry writers *before* they wrote novels and plays.

As with written images, film images go by *roles* and *rules*. They contain structural and inferential gestures, and their depth of meaning is achieved through ambiguity.

Roles and Rules

Whether you are making a narrative, a documentary, or a collage film, the rule system you set up is its key—the key to your visual language for that film. As I have already stated, creation of a rule system for any type of film other than a story film is pretty much up to the filmmaker. I say pretty much, because in a documentary you do have to collaborate with the subject to a necessary extent. Yet even here, the documentary offers an enormous latitude for techniques in rendering (invention of rule systems). The collage film absolutely waits for the filmmaker's initiative to shape it, and is inclined to "go" in any direction the filmmaker dictates. It is his universe—the universe of his personal expression—and it responds to his selections and arrangements without argument. The only argument you might get is from the people who are trying to figure out what you are up to. If you haven't made the *system* apparent to the viewer, then frustration, anxiety, and bad feelings may result. In short, the viewer is being asked to see something which he quite literally is unable to see.

[At least, the documentary has a readily understandable level for just about everyone: the informational level. This level is where we are able to concentrate our attention on the *activity* of the subject even if all else by way of sentiment to be communicated is lost. With documentary modes, at least we are able to learn something about how a ceramic pot is made, or the many ways frogs are used.]

So far, I have discussed the process of selecting images for their content, the ways to spot gestures, and ways to link them together as visually acceptable composites. At this point we are able to appreciate the need for an overall governing principle for a film.

We have the ship outfitted and under sail—but where are we going?

Each of the images you have selected, whether taped to a wall for editing or rolled up and placed in a cigar box, has a structural identity as described by its gestural configuration—by the dominant quality of its form or color. It is in the nature of these images that we will discover a clue as to how they will go together. The nature of the images, whether it can be labeled verbally, or whether it exists as an undefinable feeling, is important. What *it is* is *how it looks*—and how it appears to you is what I call its *role*. A pink flower has a pink feeling. Subjects which move in certain ways, as in dance, communicate particular attitudes. Derring-do sports events such as race-car driving may convey a sense of heroics. The meaning of any given image that is being used becomes its role.

The nature of the role tells us something about how the image should be used—that is, how it should be placed in the film with respect to its length and how it is being juxtaposed. The resulting relationship, which forms a pattern of some sort, may be called the *rule system*. The roles of images tell us how they might be placed together. In turn, when the film is viewed, it is the rule system which tells the viewer how to interpret the roles of the images. The viewer's responses are guided by what you have perceived in the images from *your* vantage. (We are, of course, talking mainly about the collage film here—although on a general level these principles can apply to all types of films.) It is the pattern you have invented and are using that enables the viewer to learn your language and receive your filmic communication. In fact, it is this system which allows us to tell whether a film is successful: whether it does indeed violate, or honor, its own governing laws. Use of a rule system makes the difference between randomness and purpose, sense and nonsense, haphazardness and intention—communication and lack of it.

Perhaps the simplest type of rule system is "theme and variation"; and perhaps the most primitive type of theme is the drumbeat (a cluster of beats and their intervals). I think of the collage film as very closely related to music. The two forms are, of course, nowhere near related in terms of content. But there are analogies we can draw between the two media, perhaps assisting in our understanding of film structure. If you are having trouble conceiving ideas for a film's rule system, it is worth trying to see its images as musical tones and beats.

One very arbitrary type of rule system is actually cutting images to sound, so that the images change in response to the change in sound tempo and mood. The real difference here is that the image has been made to serve the sound, instead of the other way around.

Another way to unify images is through comparison and contrast (placing like or unlike things together). For example, juxtaposing like movements, no matter what their inferential content, will tend to make them "go together." Movements which go, say, from left to right through the frame—such as a train—can be successfully juxtaposed to a track runner moving in the same direction. Once a "convention" of movements is established cross-screen you can put in images of birds, clouds, even water running in the same direction. Running water is certainly not the same type of movement as the train and track runner afford, yet we accept the water as a part of the rhythmic structure. The water becomes an "extension" of the basic movement—an extrapolation. Once you have successfully begun to extrapolate from the basic movement, you can stretch our acceptance of images and compound their meanings. Stretching our images, we might include a person swinging a baseball bat in the direction of the other movements—after the water. And next, you might put in an image of a person turning his head in the general direction of the movements (close-up). This succession of images illustrates theme and variation, using the configuration of gestures in a comparative way.

Use of configurations in a contrasting way involves setting up a rhythmic structure where the images' movements at intervals run counter to each other. The intervals needn't necessarily be evenly spaced: Referring to the preceding example, instead of having the person turn his head in the direction of the comparative movements, the head turns in a counter direction, and a little later on another image moves in the counter direction, and so forth. *Relative size* does have something to do with the viewer's ability to accept the amalgamation of these gestures. The closer the images appear in size, relative to the picture frame, the less the viewer will have to resolve the images visually, and the more readily he will accept them.

By this time you may have guessed that the viewer does tend to challenge certain images appearing together when they are too disparate in structure. As a footnote, it should be added that the viewer seems to accept images which are structurally related more readily than he will accept those that are inferentially (or ideationally) related. However, inferential relationships that are congruent within the viewer's set of expectations do tend to reinforce his acceptance. More skepticism is raised by faulty symbolism than faulty structure. When working with structure you are working on a physical, kinetic level which is harder to deny than "ideas" such as anti-war, pro-conservation, or doctrinaire approaches to moral values or political philosophy. But once structure is established as intentional and valid, the ideational content will at least have a chance of being entertained by the viewer—and even embraced. The old adage "seeing is believing" applies to film structure because it is the physical sensation of light and movement which is the chief persuader.

Another possible system is in comparing and contrasting gestural images which don't have a clear configurative movement. These are *passive gestures*. In this category, forms and colors can be compared: a red, round balloon can be juxtaposed to a round, orange-red, setting sun, which in turn is compared to a person wearing a red hat (extrapolation of form) and then to a red flower. In general, it seems more effective to compare colors and forms as against contrasting them. This is probably because the viewer has to go to more trouble to see the relationships. Film images go by so rapidly that unless the differences are clear in form and color, the viewer will be lost and confused.

Making your intention clear is certainly important. The acceptance by the viewer of your role and rule system is wholly contingent upon the clarity with which he can perceive it. You can have the best of ideas, but if it doesn't work at least on a structural level, it will not come across. Therefore, contrasting square items with round ones, or red ones with blue ones, will emerge as a less important contrast to the viewer than his perception of the fact that there is a constant set of *recurring* images that are round, square, blue, or red.

In a sense, the viewer of the expressionistic film has a type of expectancy similar to that of the viewer of the documentary or the narrative film. The story film viewer expects certain things to happen on the basis of conventional, familiar roles and rules woven into a conventional plot. The viewer of films where the roles and rules are unconventionally determined will find himself free of expectation *at first* (in a state comparable to Coleridge's "suspension of disbelief"); but as the film progresses he will become more and more aware that certain things *have been occurring*, and therefore will *probably occur.* His anticipation, then, is honed by the film's role and rule system itself. The film has educated the viewer to its unique language through being consistent—to the degree that the viewer feels comfortable and feels that he knows what's going on.

Inferential Gesture

I have saved exploring inferential gesture until now because its symbolic nature makes it more tenuous to describe than structural gesture. It is as if structural gesture could be thought of as an edifice—and that once it is constructed we must decide what to put into it. What is its function to be?

Where images are related in their structural movement through the frame—as in a previous example: the train, the track runner, and the running stream, all moving from left to right—we do not as yet know what to infer from them. What do they add up to in terms of ideational conclusions? Although such an extension of sense is not imperative to the collage (or to expressionistic film generally), I have suggested that the filmmaker could, if he wished, direct the latent inferential content of the images, providing us with "meaning" in addition to kinetic satisfaction. (We can find satisfaction in the simple apprehension of images placed in relation to each other with structural intention much in the way we can enjoy a roller coaster for physical thrills, even though it doesn't go anywhere in particular.

We can begin to infer what the train, the track runner, and the stream mean if other images are introduced which have more specific connotations, but which at the same time contribute to the rule system of the film. If after every image of movement through the frame you put a nonmovement image, that nonmovement image will provide a contrasting gesture. The nature of this image—the inferential content—can be determined according to the statement you choose to make. If you want to make an encouraging statement, you might insert a shot of a child running in the same direction as the three previously mentioned images into our hypothetical collage. The character of the child's image could be one of joy and exhilaration. Further reinforcement of the idea would be provided if the image of the child were exactly the same every time it is used.

The inferential effect of intercutting the child running would be to point up the more happy, sanguine aspects of motion—things in motion, nature in motion, children in motion—all of which may indicate the feeling that a world in motion is a happy world, or that movement is energy and energy is positive. (The makers of advertising films use this principle all the time.) There are a host of generalizations which might occur to the viewer from the above sequence; and it should be noted that the inferences drawn, as illustrated here, although phrased differently, do fall within the *same area of conclusion:* that movement, that is, energy, is good. The area of conclusion was directed by the child's presence. The images become mutually reinforcing in their inferential message. What you will have done in making this collage is to set up a series of metaphorical juxtapositions in which one image is interpreted as being equated with another in meaning.

But perhaps inferential gesture can best be seen in operation from another angle. We have been talking about first perceiving the image in terms of its structural possibilities, and second, seeing what inferential connotations there are which can be strengthened. There is another way: spotting inferential possibilities in an image at the outset. That means being drawn to a subject by some compelling quality it has, one that it suggests.

I saw a film once that was predicated on nothing but a series of shots of different people experiencing eating a sour pickle. Obviously, the conception of the *image* of people eating pickles came before the idea of relating the images in a structural way—through movements (biting) and form and color (green pickle shapes).

Such images having strong inferential content are often potent in their expression of joy, sadness, or surprise; so are dynamic events such as explosions, holocausts, forest fires, houses sliding down hillsides, racing car crashes, and also images of great beauty. In fact, many of these strongly inferential images could be thought of as "innately effective."

Images of strong inferential content need not be obvious, however. A child playing ball or swinging in a swing is an obvious illustration of, say, youthful joy. The subtler image of a swing swinging by itself (after a child had left it in motion) would convey somewhat the same feeling, but it might convey other messages to us too. An empty swing in motion connotes possible sadness for having had to leave such a pleasurable activity. On the other hand, through this highly controlled and subtle image, we can obtain a purer sense of the child's activity, and of childness, and, quite possibly, of joy. These are flash-back inferences, going back in time, during a past event. The image of the empty swing is certainly more ambiguous than the one of the child swinging in the swing. More is left to the imagination. It is this ambiguity that allows the filmmaker leeway to shape and mold the image (through juxtaposition) in the direction of a more personal statement.

Along this line of thought, an activity which normally produces an image of pleasure or joy can quite possibly generate an image quite the opposite in effect by the way it is photographed. Lighting, camera angle, and camera movement have much to do with the final interpretation and activity of an image. Armed with this awareness, the filmmaker can alter and transpose a subject in many ways to create images with definite and strong inferential gestures.

Bruce Connor's film *A Movie* is a good illustration of how strong inferential images can be used in ambiguous ways, pushing their innate meanings quite beyond what we would get from them had they not been juxtaposed in this film. In *A Movie* we can also appreciate how images with strong inferential content can be juxtaposed in comparison-contrast. Connor juxtaposes images of holocaust and derring-do both with images that are ridiculous and ones of lyric beauty. In this film, Connor's world seems literally bursting at the seams with disaster and human striving; irony is compounded with irony, and man's achieving constantly courts destruction and defeat.

Extrapolation of the image works in the same way for inferential gesture as it does for gestures that are structural. Extrapolation, as you will remember, involves the development of an idea by showing different aspects that illustrate it. Unlike the previous illustration where movement was used, inferential gesture uses symbol and inference rather than structure as its content. Because of this, the particular inferential theme which the image has can be manipulated, can be developed.

In the instance of Bruce Connor's film, the principal images are "achieving" and "disaster." These are the inferential themes. A motorcycle race over rough terrain is a gesture of achieving, and when the cyclist spills his bike it becomes a gesture of disaster. Just as a Wright Brothers-type airplane is about to take off, it crashes. The two contrasting inferences are linked again and again, repetitively, by theme and variation. After Connor had "conditioned" the viewer's anticipations, he might have inserted other images less obviously connoting achieving and disaster, and the emotional momentum would no doubt have carried over. Insertion of material tangential to the main theme would have deepened and developed the film's content.

There are at least two main ideas operating here. One is that repetitive images of striving and disaster leads the viewer to associate the two. This leads to the viewer anticipating disaster whenever he sees an image of striving, whether or not disaster is imminent. It also leads the viewer to presuppose that any disaster he sees has involved some degree of striving prior to the disaster. The other idea is that with clear alternatives in the mind of the viewer—that everything is either a world of achieving and/or disaster—he "attaches" these identities to *any* image he sees (in the context of the film), even if the image is something as innocuous as eating an ice cream cone. In this case, the idea of striving and disaster could take on comic proportions—especially if the ice cream were huge, or if it suddenly fell off the cone and went "plop" in the eater's lap. And what about an obese person struggling to get into clothes that are too small? With our conditioning from previous achieving and disaster images, we can practically hear the clothes tearing and bursting at the seams.

Conditioning is probably a less appropriate way to express a film's dynamics than to talk about the *rule system* of the film. If such a system is used, it will allow the filmmaker to gain greater and greater distance between the sense of the initial images and ones that come later. It is this "allowable" distance between images that permits the filmmaker to insert material of a constantly differing nature. It is a slow and methodical movement away from the initial theme, using it as a vehicle to state other themes. Let us hypothetically structure such an evolution, or development, of inferential content.

Here is a list of possible shots. Motorcyclists racing; one or two of them take a spill; a series of shots of different types of airplanes taking off, then crashing; shots of a rocket being launched, then exploding in air; shots of lovers walking hand in hand in a field; cut to a blindfolded man being shot before a firing squad; cut to a film clip from a movie where pirates are coming over the side of a ship with knives in their teeth; then to another film clip where lovers are kissing and an irate father barges in the door; cut to a child igniting a fireworks sparkler; cut back to lovers kissing; cut to girl slapping boy; cut to eagle soaring; cut back to airplane taking off, and people clapping.

In the above illustration various types of striving and disaster are seen to counterpoint one another. The overall intention of this image cluster might read: "If at first you don't succeed, try, try again." But of course the total meaning, or significance, of the illustration cannot be summarized adequately in a simplistic phrase. In a collage film of this type only the film itself can provide us with "the statement." We are talking about the language of film and images, not the language of words. So the ultimate communication to the viewer rests with the film and the clarity of its rule system.

Extrapolation of theme through juxtaposition of images can apply just as well to the documentary and story film modes as it has been shown to support the structure of the collage-expressionistic film. In using this technique, the filmmaker always should be aware of the "needs" of the form he is working in. The documentary must honor the integrity of the subject insofar as the subject cues the action and direction of the film. Cavalier insertion of tangential imagery could result in a rupturing of the subject's credibility to the point that it becomes more the filmmaker's statement than the subject's. In the story film, more liberties can be taken. Here, there are a host of possible places where extrapolation of imagery can fit in. Flash-backs, dreams, hallucinations, extrasensory perception, occultistic rites, and time compression: all these and more opportunities are implicit in the story film form. The only caution I would give is: Do not stray too far from familiar ground—the viewer's familiar ground. The rule systems for all film genres are different in specifics, yet the same principles apply among them. The manipulation of structural and inferential gestures is basic. But the manipulation of inferences is especially tricky. In this area, the film medium is a baby. There is much to be explored here, and a great deal yet to be added to the subtleties of film rhetoric.

Ambiguity

Ambiguity, the state of having more than one meaning, can either exist in an image inherently, or it can be created through manipulation of context from which meaning will generate. An image of a child laughing may in truth *look like* the child is crying. The expressions sometimes look identical; consequently, we would, as viewers, only be able to read the image as it was intended by the collage filmmaker by hearing the soundtrack, or by the types of juxtapositions which are found in the film (thus giving us a clue to the filmmaker's rule system).

An image of pregnancy, for example, can be read as either a joy or a burden for the expectant mother. Ambiguity is best illustrated by a cat eating a bird. Are we glad for the cat or sad for the bird? More than likely we would feel a bit of both. Ambiguity creates ambivalence in us. It draws us in two or more directions at once; and it is our effort, as viewers, to resolve and to rationalize these directions that generates new meaning in our minds. It is like mixing visual components, which causes a "chemical" generation of meaning, the way acid acts upon metal to produce a gas. The collage film, through its ambiguity, causes meaning *to come about*. It provides a set of circumstances into which we can project ourselves —not unlike other film genres. Where the documentary induces us with information and with fascinating facts about people, the story film provides us with a ready escape into the stylized world of fantasized lives, and the collage film forces us to become a part of its rationale in order to avoid anxiety. Where other forms provide orientation, collage requires that we orient ourselves. Because the viewer realizes that he must constantly have a "handle" on the imagery in a collage film, the filmmaker can afford to be more extravagant with his use of ambiguity. The viewer is actively trying—which makes broad, ambiguous excursions in the film's rule system permissible. The meaning which we come up with in our minds as the result of ambiguity falls within relatively predictable areas. At least the filmmaker should be able to circumscribe these areas fairly accurately through the careful use of a rule system.

As I have stated, ambiguity can be created as the result of juxtaposed images which are disparate in meaning. It sets up a resonance, a reverberation of sense which deepens the experience. (An image of a man on a hill making obscene gestures may look as if he is summoning the gods—maybe he is!) In general, ambiguity is what all bad films lack. Controlled ambiguity—that is, where the collage filmmaker, and other filmmakers, direct the ambiguity—is a condition to be hoped for, one which generates meaning experientially, rather than telling it pedantically. Uncontrolled ambiguity is what Shakespeare has termed "sound and fury, signifying nothing." It is a kind of vague poking around in significant issues in the hope that meaning will emerge artlessly, as if by accident.

Of concern to you, however, is to learn to manipulate ambiguity for maximum expressiveness in your film—and to avoid being vague or didactic. The surest way to approach this problem with a degree of confidence is through gesture, and primarily through the film's structural components. If ambiguity is well-rooted in the actual physical make-up of the collage film, and if for some reason you should be off-base in directing that ambiguity, at least a structurally strong film will deliver something of importance: visual communication with feeling.

It is not easy to direct inferential meaning in film, much less to handle multiple inferences emanating from the same image. You might wish to work first with structural considerations as your "home base," and take up inferential considerations secondly. It might then be useful to examine some of the possibilities for structural ambiguity. To put it simply, we experience structural ambiguity when we are walking home alone late at night and we perceive groping silhouetted tree branches as monsters in the dark. Shadows, especially, stimulate the imagination to conjure up all sorts of things. Film has that capacity too, being a rather shadowy medium. It plays upon our suggestibility. It can produce satisfying illusions that, for a moment, transport us into another world—the world of the filmmaker, and a world of his making. The filmmaker can now work his magic with colored shadows (no longer do they have to be gray, or black and white). Now he is able to reinforce the feelings of his "shadows" through sound, too.

In Philip Wylie's novel, *Finnley Wren*, Finnley lay on the beach and imagined forms of animals and humans taking shape in the clouds. And certainly, we are familiar with the psychologist's Rorschach test, which asks us to see pictures in inkblots. If a visual form looks *like something*, then we are yielding to an age-old human propensity to *see into things*. If a thing looks like something else, then we are seeing through the process of visual analogy. And it follows that if something looks like something else, it may also look like two or more things at once. When something can look like more than one thing at a time, then it is ambiguous.

I use the word "can" above in a certain sense. This is the way you, the collage filmmaker, have determined that a given image will look—not especially the way a viewer may interpret the image on his own. *It is of particular importance not to anticipate how others may interpret your images—but rather, to read these images confidently for what they mean to you.* Very often, how you see an image will provide a key, a way for others to see it too. (It should be remembered that we are speaking mainly of the collage film. In this particular genre, the filmmaker is in the driver's seat, and he calls the shots. This is not true with most film forms, as I have repeatedly stressed. Working in collage gives the filmmaker the most freedom, and in a way, the most responsibility.)

A visual analogy is a visual event which looks like something else—like the tree branches late at night which resemble ghostly arms. In a technical sense, an analogy exists between two things which are constructed slightly differently, but which are similar in function. Thus fishes' gills are analogous to our lungs. The veins in leaves are analogous to our veins. Water in the sea is analogous to our atmosphere. A bird is analogous to an airplane. Automobiles are analogous to houses. (Figure that one out.) Wives are analogous to girlfriends. And so forth.

But without having to perceive a similarity in function, by seeing forms as being similar in shape, color, in movement, we can successfully relate visual images because they seem to belong together. A tree, for example, resembles a human because both are long and vertical. The sun resembles the shape of a child's face—and many flowers. When forms, colors, and movements are related by placing them in juxtaposition, we tend to accept their outward similarities, and we try to associate their inferential qualities, too. When one door to the viewer's mind has been opened, others follow more easily. (This is a principle well known and well used by advertising filmmakers, so why shouldn't you use it too?) After we have been excited—stimulated is probably a better word—by purely kinetic visual events, then we are eager to draw conclusions about the inferential, or symbolic, content of the images. And this is where the real "action" takes place: the generation of meaning. Meaning is generated like gas is when acid meets metal. It is two or more images coming together which produce a meaning separate from the innate meanings of the individual images. Something new is created, something unfamiliar. It is a form of new information, like the creation of a new element except that, unlike a new element, new information is self-perpetuating. It has a way of developing and multiplying itself.

It might be worthwhile to note that all significant new meaning and information over the period of man's time on earth has been created through the process of analogical reasoning—and that it is closely linked with inferential logic. (We are led to infer things are related through their similarities.)

Language would be at a total loss if we didn't have synonyms. But why? Language, like anything else, needs to be renewed. It needs newness for life and vitality. Treading the same old path leads to lack of engagement and stultification, to disinterest and death. And since language (among the several recording media for human expression) is a part of human life, it desperately seeks to renew itself. Film is just another medium, and another method of recording expression. It, like the verbal media, has the capacity for generating new meaning; indeed, it can develop a new and useful method of human expression. It is mistaken to suppose that film will supplant words any more than autos will replace houses. Film is a medium of expression which has its own requirements and says its own things—often in spite of us.

A DESCRIPTION OF SHOTS IN STAN BRAKHAGE'S
Prelude: Dog Star Man (16mm, Color, Silent—25 min.)

Here are some things about Brakhage's film: some impressions and interpretations. Since the film is made of images, I will talk "the way" they are presented, stressing their effect on me.

The film begins with pure, clean blue; the lights appear as if on the surface of a closed eyelid—blotchy, angling-in from the corner of the picture frame—and these redouble, creating a kind of speeding rhythm . . . then the sequence explodes rapidly into flames, burning . . . geometric planes turn, topsy-turvy, turning so that the world being created is undergoing rocking, destructive, unsettled movements . . . textures, spots, and scratches on the film jiggle downward, upward, and to the sides, while superimposed intrusions of light forms, from the sides, curving planes, like planetary surfaces, round from the top, while from the bottom, from the sides, a compositional system of planes, curving, cut, slicing the picture space into sections, scooping it out . . . the feeling of elasticity . . . then a green, agonized face, like something filmed by the light of interplanetary space—eerie, nightlike the face stretches—zooming images pop out of the screen, as if pushing for freedom, out of the confines of the projected rectangle, impatient . . . next, a green man—a small solar moon-like body in his forehead, a mark of the celestial man, as resonant as the pharaohs. Textures intervene, acting to clear the specific man, to supersede him, to preempt him . . . then obscure palpitations, heartlike, mix with glitter and dullness . . . pure colors explode, intermissions of white, blue, yellow . . . then a hole, a large orifice in which cloud-things, gliding, blending, build visual intensities. Now motions, gestures. The scene twists rubbery, bending trees elongate, are pulled cataclysmically—spots of many colors dance on the screen, and the camera jiggles as it walks—the textures sweep through, destroying certainty, like passing a hand over the eyes; shapes of unknown origin slide and slip from the rectangle—disruption—sinister shapes turn lyric colors to antagonism, and mouths are everywhere, shapes almost. The shadows of the poet's world are given life—slowly proceeding into focus, then reduced to generality. This is a film about appearances: the appearance of moods, suddenness, shapes, movement—this is a speed world—peyote without loss of consciousness—here is quickness of the brain, the lightning thought, shadowy premonitions, the fleeting hint, the clipped suggestion, then crescendo—mist and clouds ejaculate from the sun-body, the arc spews and sucks black vapors . . . then a flood of light fragments, washes the mind's eye, a catharsis . . . all things become plastic and possible.

Prelude is a film about the cosmos and man. It calls up new fears, deep, embedded in the unconscious, with the moon and the sun, the signs of Isis, mother of the earth, and her attendant forces, destructive, unrelenting, unmerciful—containing the largest magnitude of earth and human mysteries. This film is about movements—cycles of birth, death, deprivation, and fulfillment. The poet uses light as nature does, giving, taking, depriving, then overwhelming . . . from the pulsations of protoplasm to bloody birth, from frosted trees to blinding tungsten, from planet smallness to the huge unmanageable man—the movements of things getting smaller, progressions of shapes, the twisting, bending trees—the film is about Brakhage.

What I have to say is skeletal—bare of actuality—the experience of the film itself. But the impressions are real and they persist. If I can carry with me impressions from this experience—reasonably accurate impressions—then others who see this film, and films like it, can do the same thing. They can experience this poetry, a talk to the visual soul. Good poetry is always conceived with personal involvement—and it can be seen that this film was made from an *intense* personal vantage, with personal emphasis, and with compulsion, agony, and pleasure. What I am saying is that those who make films and see films must recognize that film poetry is the highest attainment in the medium. And when it is successful . . . that it can be as deeply significant as anything can be.

Carl Linder
San Francisco, 1964

CARL LINDER DESCRIBES HIS WAY OF WORKING

I should start by saying how I happened to get mixed up in film. As a youngster I was fascinated by still photography—before independent filmmaking became so big. I bought a Rollei (a used one) with paper route money, and from then on I was hooked on photography. But I always thought of it as a hobby, an enthusiasm, a way to pleasurably pass the time. I never thought about making a career of it. In college I studied writing, which was another of my loves, and for a while it looked as if I would develop as a poet-playwright. About that time (in the early 1960s), movies became a big thing as a method of personal expression. I began to see quite a few older, experimental films that were available for viewing around Berkeley, California—films that played at Studios I and II on Telegraph Ave. In a way, I guess I'm indebted to Pauline Kael, because, as I learned later, she wrote a lot of program notes for the shows there; and I think she had a lot to do with the selection of films—because it was exquisite. That was when I saw the films that made me decide to give up serious writing for a while and begin to make movies. If I hadn't seen three films I probably wouldn't be writing this today. They were: Kenneth Anger's *Fireworks*, Jean Cocteau's *Blood of a Poet*, and Louis Buñuel's and Salvador Dali's *Andalusian Dog*. All three of these were true assaults on my senses. I was such a vulnerable, receptive person at the time that I felt like "throwing off my shackles" to follow the messiah, film, to what I knew was some kind of artistic nirvana. A new world of expression had been opened to me. As I said, I felt like giving up all my possessions—giving up everything—to be able to make films like that. And, in a way I did. I gave up writing and devoted my full being to making films. Somehow, I had come to feel that the theater—and words—weren't real enough, not immediate enough, and I didn't think *true* enough for my time.

I remember thinking that the Bolex Reflex (Rex) camera was the greatest thing I'd ever seen—and I wanted one. It seemed to be able to do almost anything—and on top of that it was beautifully made. It sat in a glass case in the camera store like a fine bauble. I never was a camera equipment nut, but this instrument was compelling to me beyond imagining. Oddly enough, after owning one for a year, the honeymoon was over. In fact, one night in a fit of frustration—trying to work over a film problem—I threw one of the props I was using at the camera and it fell off the tripod (although it survived just fine). For me, technology is at once a blessing and a curse. I found that I was able to perform magic, but the pains to make it happen were excruciating. I had endless trouble with the labs. To this day I believe that labs are the bane of the film artist's existence. Other filmmakers I have known have said the same thing.

When I first started filming I tried everything. My first film efforts I don't even show today. Those were made in black and white—then I turned to color. I thought I was ready for color. Even though ten years ago I could get a 100 ft. roll of factory fresh Kodachrome (with processing) for $7.50, to me that was a lot of money. Today, you're lucky to get something comparable for $15.00! But I still thought I should go easy; and it wasn't till I had formulated plans for the film *The Devil Is Dead* that I felt ready to invest all of $500.00.

The Devil was my first excursion with color, and because I was very aware of it being in color, I tried my best to make it a color-oriented film. That idea was foremost in my mind. The next thing was to get a plan down for the film. At first, I turned to one of my old short plays called *The Devil Is Dead*; but that didn't work. I just couldn't see the film in terms of a play. However, I did get some valuable feelings from it which I transposed into the film medium in the best way I knew. Finally, I just sat down and began to make notes off the top of my head. I started by trying to circumscribe in my mind what a "female character" was, then a "male character," and I worked along those general lines. The film took the following shape: Male Image; Female Image; Gluttony; Castration; Transformation; Detonation; and Fusion. Just how I arrived at all seven categories I don't know, except that they seemed primal to me—very central to my existence. Most of my notes fell more or less into that grouping. Each category eventually came to represent a cluster of images in the edited film. During the actual filming (which took maybe four or five months), I planned some of the shots, while others came spontaneously. The castration scene, for example, was very staged. The knife was sharpened to a razor cut; and the guy who was to pose for the castration turned out to be an expert knife sharpener who sharpened the knife while I recorded it to be used later on the sound track. Even though the scene was not explicit, as we think of such things in films today, it was very well done. The knife slit through the guy's blue jeans with great ease—and the long-fingernailed hands of the girl who performed the rite moved with conviction. One time the snow fell very hard outside the window, and I began to think of the Devil's death as a snowbound event. After the snowfall, I filmed a very good likeness of a burial in the snow from a mound that had formed naturally during the night; and I made it rise (through superimpositions) as if making a grand, final ascendancy—quite opposite from the way it happens in morality plays, where Lucifer *falls* (presumably to earth).

There were times when I met people quite by chance—at a party—and after having asked them to be in the film I would be busy at home writing out notes for their segment. In one case, a certain girl I met was never used in the film; but later, my notes on her were published by Dutton in *The New American Cinema*. I had forgotten she wasn't used in the film.

After I had gotten all the footage together for *The Devil*, I started to edit. How I know when I have enough footage is another hard thing to explain. I believe that my life goes in rhythms; and when a certain rhythm is completed, then I know I must edit my film and begin anew on another project. (My creative cycles last about six months.)

When I started to edit, I broke down all the footage into two basic categories. Some images were abstract, and some were representational. I began to realize the difficulty I would have in trying to make these two divergent image types relate in a juxtaposed way. It was then I realized what my *formal problem* would be. Until I was finished editing, I was conscious of trying to make the "explicit" images go with the more "general" (abstract) images. It was a challenge which provided a lot of energy to accomplish "the impossible," or what I was beginning to sense was impossible. Yet the film doesn't come off badly today—in spite of the fact that it is too long. In later films I was more sophisticated in my use of collage. I believe they are more focused and better realized.

Detonation was my next attempt at a pure collage film. I thought for some time about what roles the images would take. Again, I made notes. Here are some excerpts.

There should be many sequences of things blown apart and broken—and sequences run backwards, so that the broken things assemble and startle the eye with recognition. But these should be rapidly paced and quite varied. A sort of piñata could be one (this image is related to Pandora's box), internally composed of many lusciously colored things, having been pulled apart and out of focus will be splendid. Then, a quick assembling of it will be a denial—and the destroyed mannequin head, its broken colored parts, when it quickly assembles, the colors will turn in and disappear, leaving a black face.

Perhaps *Detonation* is about the consciousness looking at the unlookable, the forbidden, then savoring it, remembering it, until, like a programmed computer, it can recall in the excellent detail of the moment, all, in order to reprocess it as a dependable vision, constantly and indefatigably productive. How to overcome surfeit, how to keep the consciousness from becoming bloated—this is the problem, solvable only through conditioning the mind to undertake the potent, hitherto repressed, concealed detonations of experience. The mind must learn to live with harsh pleasures.

And for the explosion we must have a demonstration . . . a nude girl flaunting herself in the midst of machinery. The most drab and cumbersome surroundings must be persuaded by the girl to see and witness her beauty. A demonstration, a forcing outward of the sex to the most inanimate of life—this bunch of bolts must be made to thrive and breathe with passion . . . she will accomplish this.

It must be remembered that SIGHT IS POSSESSION—that to see is to possess—and this is the goal of detonation.

Another idea . . . on the sound track . . . that isolated phrases be coordinated with certain actions, so that a visual action is initiated by the reception of the first, initial spoken words—as if the words precipitated, or cued, an actual event.

Color will redeem the film—comedy will make it palatable—tragedy is inevitable. Let us think of significances in that order. Color will be a delight, and effortless; comedy will be planned and calculated; and tragedy will come of its own accord. Such is the basic rhythm of this film. Heroicism in color—tragedy is emitted—and the women will provide the comedy."

As you can see, my note making is often metaphorical, metaphysical, and generalized. Yet, the notes embody my *attitude* toward the film. Although they are difficult to follow as a script, they help me to surface my feelings. In some instances, however, the written imagery does find its way into the finished film. Although this particular method of writing ideas down is not standard by any means, it is the method I have evolved for myself, even if it only provides a springboard for a film.

In *Detonation* I had perfected a sound-collage technique that worked in a complementary way to the images. It was made up of short fragments of people talking (sometimes just phrases) as well as superimposed sound effects of explosions and fragments of music. Editing sound, for me, is almost as much fun as editing a film.

Another film, *Overflow*, is acknowledged by many people to be the most successful of my collage films. In contrast, it is lyrical, and lacks the ponderous, grinding quality of *The Devil Is Dead* and *Detonation*. Even so, I must say that for myself, *Detonation* contains more surprises—it is less predictable—and for that reason I find that it retains more excitement for me, even after having viewed it many times. But this is to be expected. Dramatic, abrasive material seems to hold up better than its lyrical counterpart.

Overflow is different from my other films, too, in that I can't remember filming anything special for it. As its name implies, it was made from an overflow of footage that I had acquired over a few years—filmed images I hadn't used. In one sense, it was a film built almost wholly from the editor's point of view, similar to my other films where I had begun to develop some editing and filming concepts regarding "gesture." In *Overflow* I was very excited by gestural possibilities; and it was perhaps that single consideration which guided the construction of the footage more than anything else. The basic sound I use is a stirring piece of movie background music called *Forests of the Amazon* by Villa-Lobos. I got the music in the most accidental way. I just happened to have a tape machine jacked into the FM radio when I heard the piece begin. I knew it would be right for the film so I recorded it.

With most of my films I made a "rough edit" on an almost intuitively visual basis. Then I screened what I had against the background of sounds I had collected. I did this over and over until I had evolved a piece of edited ¼" tape that played more or less exactly the way I wanted it to be in the final version. I say, more or less, because once I took the further step of transferring the ¼" tape to sprocketed 16mm tape, I then synchronized the tape and the film exactly (as to beginning and end) in a "synchronizer." I could always manipulate some of the sound *within* the film to coordinate with certain shots or scenes. I believe that this method is the simplest, from a time and money standpoint. For the kinds of films I do, this method is quite satisfactory. Purists would frown on it, if for no other reason than that I project my original film many times, rather than having a workprint made. Sometimes I get scratches on the film original; but I find that a small price to pay (if it doesn't get too bad), especially in view of the fact that prints of films always get scratched in the first few screenings anyway (no matter how careful you have been with the original).

Another thing: I have never A & B rolled my films (see glossary) and I have never had any special effects done in the laboratory. Superimpositions, fades, dissolves, and so forth were all done in the camera with the help of my trusty Bolex.

It is true that my films are imperfect from a technical standpoint. However, only in the case of one film, *Closed Mondays*, was the technical rendering (of sound) a disturbing factor. I am not defending technical imperfection. I am only saying, make your film the best way you can, and if you have something to say, your audience will make allowances. It has worked for me, and it can work for you. I haven't made a fortune on my films; I haven't even made enough money to support my filmmaking. Yet, the films have been seen all over the world, they have been reviewed in newspapers and magazines, and—most of all—people have been affected by them.

chapter 14

Working with Pure Structure

The overall progress of this book has been from the "factual" documentary type of film to the stylized "fictional" story film to an even more extreme departure from representational life—the "expressionistic" film. Within the expressionistic mode we find a cluster of ways filmmakers have found to work with "bare materials" in order to express themselves personally in film. These filmmakers seem to be taking the corpus of filmmaking apart limb from limb, examining each of the parts as an end in itself to make their artistic statements. Going further, some filmmakers choose to explore the body of film's sensual mechanisms—its eyes, its ears, its ability to make feeling from pure movement. Such films become excursions into color, form, movement, and sound as methods of operation.

SENSUALISM WITH COLOR, FORM, AND MOVEMENT

A most accomplished filmmaker in this area is Scott Bartlett. For those who haven't seen Bartlett's films, it might help to imagine what they look like. For one thing, they aren't even close to the experience most people have had with even the most "far-out" films. The closest thing I can think of is *2001, A Space Odyssey*, with its weird color effects—especially the things that look like they are "solarized" (half negative, half positive) and registered in pure blue, red, and purple colors, and so forth. Its effect on me, at least, is of something other-worldly, mythic, very distant, yet somehow it is a (past or future?) deeply experienced part of me. Something at once paradoxical, and very true.

In Bartlett's films and in *2001*, many of the special effects are achieved in the printing of the film rather than in the filming. This is why I omitted reference to it earlier in a section on "Transformation." It *is* a method (or uses methods) of transformation, and it is indeed powerful. But it is not very readily available to the beginning filmmaker—at least, not without a degree of mechanical ingenuity and a lot of patience.

In a discussion with Bartlett on his films, he had some interesting things to say. The first film of his I saw is his widely known and appreciated *Offon*, a ten minute color film with sound in 16mm said to be a milestone in expressionistic films. Other films of his I have seen are also short 16mm color films: *Moon, Serpent,* and *Metanomen.* Bartlett often works in collaboration with other people—technicians and sound people. Nevertheless, he remains the "common denominator," the one whose sensibility emerges.

In *Offon* I should say that Bartlett managed to solve the formal problem I started wrestling with in my own film, *The Devil Is Dead* (four years before *Offon* was made). In *The Devil* I tried to mix abstract and specific images. Where Bartlett succeeded was in extrapolating from the main, literal image and generating more and more abstract images from that. An analogy to this would be like starting with a medium shot of a scene and coming closer and closer, narrowing the context until it becomes abstract. However, Bartlett does this with printing methods by breaking down the image in successive stages, alternately printing with high contrast negative and high contrast positive prints, using filters of various colors. He says he tries to stay within what he calls a "watershed image," an image that is "neither recognizable nor abstract."

". . . As soon as you film something (by virtue of placing it in the frame), you already abstract the subject one level, and if you reprint the same film over and over, you will have more information from the medium itself in terms of grain and chemical change—and less and less will remain of the original image. *Moon* in particular deals with that: reprinting, reprocessing, manipulating the image to the point where it's just on the verge of being beyond recognition.

"For *Moon*, I made two A&B rolls for the background (the skyscapes, seascapes, etc.). I had another A&B roll for the foreground, the figure, and pieces that floated in space. I took prints from the two A&B rolls and mixed them in a television studio through a closed circuit console *three times* so that the three mixes plus the two sets of A&B rolls gave me seven rolls altogether—which were all the same length—but different layers, different generations. Then, with a "timing sheet" I could skip back and forth between them, dissolving from one roll into another.

"The way I mixed the print of the first A&B rolls in the TV console was to put them in a film chain, and "key" one over the other. On one "pass" I had one roll polarized so that it was negative. Then I made three passes: one was positive, and the remaining two were negative. The keying was different in each case. (In other words, the images affected on each roll were different.)"

Bartlett's process sounds complicated—and it is. It requires help, and a lot of resources. However, the beginning filmmaker who wants to try something like this need not despair. The results won't be exactly the same as in Bartlett's films, but the effect will be similar.

For most people who want to work in this area, a good place to begin would be to try refilming *a projected image* two times. For one pass you might use high contrast negative black and white film, and for the next pass you might use high contrast positive black and white film stock. (This film is available in 16mm for titling purposes, but I doubt that it can be obtained in Super 8.) After the black and white negative and positive are made, each one should be refilmed from the projected image using color film for this pass—and perhaps a blue filter for one, and a red filter for the other. (The filters can be placed over the projector lens or the camera lens—it doesn't matter.) Now you have two color prints of the same film to work from: one blue negative and one red positive. Next, with two projectors, superimpose the blue over the red, registering the two images as closely as possible, and refilm this composite on something like Kodachrome stock. If you succeed, you will have something close to the imagery in Bartlett's films. The drawbacks using this method—obtaining the right film stock and being able to sync the two superimposed projected images—are obvious. Yet just this description by itself serves to illustrate one expressionistic way of working. As the film image is submitted to successive passes, using high contrast black and white stock, there is more and more loss of detail, and the image becomes simpler and simpler—almost cartoon-like. Each generation away from the original works toward the "watershed" point Bartlett refers to, becoming more and more abstract.

[In the instance above, as the image gets contrastier, it tends to break up—and a *different* image is building up, taking the place of the original. (Also, during each refilming process, zooms can be done and frame size can be changed, permitting the image to be changed in this way as well.)]

Refilming from a projected image is basically what happens when a film is printed in the lab. Another way to accomplish this rudimentary, but controlled, high contrast printing is to build yourself a printer made from an old projector and a 16mm camera. The details on how to do it are explained in Edward Pincus's *Guide to Filmmaking* (Signet #3992).

The sounds that accompany Bartlett's films are as adventurous and arousing as his visual imagery. His work is a true assault on the senses—and in the main, it is sensual. Like the work of other sensualist filmmakers—Jordan Belson and the Whitneys—it is a celebration of sorts. It is an enchanting lyrical event.

BOB ACOSTA DISCUSSES HIS FILM

Bob is probably one of three or four students I've had out of perhaps several thousand over the years who took it upon himself to work directly on a piece of unexposed film without going through the filming (photography process) first. I should preface Bob's discussion by saying that he is an outstanding cinematographer—from the standpoint of lighting, composition, and subject emphasis. When I first saw his work, the only thing I could constructively suggest to him was to "get more drama into it." His stuff was terribly, beautifully filmed, and very lyrical. I wanted him to explore new directions, but I hadn't anticipated he would come up with such a RADICAL DEPARTURE. And, I might add, an extremely successful departure. I'll let him tell you about it.

Making a film *without the use of a camera* opened my eyes to how much of an illusion film really is . . . how easily it can be manipulated to obtain very strange effects . . . to play havoc with your mind. When I started out I was surprised to see just how long the process (working directly on film) took. After working for perhaps an hour . . . I might have completed only three feet. It takes a lot of patience. It can get very frustrating after you've worked on something for a long time, especially when you hold up the film to your eyes and look at it and say to yourself . . . boy, that's got to look great . . . but when you project it, it just isn't anything. Yet, there are times when you make two marks and a splash of color and it looks fantastic.

I tried a lot of things . . . and toward the end of making the film I attempted to put everything in a single frame—holes, scratches color—just to see how it would look. But when I saw the footage it didn't look any better—it was imperceptible.

In many ways I felt more like a painter than a photographer, because it's so emotionally draining. You have quick changes of mood. When I get frustrated, I do less and less on the film and try to finish with that session. Then, when I have a lot of patience, creativity seems to rise, and I find myself taking a lot of time at the work. When I thought I was being creative, often I wasn't . . . not as much as when I was hurrying to get the project done.

At first, I just took a roll of film, unexposed, or some white leader, and started to work on it. When I began in film I was told: Don't touch it; don't put your fingers on it; make sure there are no scratches, no dust. You get the impression that film is made of delicate silk. But after working directly on it, I found it's really pretty tough. If you mess something up you can always go back and fix it. If something doesn't come out right, you can always eliminate it. In this sense, working directly on film did away with a lot of fear I had.

In regular photography, details are not as much in your control. Whereas when you're making your own "organic photography," as I call it, I could see that making a single mark on a frame, or even two, wasn't enough. If it were a series of colors—projected at 18 fps—it was apparent that I would have to distribute each color over at least two or three frames. I found that making a different set of colors or scratches on each frame only resulted in a big blur. Each frame, I discovered, depends on the next frame, and even on the frame after that. There really can't be too much change between frames. Even if you want to indicate "emotion"—a frantic pace— and you want things to happen all at once on the screen, you have to approach things more slowly so they will have time to develop. I found that if I changed things after, say, nine frames, giving each sequence a half-second or even two seconds, it was much better.

As I worked on the film I began to get the feeling of *moving down*. When you watch a film it appears that the image is constant and it's coming directly at you. The physical reality is that the film is moving down, and the light is capturing it. When you're making marks on the film it's all moving down. It's like a big fall—like a person tumbling and changing positions as he's falling through the air. This is the feeling I got. You're constantly moving downward from the supply reel to the take-up reel. Even when I saw it on the screen I still got that feeling. I kept thinking, as I worked, of the film moving down from the supply reel through the gate of the projector to the take-up reel; this realization affected how I scored each frame or sequence.

Even now, when I see a film, I think of it as like a flowing river with different things in it . . . a real sense of the film's linearity. If you were to stand on a bridge overlooking a river and made a "frame" with your fingers looking down . . . what you would see is what I envision happens in film. As leaves, logs, or fish go by—those are like images. Realizing that the film moves downward as you are viewing it, I found it satisfying to change the direction of the scratch marks as the various lines intersected so that in the same frame, some would be moving horizontally as others moved downward. Sometimes I scratched circles instead of lines. I found that they gave off a softer feeling and weren't so tension-cocked. On the other hand, straight lines caused more anxiety. And lines that came across at an angle were like rain—in between the other two. There seemed to be an infinite potential for doing things differently—especially when I introduced various colors—a whole different dimension.

One thing I especially liked about working in this way is the ability to see what I've done instantly—without having to wait for the film to be developed. Every hour or so after working I would view what I had done—and I experienced a renewal of excitement— the way it is when you see your film just back from the lab. That's what really kept me going. I started to play games with myself. I'd work on a foot, then look at it. Other times I would wait and let it build up, and let it flow more—up to as much as five feet—and then I'd look at it.

Another aspect I enjoy about this way of working is that it can be done any time. It gives you a feeling of independence. You're not relying on the sun to be out, on actors, on unforeseen situations that might arise—or a good idea to support the film. Not only that, but you can work on it at any time of the day or night—whenever you feel like it.

NEW DIRECTIONS—ANTISENSUALIST FILMMAKING—REDISCOVERING TIME AND MOTION

Perhaps Bob Acosta was discovering the real meaning of *time* and *motion* in terms of film for the first time, but his experience is shared by some filmmakers whose most recent primary objective is to *rediscover* these important filmic components. In fact, this "current" in film roughly parallels a direction painting and sculpture took in the late 1960s—in at least one sense. Both seem to be pursuing their mediums intellectually, coming up with what has been called "intellectual art."

In my opinion, excursions of this sort certainly have a place in the total spectrum of filmmaking expression. Film, as an intellectual pursuit, is like anything pursued intellectually. The joy in it seems to be more cerebral than emotional. It is, as I have termed it, antisensual.

Most practitioners of intellectual filmmaking are dedicated to exploring miniscule "formal problems." They endeavor to get at film structure in an analytical way. Appropriately, those who follow this direction in film have been labeled "structuralists." We can get a sampling of this group from the work of Andy Warhol, Takahiko Iimura, and Mike Snow.

In Warhol's most noted efforts—the ones which puzzled audiences, bored some, and enraged others but which emerge as unique contributions to the expressionistic film—are his lengthy "one-shot" films, *Sleep* and *Empire*. These are the ultimate in a "subject interpretive" approach. In *Sleep*, the camera is fixedly stationed (like a piece of furniture), aimed at a man sleeping for eight hours. The only movement is performed incidentally by the subject as he sleeps and shifts his position in the bed. The camera is a mute observer, omniscient and objective, performing the minimal function of recording. *Empire*, a film executed along the same lines, has the camera "watch" out a window to observe and record all the phenomena attendant in and around the Empire State Building. The sun rises and sets, birds and planes fly by, a flag is raised and lowered, and lights in the building come on and go off. It is a twenty-four hour movie documenting the most trivial visual events. It is the fulfillment of an "idea" devoid of emotion, completing the requirements of subject and camera in the most minimal way. But maybe Warhol has revealed to us a tool through his (lack of effort) efforts. Perhaps someone will come along and make "art" out of his "idea." Those who participate in this type of filmmaking are, to my way of thinking, a little like white-coated technicians, toiling dispassionately, playing with their scientific toys.

Warhol's type of filmmaking seems to inspire more humor than anything else because if it is taken at face value it is ridiculous—

ridiculing the viewer for taking the time to watch a twenty-four-hour, second-hand version of a night and day in the life of the Empire State Building.

But there are structural filmmakers who have more productive intentions than Warhol's. One, Takahiko Iimura, shows us that this way of working can be shaped into a significant statement. Here are descriptions of two of his films. *Cosmic Buddha*, filmed in 8mm, projected, and then refilmed in 16mm off a screen at different speeds, has as its subject a stone-made Buddha in a temple. The original 8mm footage has been greatly expanded through refilming in 16mm. Its main concern is rhythmic manipulation of "light tones" of the originally photographed Buddha in order to generate a cosmic feeling.

In the River is footage of a man taking a bath in a sacred river in Japan. The footage is refilmed—from an editor-viewer—a few frames at a time, shifting the same "moment in time" back and forth, overlapping the same event. As a way of controlling time and movement, the event is enormously extended. The film concerns itself structurally with prolonging the time of a minimal action.

In a conversation with Iimura, he says he works on fine details regarding time, motion, light, space, form, and so forth because it is a way of preserving the memory of an event or a moment in time. What emerges is an image that is emblematic of the total event. It is a means by which to enter another reality, he said, through a detailed examination of the image's choreography—studying its gesture, seeing it from many angles suspended in time (in terms of its changes in space and time).

My evaluation of what happens in Iimura's films is that a mystical reality emerges from exploring a subject like this in great detail—in getting into it, seeing it uncommonly, focusing on it, by being forced to observe its subtle changes. It somehow enables us to *see into it*. His way of working penetrates the surface event to show a reality beyond itself. His film holds these images for the viewer to observe *through* the event, making the event seem transparent. It is as if perception were carried by a swift current, when film images are seen in normal progression; but when the film slows and eddies around a single boulder-like image, the viewer's perception sinks to deeper levels.

Such a significant effect is certainly present in Mike Snow's *Wavelength*. This film did not have a profound effect on my life; but as a total image I don't think I'll ever forget it. Here, as in Iimura's films, the "idea" generates ambiguity—and a springboard for philosophic questions. The image itself is a form of question, the kind posed by Pirandello's play, *Henry the Fourth*. Which reality are we in at any given moment—and which one is valid?

Wavelength begins with the simplicity of a Warhol film. A camera stationed outside the door of a nearly empty room looks through it and out its windows, which front on a busy industrial New York City street. The entire forty-five-minute film involves a single excruciatingly long zoom (taking the whole forty-five minutes), zooming past the doorway toward a window, and eventually ending up on a small picture of sea-waves tacked on a wall adjacent to the windows. During this epic-long zoom, while the field of vision becomes ever more limited, the viewer is aware of exposure changes (because of the light outside), and occasionally some people come into the room to move furniture out. There are even some home-movie antics by a few of the people, which come across enigmatically. As all this is "happening" (the inexorable movement from the room's outer space to the inner space of the small picture on the wall), there is a sound of fifty cycles frequency being played which gradually, finally, escalates to a piercing, barely tolerable 12,000 cycles. Some movie.

Frankly, even though I could barely wait to get out of the theater after seeing Snow's film, it did stick with me—and its idea has mellowed in my mind. Perhaps I am richer for having seen it, and perhaps it will influence, in subtle ways, my own filmmaking: Who knows? Maybe the point that comes through here is that there is much to be gained, learned, and experienced from many types of films. To acknowledge something is not necessarily to endorse it. To acknowledge a way of working in film is to be open to what it has to offer both as inspiration for your own films and as enrichment generally.

In this section, as throughout this book, I have endeavored to open doors for you to make your film—doors which might not have been discovered in quite the same perspective as I offer here.

In closing this section on the expressionistic film, I would like to recommend some books which may serve to cover this subject in greater detail for you: an excellently thorough and well-written book, *Experimental Cinema* by David Curtis (Universe Books, N.Y.); *Expanded Cinema* by Gene Youngblood (E. P. Dutton & Co., Inc.);

The New American Cinema edited by Gregory Battcock (also Dutton); and *Movie Journal* by Jonas Mekas, himself a film experimentalist (Collier Books, N.Y.).

Often I am asked what kinds of films I go to see. I can only say that I enjoy making films more than I enjoy watching them. I was an avid movie-goer when I was a kid. In those days you could get into the "show" for ten cents, or (to help the war effort) for 100 coathangers. Even a four-inch ball of tin foil from cigarette wrappers could get you in. Later on, when I was a teenager, we used to take a crowbar to a side theater exit door—and we got in that way. You might say we were dedicated. Nowadays, I like to watch the six o'clock news, and that's about it. Once in a while a movie comes along that seems worth 100 coathangers.

appendix A

Suggested Projects

The following projects are designed to help you, the beginning filmmaker, to become quickly acquainted with some practical, basic ideas behind good creative filmmaking of *all types*. They can be viewed as exercises whereby you can concretely employ certain fundamental principles discussed throughout this book, particularly in Part One. In the classes I teach, we take one of the exercises at a time—one a week—and shoot one fifty-foot cartridge of Super 8 film on each exercise. It has been very productive for my students over the years, and I recommend the same procedure to you.

INVOLVEMENT—CAMERA INTERPRETATION AND SUBJECT INTERPRETATION

Now you want to get acquainted with your camera, see what it will do, and at the same time try to start gathering material for your film.

First, pick a *subject* in which you find some degree of involvement: a subject which "projects"—one which engages you with its beauty, ugliness, uniqueness, charm—something that makes it stand out. Think of it as like type casting, where the subject you choose is to play a role. You will, therefore, have your eye out for those things which are in a sense "perfected"—like a fashion model, an extremely animated child, a well-preserved antique car, beautiful flowers, a wizened elderly person, an extremely fat person, or people dressed in outlandish costumes. The subject you choose might be an activity like skiing or hang gliding, or a place—like the desert or an oceanside reef. Such subjects are called *subject interpretive* because they are such strong subjects in their own right that they need no fancy gyrations by the camera to bring out their interesting, telling aspects. A simple documentation of this subject is sufficient.

But some things need interpretation by the camera: things which, if filmed "straight," à la Andy Warhol, would come across as "So what?" A "So what?" subject is one which is, in and of itself, uninteresting or visually uninvolving. *Camera interpretation* is any way you can utilize the camera to draw forth the subject's possible cinematic value. (For instance, how can you dramatize a stone wall visually?) The problem often presents itself with people with whom you are close—your spouse, a friend, a favorite pet—who may lack "projectability." You are challenged, then, to *extract* an interpretation from them. This exercise is designed to tax your inventiveness with the camera. For more on this, review Chapter II, "Looking at the Subject," Part One.

SCULPTURING WITH LIGHT

The importance light plays in the creation of an image is emphasized in Part One and in Part Three. It is a tool which can be manipulated to express feeling.

There is a kind of "found light," which exists naturally by the way it falls on the subject. It exists, but often it has to be discovered—and seen.

Movement around the subject with the camera assists in finding the moment when light becomes dramatic and maximally effective. When filming, you have three components: light, the subject, and you. Any movement of one of these three components relative to the other can produce a change in the image (and in its feeling).

You can look at found light in two ways: as light we did not cause, or as light we have discovered. In the first instance, light coming from the sun, from available artificial light in a home, or from spotlights in a stadium, and so forth is a light source available for reasons other than for filming. Light we have discovered, on the other hand, is light which has no appreciable effect in creating an image until we move around a subject, or until the subject moves.

There is also "manipulated light," whose source is largely, if not entirely, artificial. It involves moving the light source in relation to the subject to produce the desired image.

When you go out to shoot your roll of film, "think light" and obliterate everything else from your mind. Give it your full attention as if, indeed, you were a sculptor. Try to be sensitive to *how* it is etching your image. Experiment, try anything that comes to mind. But above all, always experiment in relation to the picture frame area. Try to experiment while experiencing light *within the picture frame*, as opposed to judging how your scene will appear before you see it through the camera. (For more on lights and lighting refer to Chapter II, "Lighting," Part One and Chapter 11, "Lighting," Part Three.)

WORKING WITH COLOR

Once, I made a color film in which I really wanted to express *color*. So, as I went about shooting the film, I simply "thought color." I made color my first consideration (the way one "thinks light"). I *conceived* my scenes in color. Just as I did, I would like you to shoot a roll of film where your main preoccupation is color. If you are successful, anybody should be able to look at your film and see the color-consciousness in it.

In looking through the camera you should sense the color of subjects: a lady wearing a bright yellow hat, the orange light of a sunset, the redness of a geranium on a foggy day, a big patch of blue sky over a green field (or a yellow field).

The importance of color is regulated by several factors: by contrast (what a color is compared with); by intensity (how bright the color is); and by volume (the shape and amount of space the color occupies relative to the frame space).

Contrast operates in a long shot, described in exercise #6, where a lone figure wearing a brightly colored skirt may be sitting on a lawn—filmed from a far distance. Wherever you have a sameness, or drabness, of setting, a single discrete color will set off the scene.

The intensity, or brightness, of a color may well determine how arresting a scene is—how attention-getting it is. You first have to let the color "work itself" on you; as it is viewed through the camera, it should yell at you.

Finally, if color is a part of an interesting form, moves in an interesting way, or occupies an interesting spatial relationship within the frame, then our attention will be drawn to it as if the color were an *event* in itself.

WORKING WITH MOVEMENT

When you turn the camera on, you should realize that every movement by you, by the camera optics, or that your subject makes, is a part of the image. *And if there is no movement, that is also a part of the image.*

In filming, we can err on the side of either not moving, moving too much, or moving awkwardly.

Not moving indicates an intense dependency on the subject to carry the weight of the image in terms of its supposed complexity: Distant scenery—landscape, ocean, or mountains—is an example. Most of the time, as in such examples of scenery, what we are seeing is resolved much more quickly than we suppose. In other words, we receive the feeling and gesture—the information of these scenes—with great speed. In effect, they are simple rather than complex images. They are images which are difficult to move in relation to with the camera, or optically, and must be treated in terms of duration (timing) of the image, rather than of movement. Moving (panning) in relation to these subjects extends their image-life, so to speak, thus extending the image in terms of scene length.

Many still photographers tend to freeze up when it comes to moving the camera. There is a definite fear of wrecking the image, perhaps by moving in an awkward way. The solution is to move anyway, even if you do wreck the image at first. This is the only common sense solution. Try to move; experiment—and let the chips fall where they may. You don't know what you are doing wrong until you do something wrong. The name of this game is trial and error. Not moving with the camera can also be the fault of "not seeing." If you see when you move, what you see will be seen importantly, and your movement will be expressive, instead of non-existent or timid.

The same is true with moving too much. Over-movement simply indicates that the filmmaker is not seeing what he is filming. Many people who move this way are trying the "scatter-shot" method in hopes of bagging an interesting image. They aren't really seeing, they are just waving the camera around. But rapid movement *can* be expressive. However, as always, it remains for the filmmaker to see in these terms: to "see rapidly." The only way for this to come about is to move rapidly while developing an equally quick awareness of the subject.

Awkward movement can be blamed either on not seeing, or on a physical problem of some sort. The most typical kind of not-seeing movement is what I call "vacuuming with the camera," the way one would use a vacuum cleaner—using the camera to "suck up" all available images. This kind of movement is characterized by aimless up and down movements sideways, and around and around. The latter is sort of a "hula hoop" movement.

A physical problem can arise from something as simple as a bad set of nerves, or from someone bumping into you, or losing your balance. You might say, well, that's what a tripod is for, isn't it? Yes and no. Tripods present their own problems. They are often hard to move when you want to obtain new camera angles quickly; and, in contrast to the hand-held camera, they are rigid in their feeling of movement. A tripod is useful when filming with a macro-close-up lens or with a long focus part of the lens, or when filming animation. It is also useful when shooting a long duration scene (story filming or documentary) with a wide-angle lens where camera movement is not necessary.

Here are some concrete things you can do to start moving. The most fundamental camera movement is the pan—a camera gesture from side to side or up or down. But beware: Camera movements can "cancel out" if you reverse a given direction, so try to confine your movement to a single sweep in a given direction. Sometimes it helps to "dry run" the movement, so that when filming begins you will be sure of moving from a point of importance to another point of equal or greater importance.

Try moving your camera *around* your subject. If a person, walk around him, get down on the floor, then stand on a table. Change the camera perspective *while filming*. You may get a few bumpy places on the film, but you can always edit those out.

Try using your zoom. Use it while moving around the subject; and if your subject is moving, then you will have a three-way compounding of movements into quite a complex image. You will have your movement, the optical movement of the zoom, and the movement of the subject. Optical or zoom movements can be most effective when they are combined with camera and subject movements.

Movement can be most expressive when the camera interacts with a subject in motion, such as when filming a dancer. The changing position of the subject causes the camera to adjust, and in doing so, there is a kind of dance that results between the camera (you) and the subject. Filmically, this can be very effective.

Traveling, or dolly shots, such as when you are filming from a moving vehicle—a makeshift dolly like a wheel chair—or just walking with the camera, can be dramatic and visually involving.

Finally, there is the motion created by filming speeds. Slow and fast motion. The former is lyric and poetical in effect, and the latter is comical (seldom used these days).

Try these suggestions with a view toward seeing what they can do, and use them to exercise your way of seeing, in motion. (For more on movement, refer back to "Seeing within the Rectangle," Chapter II, Part One.)

FILMING CLOSE-UPS

What is a close-up? If you want a close-up of a *total* person, a head shot could be termed a close-up. But it is important to realize that this is not a close-up of the head—it is a close-up of the body. A close-up of the head would be a sectioning off of the head in such a way that we could only see the eyes (or an eye), mouth, nose, and so forth in the picture frame. The same would hold true for a close-up of a fly. If you can see the whole fly, no matter how big it is on the screen, then actually it is a medium shot.

A close-up does three basic things. The first, and most apparent, is that it creates a feeling of immediacy. It also works to create a feeling of instant involvement, for it brings the viewer into the picture.

Secondly, the close-up functions as a useful descriptive device to reveal details. How wrinkly is the old woman's face? There is a tear coming down her cheek. Or, let's see: which of the ant's legs are used for digging? Details are especially important in informational films, in documentaries, and in narratives for emotional emphasis.

Thirdly, the close-up is a valuable means of transformation. It can change a subject through lifting parts of it out of context. By doing so, as I have emphasized throughout this book, you can free the subject from unwanted associations that might hinder its use in a statement. These cumbersome associations can be a considerable problem to those who are making collage films and other expressionistic film types. (The close-up is covered more extensively in Chapter II, Part One, "Seeing within the Rectangle.")

DOING A LONG SHOT

As you have seen, much of what film is about is the *control* of the in-frame context. In the close-up, we are allowed to see but a portion—the portion most relevant to the filmmaker's intentions—whether it be an eye of a person, the thorax of a bee, or the stamen of a flower. The long shot works just in reverse. It does not select optically as much as it does through the careful choice of setting into which the subject is placed.

One type of long shot is structurally composed of a *single* subject, filmed from a long distance, where the ambient visual material is nonconflicting with the main subject. The subject is filmed far enough away that it appears smallish compared to the surroundings, but not so far away that it is impossible to tell what the subject is. The ambiance should be interesting, visually, but so generalized as to allow the key subject to stand out.

The key subject, for example, could be a single white horse in a pasture, a red kite in the sky, or a person wearing a yellow hat standing on a sea-side cliff. As you can see, having a contrasting color is very important to the key subject in a long shot. Here, where the viewer must "find the subject," some form of visual identification is necessary from such a distance.

Chiefly, this type of long shot gives us an appreciation of what the filmmaker chooses to include in the picture frame—as in the close-up—yet the nature of the two types of experiences is different. Where the close-up creates a feeling of immediacy and intimacy, the "aesthetic" type of long shot I've described is subtler, more distant in feeling, more elegant. The long shot is used frequently with success, especially in story films—and the director David Lean is a consummate practitioner of this device.

Another type of long shot—the scenic shot—is the more common descriptive panoramic view of mountains, desert, or ocean from a long distance. In both types of long shot, use a tripod.

SEEKING EXPRESSIVE CAMERA POSITIONS

One of the beginner's biggest drawbacks is his lack of flexibility with the camera and his lack of awareness of the camera's expressive potential through movement, especially through the use of *camera position*.

As a rule, we do not sit and stare at objects and enjoy the feelings they convey beyond the most general of sensations. It is probably for this reason that when the filmmaker first picks up the camera, his immediate tendency is to see *as he normally would*. And that is to take what is there visually for granted. Therefore, while filming, he uses as his point of reference (selectivity) the "meaning" of the subject, in the same general sense as when seeing without a camera. A case in point is the extreme frontality with which we see in everyday situations. To us, there is always a front and a back to everything— or to almost everything. It is an attitude that we do not verbalize, but it is one that we feel, and one that directly influences our use of the camera at the outset. It isn't a particularly good attitude to have because, for one thing, it limits the filmmaker's expressive ability. In short, it limits the way a subject can be seen (and thus expressed).

For example, the top of a table is essentially its "front," because that's the part we use, and see, most of the time; and the front of a bookcase is its open side where the books are. A person's face is his front. But, as an exercise, would you be willing to say which side of a cat is its front? Try it. Cats are well known for their many-sidedness. When they are hungry they will look directly at you with a stare. When angry, they may turn their back on you and sit conspicuously ignoring you. When playful, they may display their stomachs while lying on their backs. You see, cats, unlike humans, do not think of putting their best sides forward. They are, in my estimation, truly three-dimensional animals. Can you imagine yourself, for instance, walking into a room where someone you know is sitting, perching in a chair with your backside toward them, and starting to talk with your back facing them? It would indeed be an expressive gesture, don't you think?

Although you might find it hard to be expressive in the manner above, you *can* use the camera in this way. We don't, frequently, because it seems unnatural. But the one thing to keep in mind is that seeing through the camera is in itself a quite unnatural way of seeing.

This exercise is primarily to assist you in breaking down predisposed ideas about the way things should be seen—or can be seen. And secondly, it is to show you how a given camera angle can be expressive both of *your* attitude, and that of your subject. The angle you choose is, in and of itself, an expression through selection; and it is also an act of definition (interpreting).

What, then, should you do to try out different camera positions? Try to explore them as techniques with a person as a subject. The person should be engaged in an activity—much in the way a documentary subject is filmed. It could be your wife or mother baking a cake, a child playing with a set of blocks, your spouse fixing the car, working in the garden—or something as simple as an elderly person sitting in a rocking chair.

A good thing to remember is that you don't necessarily have to move your lights with every move you make. In fact, it is desirable if you don't. Shifting lights around is an attempt to preserve that "frontality" which I mentioned earlier. What we are after in this exercise is a different point of view, and a variation in lighting will help accomplish that aim. Many very fine surprises can occur with lighting if you can have less, rather than more, regard for describing the entirety of forms.

A systematic approach might be to try dry-running the camera while moving around your subject. Let us suppose you are filming grandma in a rocking chair on the front porch. Without turning the camera on, hold it to your eye and slowly move around her at top level, a few feet from her head, moving in a circle around her. Next, hold the camera at her head level, where you are shooting right into her face on a perfectly horizontal plane, and move in a circle around her as you did before. Now move around her in a crouching position, where you are forced to shoot upward into her face. Since it will be difficult to move fluidly, without practice, I suggest you move into different positions a few feet at a time—viewing the subject in this way.

The dry-run exercise above will help you to see the various possible expressive angles you can choose when you start to shoot. It would, of course, be additionally helpful to make written or mental notes on the better angles. It is also good to keep in mind the *developing* nature of the image as you move. Although you can obtain an interesting image from a single static view, you can also film while you move so that the image develops and grows. By the same token, you can *choreograph* movements in relation to the good camera angles you have found. You can move, for example, from the top of grandma's head to the left and down, and then shift to a sudden dramatic bottom angle view up toward her face. All this in one motion, or movement.

Angle, then, can relate to movement too, as a form of wedded interpretive devices. When the two are combined they become somewhat complexly inseparable. Such a combination always carries with it a feeling of strong intentionality on the part of the filmmaker. Therefore, it is wise to use this device as if it were one of the more powerful film tools—like a loaded gun. Well-directed, it can be very expressive; and poorly directed, it can make a loud but ineffectual noise.

Another way to loosen your visual approach to subjects, especially ones which have flat, horizontal surfaces (like tables), is to film across their surfaces from the edges. Go to the end of a table, for example, and aim the camera down the length of it, resting the lens on the table top. You will undoubtedly see light glare; but you will also see a stunning depth illusion, especially if there are objects on the table.

In a way, film is quite analogous to the way the written language functions, insofar as film, like language, is a linear medium, and it is a "formal" way of seeing. And both are "discovery" media. The act of exercising the form enables us to find new and fresh ways of seeing. In film, as in language, doing *is* seeing. But the extent to which this happens depends on the exploratory verve of the doer.

SEEING WITHIN THE RECTANGULAR FRAME AND MANIPULATING SPACE

Perhaps one of the most important, yet least utilized, aspects of cinematography is the delineation of the picture frame—the rectangle. Much of what I have stressed as important to the total milieu of the film medium has been *context*. And that context is comprised of the total milieu in which the subject exists during filming (e.g., the potter's studio), the arrangement of images in the editing process, and all that exists within the picture frame itself.

The exercises dealing with close-ups and long shots have pin-pointed the uses of image size within the frame. And the movement exercise has to do with moving subjects and moving camera—all relative to the frame's space, and *edges*. Now, concentrating only on the edges (the demarcations of the frame), I would like you to shoot a roll of film thinking about this one aspect.

The first thing to do is think of the rectangular frame that delimits your subject as a screen upon which a film is being viewed.

This minor self-delusion requires some concentration on your part. But it can be done, and it is worth doing. Become the spectator of your own film. Pretend you are sitting in an auditorium. As you move the camera, be the director, onlooking, but at the same time guiding the camera. Be the critic—sensitive to movement—sensitive to what fills the space. Above all, be critical of how the shot could be done better—adjusting the camera as the omniscient director, so that it does become better.

The rectangular frame constitutes a set of tensions. Because a line drawn anywhere tends to delimit—to prevent something from escaping or to keep something from coming across it—this limiting quality is an unavoidable psychological implication of the *line*. The motion picture frame is constituted of four lines which comprise a rectangular enclosure. For our purposes, the frame could just as well be any shape. It happens to be a rectangle. All frames constitute the same tensions with regard to their edges: what they include and what they exclude.

At this point you may be thinking that this is some kind of intellectual exercise. On the contrary, it is very concrete. It has to do with the creation and maintenance of illusion. You the filmmaker are in the business of making illusions—and the rectangle is one of your tools. It is a form of power, for it can govern the tensions of the viewer as one factor, and the many other considerations of color, form, and movement as another.

Here are a few things you might try. Let things enter and leave the rectangle—such as a ball bouncing in, then out. See what happens when a person suddenly sticks his head into the frame. Or try to film in such a way that the subject is not perpendicular with the bottom edge of the frame: Film a person standing sideways, or standing in one of the corners of the frame. Try splitting the subject with one of the frame's edges. In all of these instances, be aware of the tension caused when the subject nears any of the edges, when it enters, or when it leaves.

There are numerous things to try, not mentioned here. Try to invent a few.

WORKING WITH TIME AND MOTION

Perhaps the most singular feature of motion pictures is the linked relationship between time and motion. It doesn't exist in quite the same way in other media (except perhaps in video). It can be used to render actuality, or to create an illusion of actuality. And it can be used to create a reality of its own.

In the first instance, actual time, as an event transpiring before the camera, can be recorded more or less faithfully. We see this less and less in film nowadays, and more and more in the television media. The hours-long Pasadena Rose Bowl Parade transmission is a good example, and, of course, televised ball games. In these cases, in terms of actual time, *nothing* is left out. Nothing is shortened, nothing is lengthened. But the illusion of time and motion in, say, a mystery thriller—like a Hitchcock film—can be compressed or extended at the whim of the filmmaker, creating an illusion of actuality.

Time and motion as a reality of its own can also be accomplished by shortening or lengthening scenes. Here, there is no attempt to render time and motion in a realistic way, or to convince us that what we are watching is the "real thing" or an illusion of the real thing. Such a film would call attention to time and motion as a "material," as is demonstrated in the film by Mike Snow, *Wavelength*, where a stationary camera pointed at a wall in an empty New York City loft records the passing of cars and trucks by a window. The camera, through a powerful zoom, moves inexorably in on a picture on the opposite wall. The whole experience seems very prolonged although in fact it is much shorter than the actual time that transpired (through the use of some slow motion and editing). The total experience is one of being *suspended* in time together with a feeling of relentlessness of events.

Although manipulation of time and motion is a staple of the narrative film industry, it is a highly formularized procedure, arrived at over sixty or so years. In the story film, illusionistic time must be used with care in depicting real life representations in order not to call attention to itself, thus breaking the tenuous thread of believability and rupturing the film's informational (plot) content.

For the beginner, the use of time and motion for its own sake, as a more or less pure experience, cannot only be fun, but instructive as well. I would encourage it as a useful exercise.

To begin, you might film some continuous event, such as the sun setting, in fast motion (by double framing the scene every two or more seconds). When projected, the sun will appear to sink rapidly in the west. Or, you might try extending an activity, such as eating an apple, by continuously taking different views; and by having the person eat several apples, the action will appear to be a seemingly endless feast on a single apple.

In a collage film, time is completely ruptured, as we think of real, or actual time. But while watching (or making) a collage film we do not expect that time will be real because that form of continuity is surrendered to the unique rule systems of the film set up by the filmmaker. He makes his own time. The collage filmmaker manipulates time and motion for its structural and inferential effects. But, unlike the story and documentary filmmakers, he does so mainly for metaphorical value, and for poetic use.

An understanding of the manipulation of time and motion is essential to any filmmaker. It is another way to speak. But above all, it is a most indigenous tool to the motion picture. Master it through trial and error and experimentation, and you will have mastered the medium.

CONCENTRATING ON GESTURE

As has been pointed out, all visual images have gesture; and some of these are more forceful than others. That is, there is something about them which makes them stick in our minds and which compels our attention because of their color, shape, movement, or psychological significance.

Movement on the screen, in and of itself, is a compelling phenomenon that draws and tends to hold our attention, whether it is movement within the picture frame or movement of the camera in relation to the subject (such as panning or zooming). Movement suggests a dramatic engagement of the camera with the subject, of the subject with itself, or of the subject with its surroundings. Although movement is involving, it should be purposeful and decisive, or else we feel that it is not relevant or important. Movement that is *pointless* often turns up in what are called "home-movies," which should be avoided if a strongly intentioned film is what you are making.

Movement is probably what we think of first as illustrating gesture. If you have done the exercise on "Movement," you experimented with it; and your goal was to see what it could do as an interpretive device. Now I would like you to think of movement as a gestural consideration that generates feeling and helps to characterize the image. This exercise is about *gathering gestures* almost as if they existed in isolation from the total context. In other words, as you gather an image of movement, think of the attitude it is conveying.

Next, concentrate on making this attitude decisive by obtaining decisive gestural movements. When you pan with the camera, pan decisively. If you pan hesitantly, then you should be hesitant in a decisive way. Simply make your movements purposeful whatever they are.

You can apply the same approach to the gathering of color gestures, or shape gestures, or gestures of expressions on faces. Always keep in mind how these gestures feel, what they feel like, and what they *remind* you of.

A woman wearing a bright yellow hat reminds me of a summer day—a pleasant day—and then again it might remind me of a big amorphous lemon. At times a sunset looks as if the sky is on fire. I have a pure white cat that looks as if it is naked, but its being white makes his fur look more delicate too, and more strokable.

Some shapes are generous and some look stingy. Very fat people look as if they might be warm and pleasant, while thin people might convey feelings of impatience and of being critical. Whether or not these stereotypes are correct, or accurate, is not as important as your having a definite feeling about them. If you know *how* you are using the gestures, more than likely the viewer will accept your way of seeing them. The rule system you use is an important determining factor in viewer acceptance of film imagery. (See Part Four, "The Film as Subject.") An important point here is to recognize that what is true in a film may not be valid at all as a general truth, or as generally applied.

Gestures with psychological significance (inferential gestures) tend to be on the order of events such as violence or love; they tend to arise from any image that contains strong associational content involving heroics, passion, life, or death. For example, facial expressions tend to have this kind of associational content. (For more on gesture, please refer to Part One, "Shooting Your Film," Part Two, "Filming with Gesture," and Part Four, "Inferential Gesture."

SHOOT A ROLL OF DOCUMENTARY FOOTAGE

Everyone, at one time or another, has the inspiration to film people naturally—to extract meaning from subjects as they exist in actuality. Home-movies are an attempt at this; they are, in fact, what one might call "uninformed documentaries."

On the other hand, a reason for setting about to try to film an *informed* documentary—even if your footage consists of only one roll—is to offer you an occasion to use fundamental filmic principles which, when assimilated into your technique, can be profitably used as a basis for any type of filming. The documentary is the forerunner of all film genres. It is, in short, "what comes naturally" with the camera. Although it is a form of expression native to the camera, it is a very abused form: Many people think all you have to do is turn the camera on and let it run, aimed at the subject. This is all right if your subject is compellingly interesting. The trouble is, very few subjects are so engaging. More often than not, the "substance" of a subject has to be brought out with the camera.

The best way I've found to understand the documentary is to shoot a roll of film based around a single person. One person, as a subject, affords maximum exposure to subject movement, without the special problems that come with working with groups.

Your aim should be twofold: to reveal some of the purely informational content; and to reveal, through camera technique, something of your subject's personality that makes him distinctive. I call this an *intimate* approach to the documentary because it is a close working between you and another person. It has the advantage of minimizing logistics while maximizing content.

For instructional purposes, I have termed the how-to-do-it part of a film *informational*. It is that part of the film's content which allows us to know how shoes are made, how glass is blown, or how saws are sharpened. It lets us know the details of the subject's "activity."

But revealing something of your subject's personality gets beyond the purely informational level. Who is this person? Why is he drawn to his occupation? What makes him an individual?

The first step is to find a subject. He may be your spouse, a friend, possibly someone who provides you with a service. It may be a professional fashion model with whom you are acquainted, a woman who instructs deaf mutes, or a neighbor who takes special pride in her garden. And try to find someone who has an occupation with visual possibilities. A secretary, for example, has a limited range of activity as a subject, and so might a mailman. But as you know, a child can be a superb subject. The next thing is to show what this person is doing occupationally, as an activity, through interpretation with the camera, at the same time revealing something of the person as an individual.

When you have succeeded in shooting a roll of film like this, you might wish to pursue the film further, making a complete documentary, or you might want to use the footage in a collage film. However you use the film footage, the experience of having tried this exercise should provide dividends in many films to come.

DO A MINI-STORY FILM

Making a story film is simple if you think simply about it. A very short story film is like a vignette, or a "slice of life." It can be made with one actor, or none! The action (plot) can take place in the most ordinary familiar surroundings—a living room, or a backyard. The plot can be a simple line of action: someone preparing to go to bed, a person fishing, baking a cake, strolling down a street and looking into shop windows, or waiting for a bus.

I have seen story films where there is no actor, except for the filmmaker himself. Holding the camera in one hand, he opens the door to his apartment, and with the camera still running, he walks from one room to another, pausing for a moment for the camera to scan the room's furnishings, along with objects which may help to reveal the subject's taste and personality. Everything from turning on the TV to cooking dinner is done from the subject's point of view. It looks as if this is going to be a run-of-the-mill evening in the life of the filmmaker, when we are surprised, as he is, to discover there is a girlfriend of his taking a shower. We don't even have to show her because he discovers her underwear on his bed; and when he opens the bathroom door, steam escapes. At this point, we see his hand taking off a shoe, presumably to join his girlfriend in the shower. The last shot is the bathroom door opening again, as the camera enters through the steam. Fade out.

Putting a little story together is fun. When you edit, it's like constructing a puzzle, the pieces of which you made yourself. In a short film of this type, it is possible to exercise virtually all the narrative devices—such as subject point of view, reaction shots, cut-aways, expansion and compression of time, and so forth. Give it a try.

USE A POEM AS A SCRIPT

A script is nothing more than a guide to the making of a film. It usually contains suggestions for images, with a plot for the progression of the images. Poems can be very useful guides as makeshift scripts because they are often rich in imagery already, and because they are very suggestive of meaning.

If a poem is used, it should be thought of as *an occasion* for making your film. And it is important to realize that your film can never be exactly like the poem. The media of writing and film are distinct in themselves with their own special requirements and messages. A written poem can be used as a schematic, the film interpretation of which will be *adjacent* to the words, and will have a slightly different character, as interpretations always have. An interpretation, after all, is only *a way* of looking at something. Understanding this, you should not be too worried about being absolutely faithful to the poem, because that is impossible anyway.

Therefore, the film you are about to make from a poem will, in actuality, be *your* film, and you will be free to emphasize what you wish, taking full interpretive license. You may wish to make a visual image of every word, or to make an image of every line or stanza. How general or how specific you make your film images is up to you.

The word love, for example, may suggest a mother holding her child, a couple in embrace kissing or running together or holding hands, a woman putting food on the table, or two kittens nuzzled together sleeping. It might also be a simple image of a flower.

Finally, you may wish to have a reading of the poem to use as the film's soundtrack—or you may want to have your film stand independent of the poem, using your own idea for a soundtrack.

EXPERIMENT WITH SOUND

This exercise is about "playing around" with sound to find out how it affects the visual image, and what is possible to express with it.

Let us assume that you have finished your film and are ready to put sound with it. You may want to use music, since it is the easiest to obtain and the most effective type of sound track. Its constancy will tend to weld the images together. And, as you know, any sound, whatever it is, tells us *how to feel* about a film. I would suggest trying a wide range of recordings at first, to get the effect different sounds have on the images. You will find that baroque-classical music will have a different effect from romantic-classical, and that jazz has a different effect from rock music. In addition, within these individual classifications, each piece has its own mood apart from its general classification.

To be aware of sound qualities is the first step. Apart from music, there are sound effects—clicks, buzzes, sirens, explosions, footsteps, birdcalls, gongs, and so forth. Sound effects records can be obtained at any well-equipped record store, or you can make your own sound effects and record them. You can obtain many sound effects by taping them off your AM-FM radio (by jacking directly into the amplifier).

By slowing down the recorded sound from, say, $7\frac{1}{2}$ ips to $3\frac{3}{4}$ ips, and rerecording it, you can change it to sound like something else. For example, a cough slowed down tends to resemble a lion's roar. Bird calls slowed down take on the character of jungle apes! A cat's purr can sound like a tractor.

Once you have taped the sounds, you should try to see how they work with your film when projected. It is important to try a lot of different sounds in order to see how they can swing the meaning of an image one way or the other.

Sound editing is a simple matter and can be quite exciting in itself. This is an area every filmmaker should explore. (For specifics on sound and sound editing, see "Introduction to Sound," Part One, "Documentary Sound," Part Two, and "Some Things You Should Know about Story Film Sound," Part Three.)

TRANSFORM THE SUBJECT

Transformation results whenever a subject is seen and filmed with a point of view. It occurs both in minor and in spectacular ways. As has been pointed out, a point of view is inevitable whenever we are required to see a subject in a specific way, such as through the rectangle of a camera viewing system. Also, whenever the filmmaker controls what we are seeing optically, through subject size or manipulation of the lens focal lengths, we are experiencing a transformed subject. In short, the image of the subject is altered from the way we see the subject in actuality. The transforming process that the camera allows us calls attention to how the filmmaker sees as opposed to how everyone else sees. This is why it is so important to be aware of the camera's special potential—its range of transforming devices.

A good way for the filmmaker to build his expressive power is through some of the more spectacular ways the camera can transform a subject. Expressive power implies a strong point of view toward the subject—a particular way of seeing it. This exercise on transformation could be regarded as a point of view "sharpener."

Let us begin by changing and distorting subjects for the sake of changing them. Amuse yourself with the many possible visual "alterations" using items you might find in your kitchen cupboard. Change the shape of your subject by using the bottoms of glass tumblers or bottles, prisms, magnifying lenses, and tear drops from chandeliers. Just hold these in front of the lens while filming. You can even strap devices to the lens using black masking tape (over a skylight filter in front of the lens element).

You can change the color of your subject through the use of filters, not necessarily the fancy expensive kind you can buy at a photo store, but pieces of glass from broken bottles, or transparent colored plastics (sometimes found on children's toys). Just hold these items over the camera lens while you are filming. Whether using prisms or filters—or whatever you use—try not to let us see the *edges* of the device. After all, it is the image we are concerned with, not an awareness of the transformational gimmick you are using.

Experiment with the distortions which can occur when filming into pond reflections, plate glass windows, all sorts of chromium-plated devices such as toasters, electric irons, hubcaps, and polished surfaces such as car fenders, table tops, and so forth.

You may even wish to try combinations of these devices—such as filming a reflection through a filter. The rule is: If you can see it through the camera, you can film it. There are exceptions, of course, where there is not enough light to permit exposure. One way to overcome this is, when using filters and various glass thicknesses, to adjust the camera angle so that the light source obliquely backlights the subject, allowing for the maximum amount of reflected and transmitted light. (For a complete run-down on transformation, please see Part Four, "Methods of Transformation.")

MAKING A MONTAGE IN THE CAMERA

Making a montage in the camera is possibly one of the most fun and instructive things you can do. The way to go about it is to take a single subject, preferably a person who is engaged in a series of actions that are related. For example, your wife comes out of the house in her bathing suit, steps into the pool, swims around for a while, gets out, dries herself off, sits in a deck chair and proceeds to apply suntan lotion to her body—legs, stomach, face, shoulders, and so forth. Then she reads a book, after which she again enters the pool, swims for a while, gets out, and enters the house. Here is a series of actions with a beginning, middle, and end which can be filmed and edited in the following manner to create a montage.

First, as you know, the main reason for montage is to describe a scene interestingly, with drama and flair, and yet to create the illusion of continuity of action without having to film the action in sequence, the way it actually happens. Montage is a form of brevity, but also a form of emphasis.

A simple exercise that anyone can do is: Take the above situation with your wife at the pool and choose your opening shot in order to best describe the total situation—wife, house, pool, deck chair, and so forth. This is called an *establishing shot*. This type of shot lets us know what is happening, and where everything is. One can depart from this procedure, of course, but it might be profitable for the beginner to start simply.

After the establishing shot you can document everything else that happens—with unusual angles, close-ups, zooms, and so forth—and the viewer will be assured that everything following is relevant to the opening scene.

A handy procedure (to preserve action continuity) is to have your wife stop every time you decide to change camera position, suspending the movement of her arms, legs, and general bodily attitude, until you can get a new camera position and resume shooting. If you are careful to remind your subject-wife to maintain her posture while you search for a fresh view, then later, when you are ready to edit, you will be able to cut on matching movements. (See "Filming for Continuity and Emphasis," Part Three.)

In editing, you can put close-ups with medium distance shots, and they will match perfectly if the action matches. If, for instance, she is applying oil to her legs, you would have her stop the motion of her hand and hold it in place until you had set up the camera with another view. Then you would have her continue her movements for the next scene. When you edit the film, you will be able to cut on the precise place where the camera position changes without interrupting the flow of movement.

A more complicated procedure than the one above is not to adhere to the exact movements of the subject, but to find, instead, other subjects that will allow you to cut-away from the main action. The cut-away can be thought of as an "escape hatch" that allows you to skip around without having to follow the flow of the action in minute detail. The cut-away allows you more freedom and latitude. It could be a close-up shot of your wife's feet or her mouth, or possibly of an object floating in the pool. Whatever you use for a cut-away should be relevant to the scene, and understood by the viewer as a part of the overall context.

Now let us use montage for the purpose of giving an *impression* of the action. That is, instead of being faithful to the action as it occurs, we will use highlights of the event, allowing us to get a sense of what is happening through a few carefully selected details. In the film classic, *Citizen Kane*, days and even years are compressed into a few moments of images, suggesting the passage of time and the occurrences therein. One use for this kind of montage technique is in filming a parade or a children's birthday party—where only a few moments may be worth seeing—and where your principal aim is to preserve the sense of the event.

MAKE A COLLAGE IN THE CAMERA

After having experienced making a montage in the camera, you are ready to see what happens when you make a succession of images in the camera which are not unified by a common subject. It is a useful exercise to try to put images together which are disparate in content in order to see the possible metaphorical relationships between images, and their power to communicate in this way— rather than linearly, as is more the case in montage.

To appreciate an image for its linear content only is to know the communicative potential of only half the image. It is rather like appreciating an automobile for its use as transportation to work, and not for its use as a pleasurable experience. Collage is a means of communicating in film more for the images *in themselves,* and how they affect images around them, than for using images to promote ordinary information and conventional emotions. Collage is a poetic mode, and it is likely that an understanding of how it works will intensify your understanding (and use) of montage—the prose mode.

Collage can best be controlled at the editing bench, but many times when a beginner attempts a collage he finds that he is lacking many images which would make it better—or perhaps he does not have the command of "possibilities" in putting the images together. It isn't a bad idea, therefore, to make a collage in the camera, on one roll of film, just to "get the hang of" how collage works.

Believe me, making a collage in the camera can be hard work; but it can be fun too. It causes you to compose your film *as you shoot*—similar to the technique of making a montage in the camera. The difference here is that with collage, you don't have to consider a conventional theme as a point of reference. You can shoot anything that suits your whim. However, your experience will be more worthwhile if you should consider unifying the images you are placing in juxtaposition according to movement, shape, color, and other gestures.

Wherever you choose to shoot your collage film in the camera, it should be where there is an abundance of material for images. An excellent place is at a swap meet, or an outdoor festival, where there is likely to be an immense variety of objects and people—all in the area of a few blocks. An amusement park is another good choice. The main thing to remember is that in making a collage you don't want to feature the atmosphere of the place. It is unimportant, in this type of film, for the viewer to be aware of the nature of the occasion or event. If you feature the place where you are shooting, your film will take on a unity of "place," and therefore will become a montage. The way to avoid this is to use plenty of close-ups, filters, reflections, optical distortions, and other transformational devices. (More on the collage film can be found in Part Four, "Making a Collage Film.")

SHOOT A ROLL OF AMBIGUITY

Use of ambiguity will deepen the meaning of your film, especially if it is your aim to get as much into it as you can.

I am aware that the word ambiguity is loaded with *possible* bad connotations. There is no questioning the fact that when ambiguity works to hamper communication to the detriment of getting across clear messages when clarity is desired, then it should be avoided— as, for instance, in the case of the educational film.

An educational film is not what one would call an "expressive" film as such—although many educational filmmakers might disagree. An expressive film is one that works as freely as possible in relation to the particular *needs* of the subject. By this token, an educational film is perhaps more hamstrung by *a priori* necessities than any other type of film. Such a film must conform to a host of basic requirements even before it can be garnished with interesting forms of imagery. It is not to berate the educational film that I use it as an example. Rather, it is to show a type of film which cannot tolerate ambiguity. Therefore, if it is your wish to make such films professionally, this exercise may not be directly useful to you.

On the other hand, more creative film forms, such as the story film, documentary, and the expressionistic film, will not only bear ambiguous content, but will benefit immensely from it.

All you have to do to create an ambiguous image is to film something that looks like something else other than itself. For example, close-ups of insect appendages may resemble parts of machines in motion. The peeling of an orange may appear to be a sexually suggestive act, and the cutting of a cake can suggest aggressiveness, even violence. The potter's studio, when darkly lit, may resemble an alchemist's laboratory. An expression of crying may appear as laughing.

One way of becoming sensitive to ambiguity in daily events is to watch television with the sound turned off. Then try to imagine what the program is about, or what the attitudes of the people are. See how active your fantasies can be about what you see, if you are not told what they are *supposed* to be. The point here is that ancillary meanings exist in all things as we perceive them, but that we select the meaning which is dominant, or intended, by the communicator. Thus, a bit of demagoguery can be perceived in *any* political address, but we don't consider it important unless we should disagree with the speaker's platform or methods. The possibility for wildly different interpretations, if not for the reverse of what is intended, is inherent in all situations. Seeing these possibilities allows more creative latitude, not only to swing the communication-to-be-projected to favor your view or attitude, but to use the ambiguity to create a "controlled tension" in the viewer. Tension is constructive of mind expansion and of fantasies in the viewer; and it is most desirable to the filmmaker, who is a creator if illusions and a creator of "belief."

One of the main functions of ambiguity is to release the viewer's hold on his own attitudes and beliefs so that he will embrace yours for the time that you are presenting the film. When you present attitudinal choices to the viewer which are equally suggestive in terms of meaning and interpretation, then he suspends his belief (or disbelief) until he can get himself organized in his thoughts again. It is during the viewer's constructive period that the filmmaker has the opportunity to inflect or control the ambiguous content so that the film is maximumly effective relative to his intentions. Film is considered to be one of the more compelling and powerful media in controlling attitudes. Manipulation of ambiguity is one of the ways.

Because this is one of the more complex ideas filmmakers work with, there is no glib or easy way to explain what you might do to experiment with it. Therefore I should like to refer you to Part Four, "The Film as Subject: Ambiguity," for some more background and practical suggestions.

SHOOT AND EDIT A SHORT FILM TO ILLUSTRATE EXPANSION AND COMPRESSION OF TIME

I contend that if you do this exercise successfully, it will put your film in the Big League, and out of the beginner, amateur class. Expanding and compressing time is what most professionals use all the time—and it is what some "professionals" don't understand completely enough. It is the backbone of film rhetoric.

Take an extremely simple line of action, film it, and then edit it in two different ways. The action should be continuous, and it should have a somewhat fixed, understood time limit in terms of how long the action normally takes to be completed. Changing a tire is a good example. We know we can compress the time this activity takes or we can expand it according to the function of this scene in our film.

We can compress time by eliminating unnecessary details. A girl is stuck on the highway; her car has a flat tire. The point of the sequence is to show how adept she is at what would chauvinistically be considered a "man's activity." In this case, we tie every shot to smooth gestures—such as stopping the car, standing, looking at the flat tire and shrugging nonchalantly, opening the hood, wheeling out the spare, her hand jacking up the car, a shot of her deftly twisting off a lug, pulling the flat tire off, pushing the new one on, twisting a lug on, spinning the tire with her hand, lowering the car, a side shot from inside the car as she pulls out onto the highway again, and a close-up of her satisfied smile.

We could expand this activity in order to show her frustration and exasperation. She's late for an appointment. She looks at the flat tire, looks at her watch. She gets the car manual out, opens the hood with some difficulty, has trouble with everything—every detail is shown, every grease smudge is recorded. The whole event takes three times longer because more details are included than in the first version, together with longer duration shots. It becomes a long, drawn-out story, but it serves the filmmaker's purpose. (For more on this subject, refer to Part Three, "Filming and Editing for Continuity and Emphasis."

A FEW MORE IDEAS TO TRY

Try taking a single subject and treating it in terms of the three principal film approaches—documentary, story, expressionistic. For instance, a person building a boat can occasion an intimate documentary showing the man's dedication and determination as he works. A good story film could also be extracted from this action because there is a romantic component here—the fulfillment of a life-long ambition. There is the possibility for conflict—in anything that might thwart his ambition. Will he succeed? Where is the fly in the ointment? And, as an expressionistic film, you could play around with filters and distorting devices such as prisms, and so forth; or a time and motion study could be done à la Mike Snow. (See Part Four, "New Directions—Antisensualist Filmmaking—Rediscovering Time and Motion.")

Try using various sorts of continuity devices: a repetitive subject that threads the action, a common action or activity (people running, eating, smiling, and so forth), a common setting (the park, a carnival, the beach), a common visual feature (a dominant color, a dominant form, a dominant rhythm).

Do a *single subject film* on, say, flowers, sports, faces, or a close-up exploration of the nude body—anything that is tied together by a single subject.

Try to change the rectangular picture frame by shooting through something like a large sewer pipe or a chink in a wall. In other words, try framing the subject in an unusual way, thus obliterating the frame as we normally think of it.

Try to set up your action, if you are making a story film or documentary, so that there are related things happening, either in front of or in back of the main action. Set up *levels of the action*. (See Part One, "Seeing within the Rectangle.")

appendix B

Suggested Reading

USEFUL ARTICLES FROM THE *FILMMAKERS NEWSLETTER*

The *Filmmakers Newsletter* is a magazine I founded in 1967 (and edited for the first few issues). Over the years of its phenomenally successful development—after I left the publication—it has retained most of the original format and purpose. I myself subscribe to it, and I have every issue to date. Therefore I thought it appropriate to share a knowledge of some of the useful articles that have appeared since the magazine's inception.

Below is a list of articles that bear, more or less, on the material in this book, and that will provide you with relevant supplemental reading. The *Newsletter* can be obtained from many large libraries, and especially from school libraries with film programs.

Additional information and subscriptions can be obtained by writing to the

Subscription Department
Filmmakers Newsletter
P.O. Box 115
Ward Hill, Massachusetts 01830

or to the

Editorial Office
Filmmakers Newsletter

41 Union Square West
New York, New York 10003

Animation

"Interesting Animation Techniques," Vol. 2, No. 11, p. 4.
"Building an Animation Stand, Part I," Vol. 5, No. 2, p. 39.
"Building an Animation Stand, Part II," Vol. 5, No. 3, p. 39.
"Building an Animation Stand, Part III," Vol. 5, No. 4, p. 36.
"Animation Kit" (a continuing series of articles), Vol. 5, No. 5 to the present. All about animation.
"Animation Cycles," Vol. 5, No. 4, p. 46.
"Abstract Animation," Vol. 5, No. 9/10, p. 46.
"Oxberry," Vol. 5, No. 12, p. 24. On the Oxberry Printer.

Documentary Filming

"Making a Personal Documentary," Vol. 4, No. 9/10, p. 53.
"Gimme Shelter," Vol. 5, No. 2, p. 20 & p. 29.
"Filming in China," Vol. 5, No. 6, p. 27.
"What Is the Documentary Film?" Vol. 6, No. 6, p. 25.

Editing

"Multi-card Editing," Vol. 2, No. 4, p. 22.
"A&B Roll Editing," Vol. 2, No. 6, p. 19.
"Mixing B&W Film with Color," Vol. 2, No. 9/10, p. 19.
"How to Make Good Splices with a Maer-Hancock Splicer," Vol. 3, No. 1, p. 24.
"So You Think You Know How To Splice, Part I," Vol. 3, No. 1, p. 24.
"The Art of Splicing, Part II," Vol. 3, No. 7, p. 26.
"Making Trim-bins and Other Things," Vol. 3, No. 4, p. 16.
"Edge Numbering," Vol. 4, No. 9/10, p. 42.
"Cutting Scene 277," Vol. 5, No. 3, p. 44.
"Cutting News Film," Vol. 5, No. 12, p. 45.
"Quick Negative Cutting," Vol. 6, No. 12, p. 60.

Film Economics

"Making $$$ in Filmmaking" (a continuing series of articles), Vol. 4, No. 8 to the present.
"16mm Film Budgeting: Art or Survival?" Vol. 4, No. 11, p. 32.
"A Rap Session on the Distribution Game," Vol. 5, No. 12, p. 8.
"Buying a Used Camera," Vol. 6, No. 5, p. 55.
"Checking a Used Camera," Vol. 8, No. 3, p. 61.

Filming Technique

"Close-ups and Macrocinematography with Non-reflex Cameras," Vol. 3, No. 2, p. 8.
"Time-lapse Cinematography," Vol. 3, No. 4, p. 26.
"More about Time-lapse Cinematography," Vol. 3, No. 6, p. 44.
"Advice on Panning," Vol. 3, No. 12, p. 51.
"Deep Focus Cinematography," Vol. 4, No. 7, p. 19.
"Filming in Different Weather Conditions," Vol. 4, No. 8, p. 40.
"Filming at Night," Vol. 5, No. 6, p. 45.
"The Use and Abuse of the Zoom Lens," Vol. 5, No. 12, p. 20.
"Lens Gimmicks for Special Optical Effects," Vol. 6, No. 2, p. 42.
"Depth of Field," Vol. 6, No. 2, p. 55.
"Depth of Field," Vol. 6, No. 3, p. 33.
"Depth of Field," Vol. 6, No. 4, p. 51.
"A Discussion with James Wong Howe," Vol. 6, No. 4, p. 20.
"Sight and Sound: Counterpoint or Entity?" Vol. 6, No. 7, p. 27.
"Life on a Thread," Vol. 6, No. 8, p. 33. Filming a spider building his web.
"Production Continuity," Vol. 7, No. 3, p. 53.
"Shooting Day-For-Night," Vol. 7, No. 4, p. 62.
"Do-it-yourself Special Effects," Vol. 8, No. 4, p. 59.

Lighting

"Electricity and the Filmmaker," Vol. 3, No. 5, p. 8.
"A Natural Look at Artificial Light," Vol. 4, No. 5, p. 36.

"Basic Electricity for Filmmakers Part I," Vol. 6, No. 2, p. 51.
"Basic Electricity for Filmmakers Part II," Vol. 6, No. 3, p. 53.

Sound

"Mechanics of Sound Sync," Vol. 2, No. 4, p. 1.
"Use of Sound Effects," Vol. 2, No. 12, p. 28.
"Types of Sounds to Go with the Image," Vol. 3, No. 7, p. 16.
"A New Approach to Film Sound," Vol. 3, No. 12, p. 4.
"Basic Elements of Sound Recording," Vol. 3, No. 12, p. 36.
"The Acoustics of Recording," Vol. 3, No. 12, p. 52.
"Choosing the Proper Microphone for Film Sound," Vol. 4, No. 2,
    p. 40.
"Optasound," Vol. 4, No. 3, p. 38.
"Microphones and Sound Characteristics," Vol. 4, No. 7, p. 36.
"Recording a Narration Track," Vol. 4, No. 12, p. 48.
"Sound Graphics," Vol. 5, No. 2, p. 45.
"Film Sound Recording," Vol. 5, No. 7, p. 50.
"One Person Sync-Sound; A New Approach to Cinéma Verité,"
    Vol. 6, No. 2, p. 24.
"The Art of Dubbing," Vol. 6, No. 6, p. 56.

Story Filming

"The Sweet Love Bitter Affair," Vol. 5, No. 5, p. 28. Some problems
    in making this story film.
"Filming Andy Warhol's *TRASH*," Vol. 5, No. 8, p. 24.
"Stacy Keach: Acting for Films," Vol. 6, No. 8, p. 28.

Super 8 and Super 16

"Superserious 8" (a continuing series of articles), Vol. 5, No. 6 to
    the present.
"Preparation for Lab Duplication," Vol. 6, No. 1, p. 53.
"The Emergence of Super 16," Vol. 5, No. 11, p. 24.
"The Emergence of Super 16, Part II," Vol. 6, No. 3, p. 24.
"A Super 16 Production Experience," Vol. 5, No. 11, p. 30.

"Super 16 Production," Vol. 6, No. 3, p. 28.

Videotape

"Videotape versus Film," Vol. 5, No. 6, p. 40.
"Videotape Technology and Film," Vol. 5, No. 7, p. 44.
"Electronic Cincmatography," Vol. 6, No. 6, p. 42.

Miscellaneous

"Equipping a Gadget Bag," Vol. 2, No. 1, p. 7.
"Develop Your Own," Vol. 2, No. 5, p. 20. Developing your own film.
"Physics and Film," Vol. 2, No. 8, p. 1.
"Solarization," Vol. 3, No. 11, p. 18.
"Overcoming Parallax Problems with Non-reflex Cameras," Vol. 3, No. 12, p. 24.
"Making High-contrast Negatives for Titles," Vol. 3, No. 12, p. 26.
"There are Film Festivals and There are Film Festivals," Vol. 4, No. 8, p. 19.
"Film Festivals from the Other Side," Vol. 6, No. 6, p. 59.
"More Applications of High-contrast Negatives in Making Titles," Vol. 4, No. 8, p. 38.
"Incorporating Color Transparencies in a Film," Vol. 4, No. 11, p. 41.
"Equipment & Services Directory for Independent Filmmakers," Vol. 4, No. 9/10, p. 34.
"Special Filmmakers' Services," Vol. 6, No. 4, p. 30.
"4th Equipment and Services Directory," Vol. 7, No. 9/10, p. 48.
"Unmasking the Matte," Vol. 5, No. 3, p. 42.
"Color Conversion Filters," Vol. 5, No. 4, p. 41.
"Exposure Meters," Vol. 5, No. 5, p. 43.
"Exposure Meters, Part II," Vol. 6, No. 4, p. 45.
"Showing Your Films in Europe: A Journal of a Traveling Filmmaker," Vol. 5, No. 9/10, p. 31.
"Using Your Camera as a Contact Printer," Vol. 5, No. 12, p. 16.

"Beware of Underground Film Festivals Bearing Entry Blanks with Small Type," Vol. 4, No. 8, p. 22.

"A Look at Lenses," Vol. 6, No. 8, p. 47.

"The Art of Make-up—*The Exorcist*," Vol. 7, No. 6, p. 18.

SELECTED BOOK LIST

The New American Cinema by Gregory Battcock (Dutton). An anthology of writings by experimental filmmakers and observers of the film scene vis-à-vis the film-as-art, independent, and underground film. This book enjoys much popularity for its rich diversity of content, ideas, and objectivity. Inspires adventurous thinking.

Elements of Film by Lee R. Bobker (Harcourt, Brace & World, Inc.). Pretty thoroughly covers all aspects of story film production, with a liberal sprinkling of aesthetics. Widely used by the student-professional.

Experimental Cinema by David Curtis (Universe Books). A chronological history, as well as being organized according to "schools" of the experimental film. Is more interesting and more accurate than the Renan book below.

Young Filmmakers by Rodger Larson (Avon Books). Interestingly written. But half of the material is overgeneralized, or not relevant to the beginning filmmaker. I picked this book because of its simplicity of presentation, and for its useful illustrations of various types of films.

Independent Filmmaking by Lenny Lipton (Straight Arrow). Everything you wanted to know, and some things you didn't want to know, about filmmaking. Completely technical, minus aesthetics.

Cinematography by Kris Malkiewicz (Van Nostrand-Reinhold). A comprehensive film production guide, especially good on lighting.

The Five C's of Cinematography by Joseph V. Mascelli (Cine/Grafic Publications, Hollywood). A very detailed, practical book covering camera angles, cutting, composition, close-ups, and continuity. An excellent book on the above subjects.

Guide to Filmmaking by Edward Pincus (Signet). A clear, simple and useful film production handbook for Super 8 and 16mm. It is the book I have been using in my classes.

An Introduction to the American Underground Film by Sheldon Renan (Dutton). A chronological history of the American experimental film. Informative, but hastily written and incomplete.

A Primer for Filmmaking by Kenneth H. Roberts and Win Sharples, Jr. (The Bobbs-Merrill Co., Inc.). Geared to the would-be professional filmmaker, this is one of the best all-round books of its type.

Creative Filmmaking by Kirk Smallman (Bantam Books). Interestingly written, and a good film production guide, especially for the "advanced" beginner.

Expanded Cinema by Gene Youngblood (Dutton). Could be considered a sequel, or update, to David Curtis' *Experimental Cinema*. It discusses many of the creative things that can be done with both film and video.

A & B ROLLS Used in professional work to avoid splice flashes and to facilitate fades, dissolves, wipes, and other effects when the original is printed. The original is "broken down" into two separate rolls by the editor, where each scene is staggered (and slightly overlapped) with black leader in checkerboard fashion. A scene on the "A" roll is opposite black leader on the "B" roll and vice versa. (There can be A, B, C, D, and E rolls, depending upon how much specialized work needs to be done.)

ACTIVE GESTURE A movement by the subject, or by the camera, which has a clear beginning and end.

ANGLE OF VIEW The amount of a scene that is "taken in" by the lens, usually expressed in degrees.

ANIMATION Giving the appearance of movement to either drawings or magazine cut-outs by filming them a couple of frames at a time in various positions. Inanimate objects can also be animated in this way.

ANSWER PRINT Sometimes called a trial print; it is a print to see if the lab work requested was accomplished (and is satisfactory) before a "release print" is ordered.

ANTITHETICAL SOUND Sound that, instead of reinforcing the image, plays off against it.

APERTURE The iris diaphragm opening that permits the passage of more or less light through the lens.

ASA RATING A film stock's degree of sensitivity to light as designated by the American Standards Association.

BACK LIGHT A light coming from in back of the subject toward the camera lens, sometimes causing the subject to be silhouetted.

BALANCED LIGHT A light source which has been corrected for either the color red or blue. Sometimes the correction is "built in" to a bulb, and sometimes it is accomplished by placing a filter gel over the light source.

BLOCKING Preplanned movements of actors, often "chalked off" on the floor, to keep the performers within range of the camera lens.

CAMERA GESTURE Any movement of the camera, whether a pan, dolly, or zoom shot, which has a definite configurative movement—a clear beginning and end.

CAMERA INTERPRETIVE Where the camera acts as interpreter by moving selectively in relation to the subject, or else by assuming selective, descriptive positions relative to the subject. Also, any camera "manipulation" relative to the subject causing it to be interesting.

CAMERA MOTOR SPEED The speed at which the camera motor runs, which directly affects the filming speed (frames per second).

CAMERA POINT OF VIEW How the camera sees the subject.

CAMERA POSITION Wherever the camera is placed relative to the subject.

CATCH LIGHT A light placed in such a way that it reflects in the eyes of the subject, providing a "gleam."

CINEMATIC PRESENCE This is created when cinematic devices are used—such as camera or subject movement, subject size (close-ups and long shots), and manipulation of the picture frame. A condition as differentiated from "theatrical presence."

COLLAGE A term used in painting after the turn of the century to denote a school of art which combined a variety of disparate materials pasted on a surface. The materials consisted of cut-outs from old medical and phrenology journals, as well as pieces of newspaper and fabrics.

COLOR TEMPERATURE A man by the name of Kelvin discovered that as a black metal bar was heated it first turned red, then as it got hotter, it turned blue. Hence the concept of color temperature. Blue light is "hotter" than red light, and this contrast is expressed in Kelvin degrees.

COMPOSITE PRINT When two or more rolls of film, and/or a sound track, are combined on a single roll. More commonly thought of as the "sound" and "picture" wedded on a single print to make a "release print" to be distributed to the public.

COMPRESSION OF TIME Whenever actual time is shortened, becoming "screen time"; and when a filmed event is shortened to eliminate unnecessary details of an action.

CONTINUITY A common thread which holds a film together. Subject, theme, plot, film technique, and sound are some forms of continuity.

CONTRAST GLASS A monocle-like device used by directors to get a true sense of the contrast between light and shadow on a movie set as it will appear in the filmed image.

CROSS SCREEN Any movement from left to right, or vice versa, across the motion picture frame.

CUT-AWAY Any shot used, while editing a film, as an insert which departs from the main line of action, and which allows for the editorial freedom needed to expand or compress actual time into "screen time."

CUTTING ON THE ACTION Cutting on a shot as the action begins, and again as the action ends.

DAILIES These are "work prints" of the film shot during a single day. They help the director see the immediate results of the day's shooting, and they are also used to edit the film instead of using the original negative.

DEEP FOCUS When depth of field extends for an unusually long distance.

DENOTATIONAL UNIT When a given activity is broken into segments called gestures. Each gesture can be considered a denotational unit, in that one movement gives rise to another.

DEPTH OF FIELD The amount of the picture image in acceptable sharp focus, both in front of and in back of the subject focused on.

DEPTH OF FOCUS The area of the picture image in *critical* sharp focus rather than merely in *acceptable* sharp focus.

DIOPTER A close-up lens placed on the front of a regular lens to permit filming closer to the subject.

DISJOINTED NARRATIVE A story film where the line of action is nonsequential.

DOLLY SHOT A shot accomplished while the camera is moving as opposed to a "pivotal" pan shot where the camera remains stationary.

EDITOR-VIEWER A device used, in editing, to view the film, enabling the editor to select the exact frame on which to cut a scene.

EPISODIC A type of story film where the main action takes place in a series of locations as opposed to a single location. Often one person's adventures or experiences.

EXPANSION OF TIME When the actual time an activity takes is expanded to a longer "screen time" in order to create mystery or suspense. This is done by filming the same event with multiple cameras or by using cut-aways in order to provide the necessary film to extend the action.

EXTRAPOLATION OF FORM Where similar forms are used in a film—and they gradually become more and more different—eventually departing from the original shape. Frequently used in abstract and animation films.

EXTRAPOLATION OF THEME Where the central theme is altered, deepened, and transformed by other, related themes.

F/STOP A numerical designation (such as f/5.6) which indicates the size of the aperture opening.

FADE IN The gradual brightening of an image from pure black.

FADE OUT The opposite of fade in—where the image gradually goes black.

FAST MOTION Created when film is shot at any speed less than the speed at which it is to be projected. The motion becomes speeded up, Chaplinesque style.

FILL LIGHT The light which is used to fill in shadow areas of a subject, allowing for detail to be seen in those areas.

FILM DENSITY   Has to do with how "dark" the film image is, allowing more or less light to pass through it when projected.

FILM EMULSION SPEED   The degree to which a given film stock is sensitive to light, expressed in terms of the ASA rating.

FILM ORIGINAL   The film that is shot in the camera, as opposed to a print of that film. Sometimes referred to as the "negative."

FILTER GEL   A filter made of gelatin or clear colored plastic, for the purpose of changing the color temperature of the light source.

FIRST TRIAL PRINT   Sometimes called the first "answer print," where "timing" and color changes are viewed for the first time in a print back from the lab.

FIXED FOCAL LENGTH LENS   A fixed lens of a specific focal length that can only be changed by switching to another lens, unlike a zoom lens that itself is variable in focal length.

FOCAL LENGTH   Expressed in millimeters, it indicates whether a zoom lens position is wide-angle, normal, or telephoto. Any position less than 13mm for Super 8 is wide-angle, and any position more than 13mm becomes telephoto.

FOOTCANDLES   Units of measurement used to gauge the intensity of light. Most light meters measure the light in footcandles.

FRAMING THE SUBJECT   Anything appearing in the foreground of a scene used to "set off" a subject—such as tree branches.

GESTURE   A dominant color, form, or movement of an image (or scene) that provides the editor with a basis on which to cut. In this sense *sound* is also a gestural factor.

GRAIN   The sandy-like particles in a projected film image that are larger and more noticeable in "fast" films with a high ASA rating.

HARD LIGHT   A very intense, focused light, like the sun's, that creates sharp, harsh shadows. The opposite of "soft light."

HIGH KEY LIGHTING   An overall bright illumination of a scene.

HORIZONTAL PAN   A pivotal sideways movement of the camera.

IMAGE   The results of a subject rendered on film, not always a likeness of the subject. Also, any visual event, in terms of color, form, or movement registered on film, that can be used for expressive purposes.

INCIDENT LIGHT   The amount of light *falling* on the subject, as opposed to light reflected from it.

INFERENTIAL GESTURE   The "meaning" a film subject projects. Ideas which are associated with a subject.

INTERCUTTING   Placing a shot, or scene, between two other shots or scenes.

INTERNAL MONOLOGUE   A voice heard "over" a scene reflecting what a subject is thinking.

INTERNEGATIVE   A negative made of the picture original—often a composite of A & B rolls—from which "release prints" are struck.

INTERVALOMETER   A device used in time lapse photography, allowing the camera to film over long periods of time unattended. It automatically triggers the single-framer at predetermined intervals.

INTIMATE DOCUMENTARY   An in-depth film portrait of a single individual.

JUMP CUT   Occurs in an edited film where a "piece" is missing from a line of continuous action, causing the subjects to "jump." Most often seen where movies have been badly edited for TV. Usually, a jump cut can be avoided by inserting a cut-away, which diverts the viewer's attention away from abrupt changes in subject position.

JUXTAPOSITION   Two shots which are joined together are considered to be juxtaposed.

KEY LIGHT   The main source of illumination while filming.

KICKER LIGHT   Sometimes called a "hair light," it is a small intense spotlight, often coming from behind or from the side of a subject, aimed at the hair in order to give zesty highlights.

LAP DISSOLVE   A transitional device between scenes which can be performed in many Super 8 cameras. It is a double exposure, where as one scene fades out, another simultaneously fades in. The out-going scene dissolves away, while the in-coming scene dissolves into existence.

LENS SPEED   The "faster" a lens, the more light it admits to the film. Lens speed is designated by any given camera's smallest f/stop. F/1.2 is considered a fast lens for Super 8 cameras.

LEVELS OF FILMIC REALITY   The several changes a filmed subject undergoes from the time the camera rolls until the time the film is projected, the point being that some transformational changes in the subject are inevitable.

LEVELS OF THE ACTION   This is experienced when, in the same film frame, different activities are going on simultaneously at various distances from the camera. Used almost exclusively in story films to counterpoint a scene's main subject.

LIGHTING RATIO   Basically, the difference between the lighting intensity of the key light compared to the fill light.

LINEAR DISTORTION   This occurs when straight lines—horizontal or vertical—are filmed with lenses of *extreme* focal lengths. These lenses cause lines to bend. An extreme wide-angle lens can turn a flat ceiling into a dome, and an extreme telephoto lens can turn a domed ceiling into a flat one.

LIP SYNC   Where the voice on the sound track is synchronized with the subject's lip movements.

LOW KEY LIGHTING   Where the subjects in a scene are lit selectively, so that some portions of a room are more brightly illuminated than others and where some portions of the subjects, usually the head and shoulders, receive the most light.

MANUAL OVERRIDE Allows the filmmaker to bypass the automatic controls of the exposure meter or the zoom, and to operate them according to his judgment.

MASTER SHOT A shot of the overall view of a given scene—sometimes called an "establishing shot" because it establishes all the important scene components in the viewer's mind.

MATCHING THE ACTION Where different angles of the same scene are joined in a way that will avoid interrupting the flow of action.

MIXING The term is applied, usually to sound mixing, where different parts of a sound track are brought together on a single sound roll. At the outset, there are separate rolls for each type of sound. There may be a "presence track," a "dialogue track," a "music track," and a "sound effects track," which are then combined on one roll.

MONTAGE Where shots are related as to subject, theme, location, or time, or where they are juxtaposed for story telling purposes, or to create an impression. There are other uses for montage, but in the main, it is a basic editing "strategy" in all story films.

MOVIEOLA A large, cumbersome, and sometimes awkward motor-driven machine used in editing—where a separate roll of sound and one of picture (the work print) can be played in sync. Used for viewing, cutting, and synching sound pictures.

NATURAL LIGHT Usually comes from the sun, as opposed to "artificial light," which is generated by man-made bulbs.

NATURAL LIGHTING Light which exists under normal circumstances—whether from the sun or electrically generated—that the filmmaker hasn't contrived intentionally. Under this category would come car headlights, house lamps, candlelight, street lights, and stadium lighting.

NORMAL LENS A lens which most closely approximates the way we would normally see. For the Super 8 camera it is 13mm in focal length.

OMNIDIRECTIONAL MIKE A microphone that is sensitive to sounds in a full circumference around it, as opposed to a unidirectional mike that is sensitive mainly to sounds coming from one direction.

OPTICAL EFFECTS Effects created by the lens of a camera, or by an optical printer.

OUT-OF-FOCUS DISSOLVE A way of making the subject blur into oblivion by turning the distance setting quickly while filming. For best results, the lens aperture should be as wide open as possible, and the longest focal length lens should be used, giving extremely shallow focus.

OVERLAPPING THE ACTION This is done as a natural concomitant to "matching the action." As the camera assumes a different angle, the subject is requested to go through the "tail end" of the last section again, thus providing an overlap with the preceding shot and giving the editor a way of matching the action of the different camera angles when they are joined.

PAN Any pivotal movement of the camera—up, down, or sideways.

PARALLEL CUTTING Involves the intercutting of two or more actions which are understood to be happening at the same time.

PASSIVE GESTURE Either a shot of a subject not in motion, or of a subject moving so rapidly (and rhythmically) that its movements are neither easily distinguishable nor important as individual movements.

PIXILATION A moving subject filmed while single framing. The effect is highly speeded up, spastic, and comical.

PLANE OF CRITICAL FOCUS The sharpest area of a picture in terms of focus.

POST PRODUCTION All the details attended to after the film has been shot and developed. Editing, titling, mixing, and so forth are all facets of post production.

PROCESS OF MUTUAL INFORMATION During filming, the filmmaker's selective response to the subject, and his altering that response according to what he *learns* from the subject. A kind of "feedback."

QUARTZ HALOGEN A type of lamp used in lighting that is intensely bright for its size, and unlike many other types of bulbs, does not change color balance as it nears the end of its life.

QUICK CUT A very short piece of film (of a shot or a scene) only a few frames long—anywhere from three to ten frames in length—depending, of course, on the projection speed. (Don't forget that, at 18 frames per second, nine frames equals ½ second, which is still a long time in film terms.)

RAW STOCK Film stock that has not been exposed.

REACTION SHOT A shot of a subject's reaction to what is going on in a scene.

REFLECTED LIGHT Light *bouncing off* a subject, as opposed to incident light *falling on* a subject.

REINFORCING SOUND Sound which goes with the image, such as romantic music with love scenes.

RELEASE PRINT The final, perfected print of a film which is ready to show to audiences.

RESOLUTION The ability of film and/or camera optics to reproduce sharp lines in a film image.

REVERSE SHOT Accomplished by reversing the camera position in relation to a previous shot of a subject.

RIM LIGHT Usually a small spotlight placed in back of a subject causing it to be slightly "haloed" or rimmed in light.

ROLE SYSTEM The roles assigned to performers (if a story film), or to images (if an expressionistic film).

ROTARY SHUTTER A shutter in many motion picture cameras that is a disc with a pie-shaped hole cut out of it (to admit light) that spins in a rotary fashion.

RULE SYSTEM In a story film it would be the plot; but in an expressionistic film it would be the pattern of recurring images, or the rhythm of the cutting.

RUNNING FILM   A film having an episodic structure where the hero (of a story film) "runs" from one predicament or adventure to another.

SCREEN TIME   The illusion of time being "normal" even though, filmically, an event may have been stretched or shortened to suit the purposes of the filmmaker.

SCRIM   A gauze-like material—nylon, cheesecloth, window screening—held in front of a light source in order to diffuse light.

SHALLOW FOCUS   The opposite of deep focus, where depth of field is minimal.

SHOOTING RATIO   The ratio of film used in the editing to the amount of film shot.

SHUTTER SPEED   The amount of light "chopped off" by the rotary shutter. This is determined by how fast the shutter is spinning, which in turn is determined by the camera's frames per second. (The exception to this is when a "variable shutter" is used—with which only a handful of cameras are equipped.)

SITUATION FILM   Takes place in a single setting or situation, as opposed to a "running film."

SLOW MOTION   Whenever a film is shot at a greater frames per second rate than the rate at which it is to be projected, it slows down the motion.

SOCIAL DOCUMENTARY   A journalistic film of a group of people who share in common some aspects of their background as well as common goals.

SOFT LIGHT   Usually, diffused light that does not cast harsh, sharp shadows—in contrast to sunlight.

STORY FILM   A film based upon a fictional story.

STRUCTURAL GESTURE   The *general feeling* conveyed by such pictorial structural elements as color, form, and motion. The dominance of these elements as opposed to the dominance of "ideas" associated with "inferential gesture."

SUBJECT   A person or thing at which the camera is aimed.

SUBJECT GESTURE   Where a subject performs the gesture, as differentiated from gestures performed by the camera.

SUBJECT INTERPRETIVE   Where a subject is characterized by such compelling aspects—through appearance or actions—as to "project" them in a way that simple documentation of them with the camera is sufficient.

SUBJECT POINT OF VIEW   A filmed view which allows us to see what the subject is seeing—sometimes called "subjective camera," or "subject view."

SUPERIMPOSITION   Otherwise known as double exposure. This is where one image is laid over another (by winding back the camera and refilming). Can be performed in some cameras, or in the printing process.

SURREALISM   Where the juxtaposition of people, things, or events *within the picture frame* is out of place with the general setting or mood.

SYNC   Where the picture image coincides intentionally with a given sound.

SYNCHRONIZER   A device with sprocketed wheels that are interlocked, together with a footage and frame counter, that enables the editor to sync sound with picture, or to align two or more reels of film, as in A & B rolling.

(A) TAKE   One or more filmed versions of the same scene.

TAPE SPLICE   Where two ends of film are joined—butt-end to butt-end —by a piece of mylar tape.

TELEPHOTO LENS   The long focus position of a zoom lens.

THEATRICAL PRESENCE   Characterized by three dimensional "happenings," such as stage plays, street corner scenes, dinner with the family, or classroom presentations. Anytime when people either seem to be "on stage" or "performing" for other people, there is a high degree of theatrical presence.

TIME LAPSE PHOTOGRAPHY   Through the use of single framing at predetermined intervals, events which take days, weeks, or months to transpire can be compressed into seconds or minutes of screen time. The growth of plants, or the opening of flowers, are classic examples.

TUNGSTEN LIGHT   Most light bulbs. These have tungsten filaments which glow, causing the bulb to emit light.

UNIDIRECTIONAL MIKE   A microphone sensitive largely to sound coming from the direction at which it is pointed.

VARIABLE FOCAL LENGTH LENS   A zoom lens.

VERTICAL PAN   A pivotal movement of the camera up or down.

WET SPLICE   Where two pieces of film are overlapped and welded with solvent cement.

WIDE-ANGLE LENS   The short focal length position of the zoom lens.

WILD TRACK   Sometimes called a "floating track," this is sound intended to go with the image but unsynchronized with it.

WORK PRINT   A relatively inexpensive one-light print* of a film used in the initial editing process prior to the cutting of the original negative. It is used *in place* of working with the picture original. (* A one-light print means that one printing light is used for all scenes in a given roll of film, as differentiated from a "timed print," which means that each scene is given an individual exposure in the printing.)

Index